SHAPES

2D Shapes

Rectangle

Parallelogram

Triangle

Semicircle

Square

Circle

Oval

Rhombus Trapezoid Pentagon Hexagon

3D Shapes

Sphere

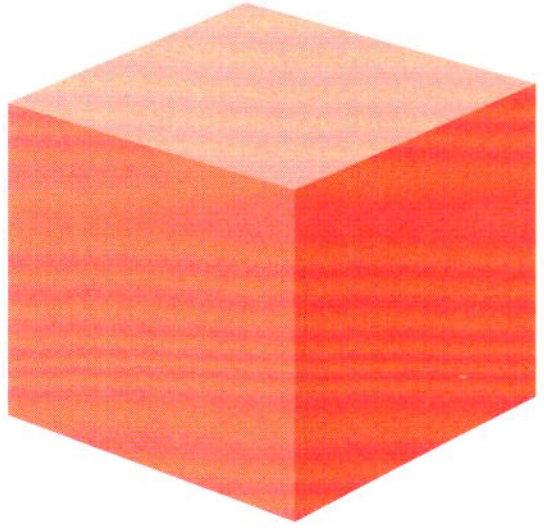

Cube

Pyramid

Triangular Prism

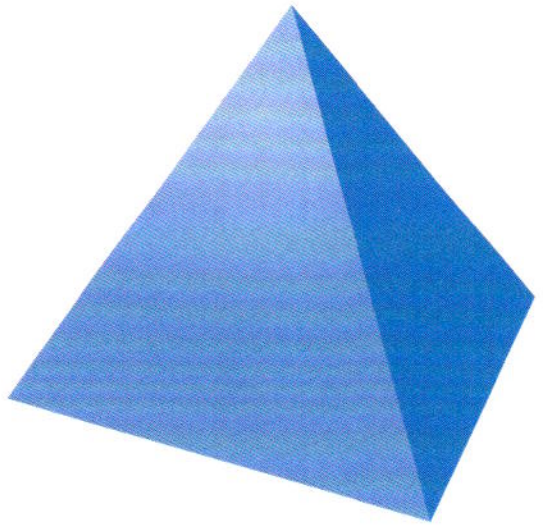

Cuboid

Cone

Cylinder

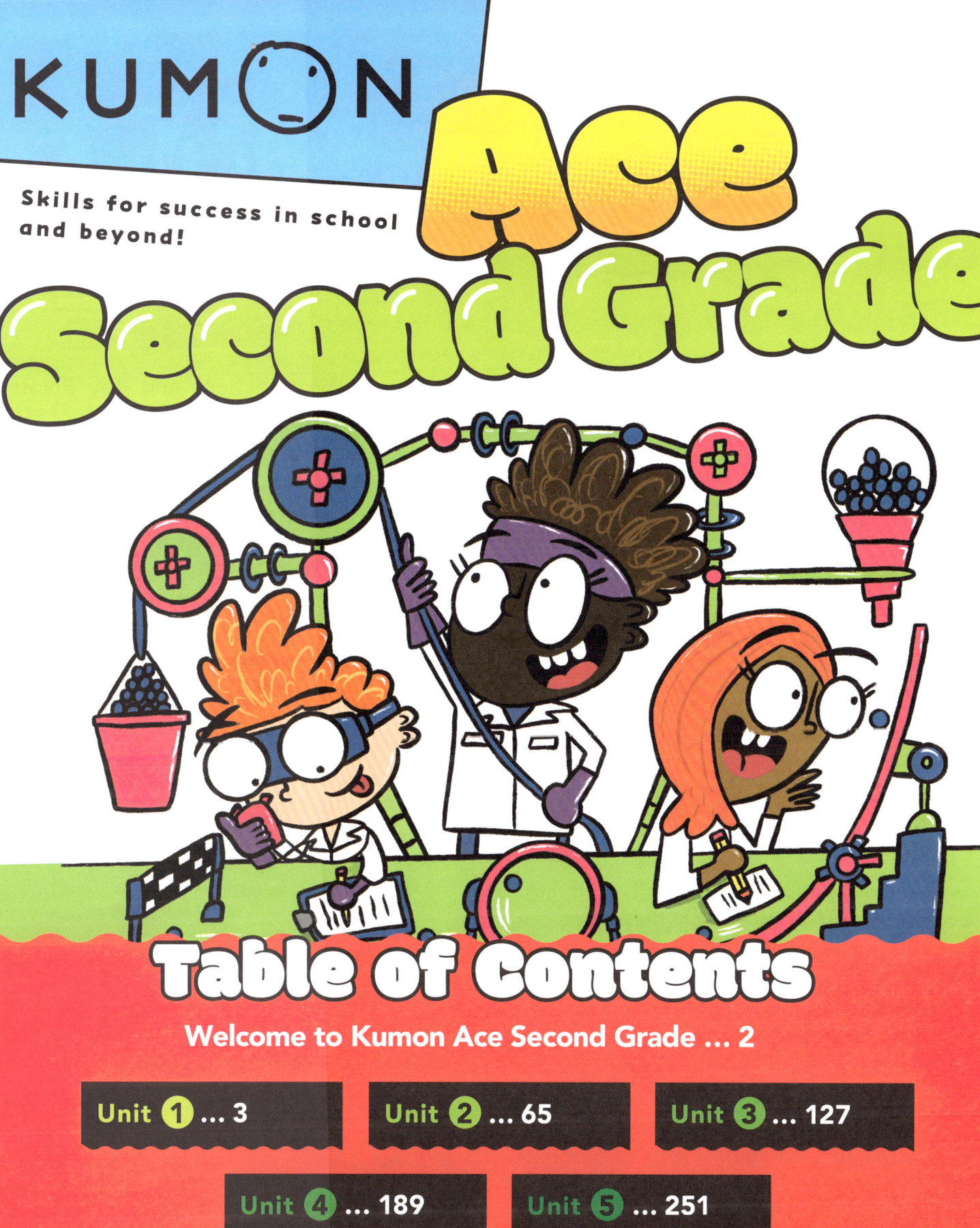

KUM☺N

Skills for success in school and beyond!

Ace
Second Grade

Table of Contents

Welcome to Kumon Ace Second Grade ... 2

Welcome to Kumon Ace Second Grade

KUMON Ace Second Grade — Grade 2, Ages 7–8

Skills for success in school and beyond!

Language Arts / Reading / Math / Science / Social Studies / Technology / Personal Finance / Thinking Skills / Art / PE / Social-Emotional Learning

Includes
- ☆ Study Poster
- ☆ Great Job Stickers
- ☆ Award Certificate

❶ Write the date at the top of each page.

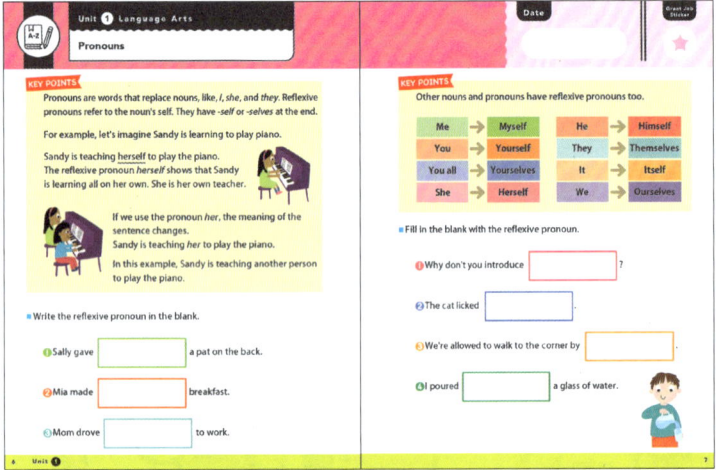

❷ Read the directions and Key Points on each page. Then complete each activity.

❸ When you complete a section, check your answers with the Answer Key in the back of the book. Try again if you got any wrong.

❹ When you are done checking your answers, place a "Great Job" sticker on the top of the page!

Let's study!

☆ When you have finished studying each unit, put a sticker on the sheet on page 319.

☆ When you have finished all of the units, place the largest sticker at the bottom of the same sheet.

☆ Then have your parent or guardian sign the Certificate of Achievement and present it to you!

Cut out the study posters and hang them up for further study!

Unit **1** Table of Contents

Use this page to keep track of your progress throughout the book. Place a check mark in the box when you have completed a section.

Nouns

KEY POINTS

A noun is a person, place, or thing.
Collective nouns describe a group. Here are some examples:

team

flock

bunch

class

■ Write the collective noun that best completes the sentence.

❶ The basketball  has a game later.

❷ Our [   ] has a field trip on Friday.

❸ A [   ] of geese flew overhead.

❹ There is a [   ] of grapes in the fruit bowl.

KEY POINTS

Usually, when we want to show that there is more than one noun, we add an s on the end. But some nouns are different. We call these irregular nouns. Here are some examples:

Tooth ➡ Teeth   Child ➡ Children   Fish ➡ Fish

Foot ➡ Feet   Mouse ➡ Mice   Moose ➡ Moose

■ Fill in the blanks.

❶ Every morning I brush my  .

❷ When I jump, I lift both  .

❸ All of the [   ] in the class like recess.

❹ Eek! I thought I saw two  .

Pronouns

Pronouns are words that replace nouns, like, *I*, *she*, and *they*. Reflexive pronouns refer to the noun's self. They have *-self* or *-selves* at the end.

For example, let's imagine Sandy is learning to play piano.

Sandy is teaching <u>herself</u> to play the piano.
The reflexive pronoun *herself* shows that Sandy is learning all on her own. She is her own teacher.

If we use the pronoun *her*, the meaning of the sentence changes.
Sandy is teaching *her* to play the piano.

In this example, Sandy is teaching another person to play the piano.

■ Write the reflexive pronoun in the blank.

① Sally gave [ ] a pat on the back.

② Mia made [ ] breakfast.

③ Mom drove [ ] to work.

KEY POINTS

Other nouns and pronouns have reflexive pronouns too.

Me	→	Myself	He	→	Himself
You	→	Yourself	They	→	Themselves
You all	→	Yourselves	It	→	Itself
She	→	Herself	We	→	Ourselves

■ Fill in the blank with the reflexive pronoun.

❶ Why don't you introduce [ ] ?

❷ The cat licked [ ] .

❸ We're allowed to walk to the corner by [ ] .

❹ I poured [ ] a glass of water.

Verbs

KEY POINTS

Past tense verbs show an action that has already happened. Many past tense verbs end with -ed.

play → **played**

But some verbs don't follow this pattern. These are called irregular verbs.

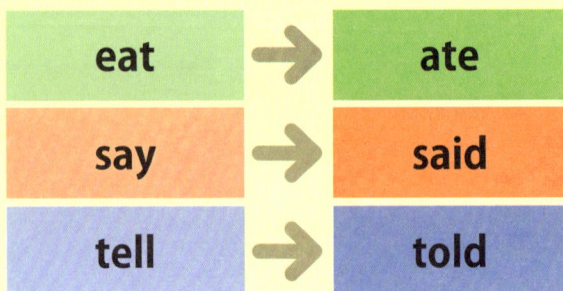

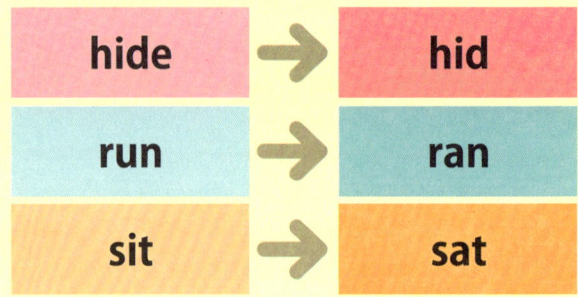

eat → ate	hide → hid
say → said	run → ran
tell → told	sit → sat

■ Fill in the blanks.

❶ We _____ a race in gym class.

❷ I _____ a slice of pizza.

❸ She _____ me a funny story.

❹ My cat _____ in a box.

■ Match the present tense verb with the correct past tense verb.

swim ●   ● sang

sing ●   ● swam

sleep ●   ● won

write ●   ● stood

stand ●   ● wrote

win ●   ● slept

Adjectives / Adverbs

Adjectives describe nouns.
For example, here are some adjectives that could describe a horse:

big   beautiful

brown   friendly

fast

■ Circle the adjective in each sentence.

① I wore a (yellow) shirt.

② The tiny dog played with a stick.

③ The mask was scary.

④ We heard some loud music.

KEY POINTS

Adverbs describe verbs or adjectives.

When they describe a verb, they show how the action happened. For example, *happily* and *quickly* are both adverbs.

We played *happily*.

She walked *quickly*.

When they describe an adjective, they show the degree or amount. For example, *very* and *really* are both adverbs.

An elephant is *very* large.

This food is *really* salty!

■ Circle the adverb in each sentence.

1 Lucas   wrote   his   name   (neatly.)

2 Mary   played   piano   beautifully.

3 The   ice   cream   was   extremely   cold.

4 They   sang   loudly.

■ Fill in the blanks with the correct part of speech to tell a story.

Today I had to go to [_____].

place name

I felt [_____] **, so I brought some**

adjective

[_____] **with me. On the way,**

plural noun

I [_____] [_____] **. I met my friend**

past tense verb *adverb*

[_____] **and we** [_____] **.**

name *past tense verb*

Next time I will [_____] [_____] **.**

verb *adverb*

■ Trace your finger around the square and breathe in and out along the sides.

Start Here

Breathe in

Breathe out

Breathe out

SQUARE BREATHING

Breathe in

Short and Long Vowels

Vowels can be long or short. Let's start by looking at *A*, *E*, and *I*.
Say each word aloud to hear the difference.

Long A gr**a**pe

Short A **a**pple

Long E p**e**a

Short E **e**gg

Long I **i**ce cream

Short I f**i**sh

■ Read the words in the word bank.
  Then write them in the correct space below.

pack, leg, like, rake, sick, teeth, mint, well, wheel, fin

Long Vowels

Short Vowels

KEY POINTS

Now let's look at *O* and *U*.
Say each word aloud to hear the difference

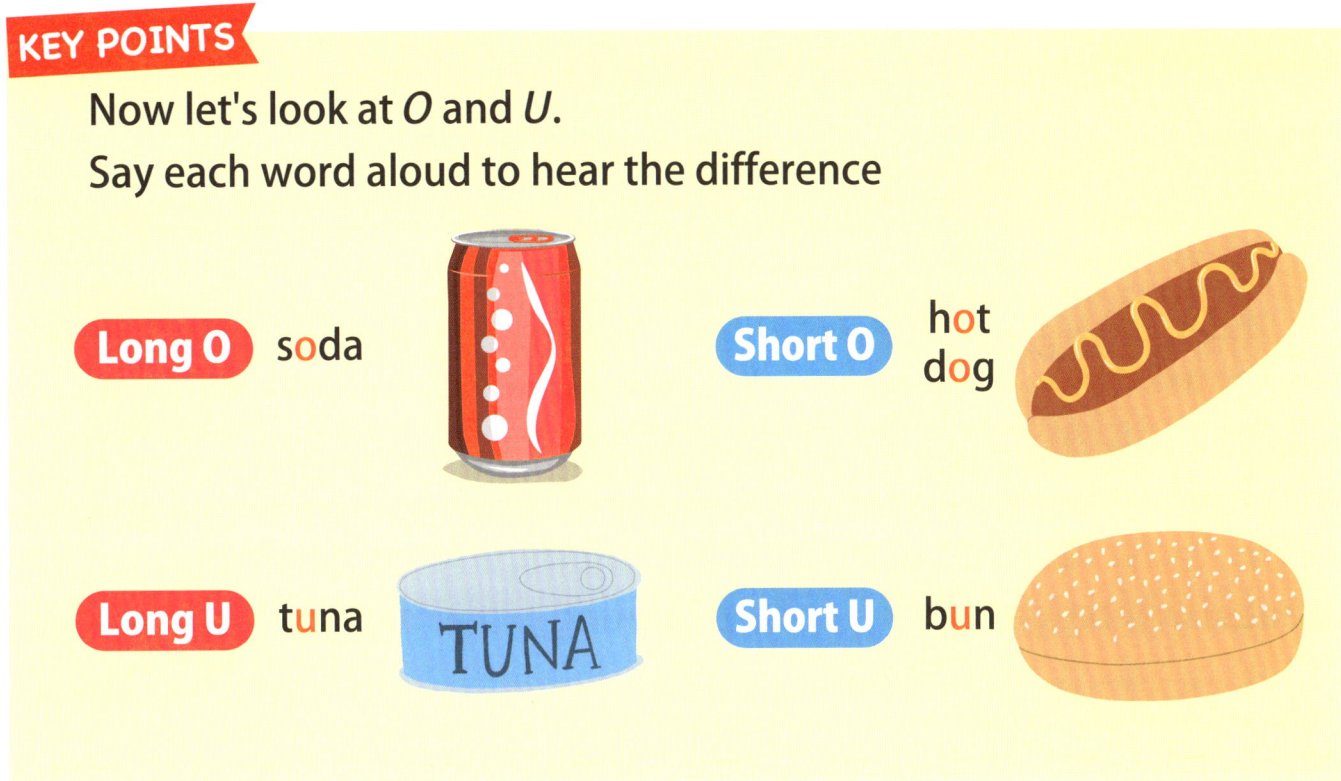

Long O soda

Short O hot dog

Long U tuna

Short U bun

■ Read the words in the word bank.
Then write them in the correct space below.

shone, shut, rock, luck, pole, stone, stuck, rug

Long Vowels

Short Vowels

Decoding Two-Syllable Words

Breaking a word into syllables can help readers decode the word. Read the words below out loud. Clap as you say each syllable.

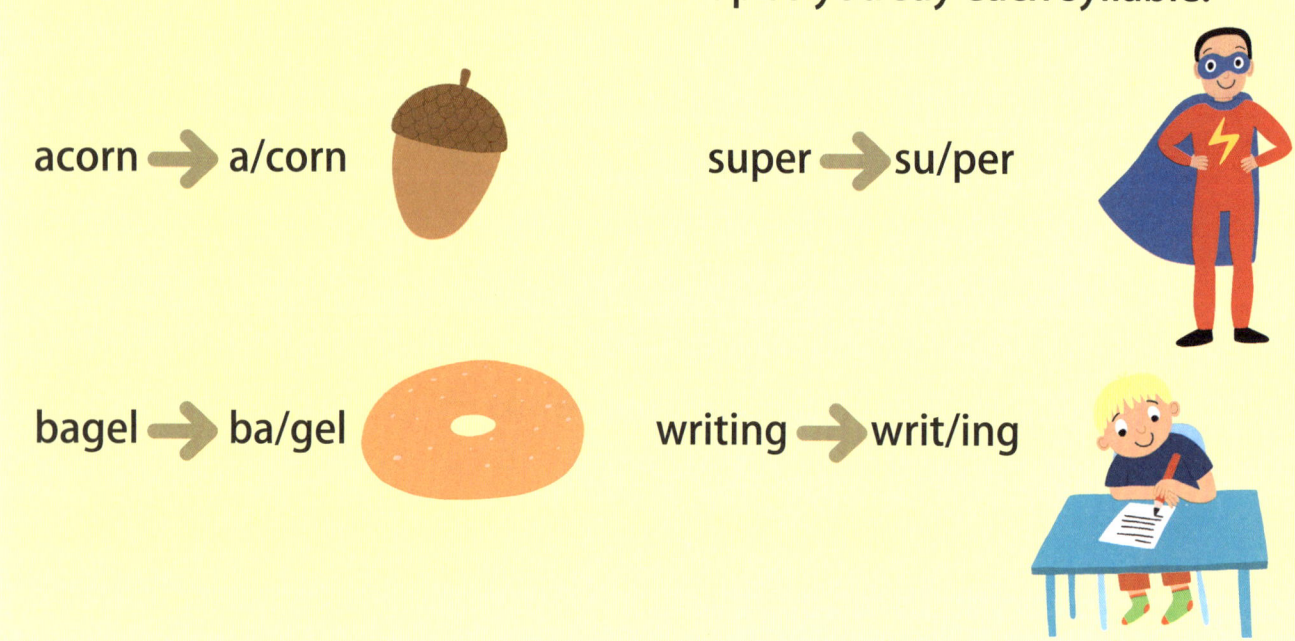

acorn ➡ a/corn

super ➡ su/per

bagel ➡ ba/gel

writing ➡ writ/ing

■ Read the words below. Practice breaking each word into two-syllables. Draw a line between them.

r a i n | i n g   c o o l e r

t i g e r   e a t e n

s p o k e n   b i k i n g

■ Choose the word from the box that best completes the sentence, and write it below.

> traced, voted, playing, spider, student, feeding

1 Our cat is hungry, so we are [ ] her.

2 I [ ] this picture from my favorite book.

3 We are [ ] hide and go seek.

4 Eek! I saw a [ ] .

5 Our class [ ] on which activity we will do next.

6 The teacher helped the [ ] find their book.

KEY POINTS

A prefix is a word part that can be added to the beginning of a word. Prefixes have meanings. Here are some examples:

Prefix	Meaning	Example	
pre-	before	preschool →	Before kindergarten, I went to *preschool*.
re-	to do again	reread →	I've read this book before, but I love to *reread* my favorites.
un-	not	unhappy →	I was *unhappy* to hear that we had a pop quiz!
dis-	not	dishonest →	He was being *dishonest* when he said that.

■ Combine the prefix and the word to create a new word.
  Then write the meaning.

❶ dis- + appear   disappear   to go away

❷ un- + kind

❸ pre- + view →

❹ re- + write

KEY POINTS

A suffix is a word part that can be added to the end of the word. Suffixes have meanings. Here are some examples:

Suffix	Meaning	Example
-er	more	higher: My kite flew *higher* than hers.
-est	most	biggest: Our class is the *biggest* in the grade.
-less	without	thoughtless: I made a *thoughtless* mistake.
-ly	turns adjective to adverb, describes action	quickly: We ran away *quickly*.

■ Combine the suffix and the word to create a new word. Then write the meaning.

❶ **thank** + **-less** →

❷ **kind** + **-ly** →

❸ **tall** + **-est** →

❹ **small** + **-er** →

■ Read the passage below and circle the words that are spelled incorrectly. Then spell them correctly in the space below.

Today I went to the park with my

~~frend,~~ Ben. Our moms sed we could

friend

stay for one hour. It was a little

coled out, but we didn't mind. I had

sutch a fun time. I hope we can go

agin soon.

■ Choose the word from the word bank that best completes each sentence.

> because, other, what, use, give

❶ I didn't know _____ to do!

❷ Can you pass the _____ book?

❸ I like cake _____ it's sweet.

❹ It's her birthday, so I will _____ her a card.

❺ I will _____ a fork to eat my dinner.

Brain Break
Maze

■ Draw a line from the start to the goal by connecting the long vowel words.

START

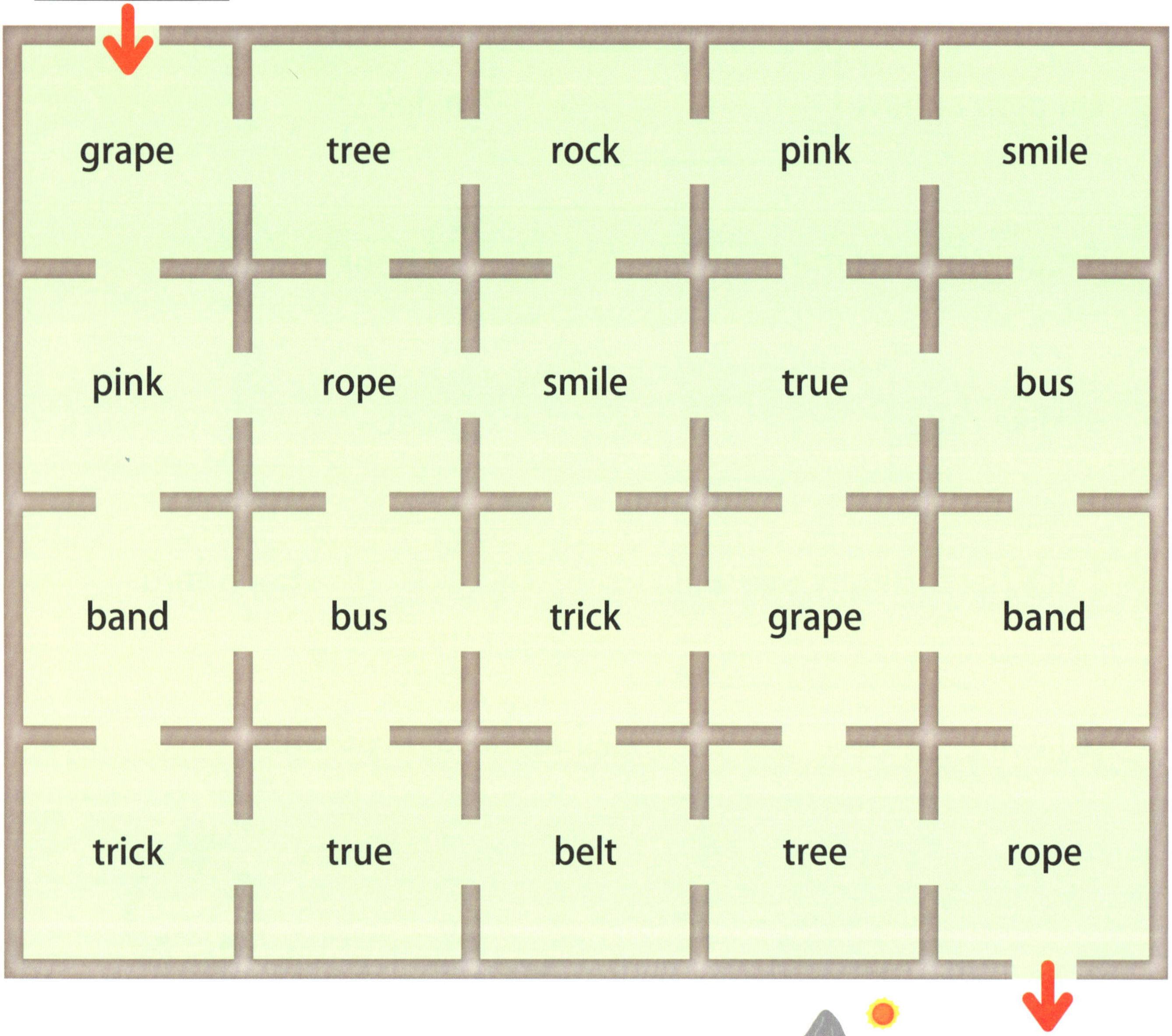

grape	tree	rock	pink	smile
pink	rope	smile	true	bus
band	bus	trick	grape	band
trick	true	belt	tree	rope

GOAL

Mindfulness Break!

A positive affirmation is a sentence that is thought or said out loud to help a person feel more positive or optimistic about a situation.

■ Write a postive affirmation for each situation.

❶ Joining a new sports team and meeting new players.

_____

❷ Standing up in front of the class for Show and Tell.

_____

❸ Trying a new food.

_____

Place Value 1

■ How many colored sticks are there in total? Look at the numerals and words, then write the numbers.

1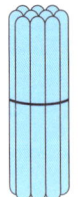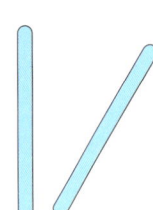

1 ten   **2** ones

| 12 |

4

4 tens   **3** ones

| |

2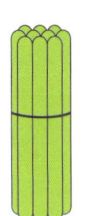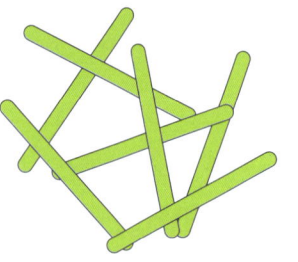

1 ten   **7** ones

| |

5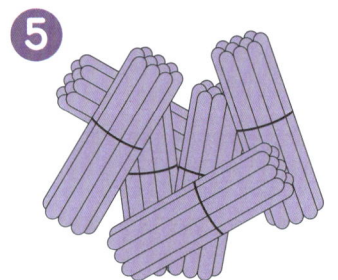

6 tens   **0** ones

| |

3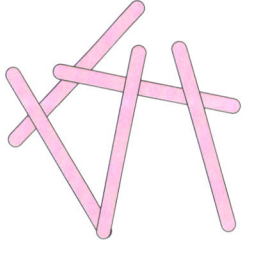

2 tens   **5** ones

| |

6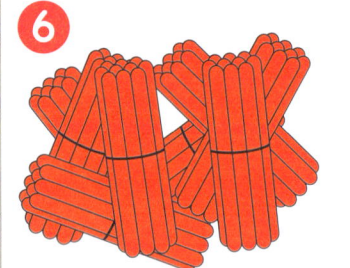

8 tens   **9** ones

| |

7

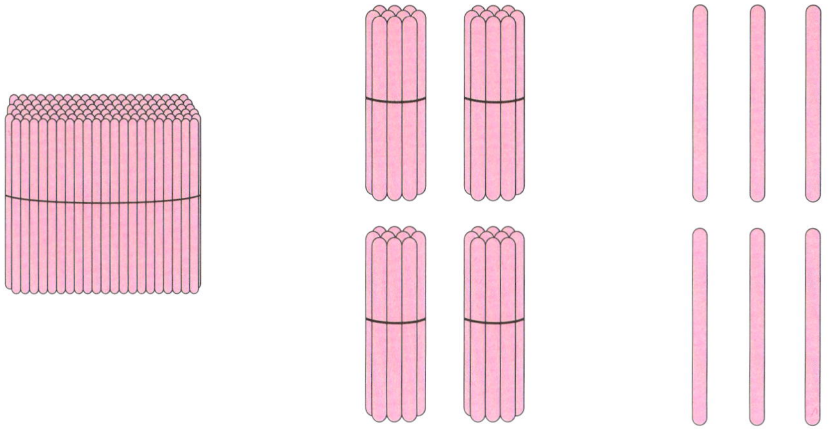

1 hundred   4 tens   6 ones

8

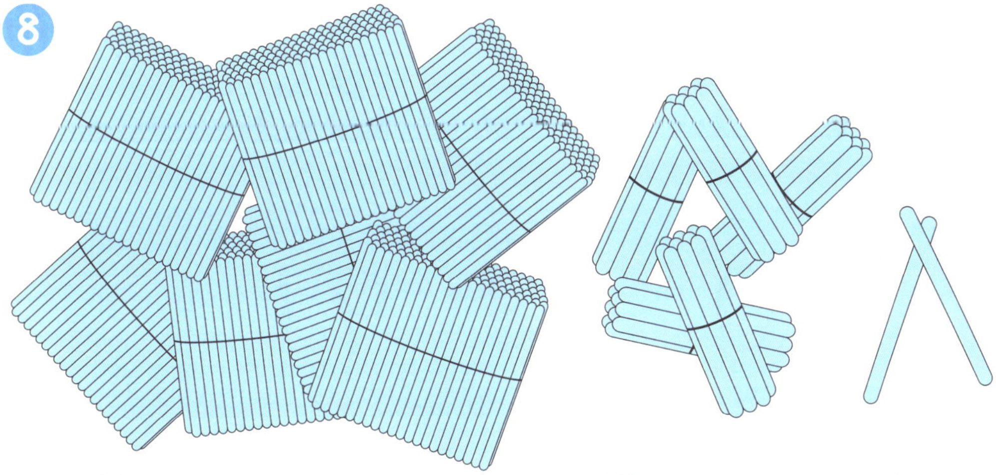

7 hundreds   5 tens   2 ones

9

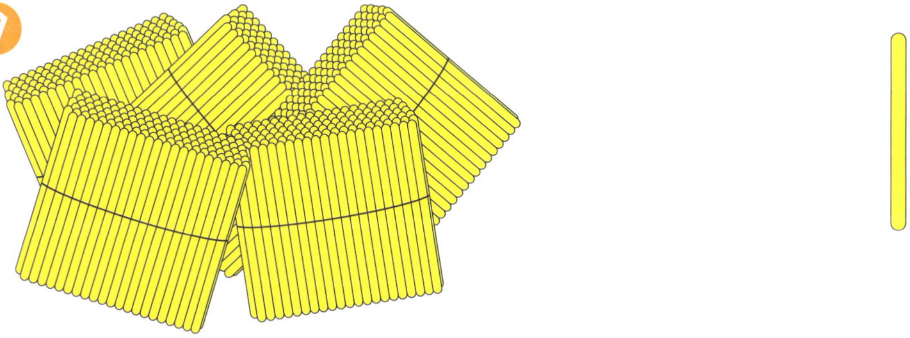

5 hundreds   0 tens   1 ones

Place Value 2

2-digit number

1	7
↑	↑
tens	ones

3-digit number

5	9	3
↑	↑	↑
hundreds	tens	ones

■ Circle all the numbers that have a 3 in the ones place.

(23) 53 14 38

79 30 63 91

■ Circle all the numbers that have a 7 in the tens place.

67 19 70 77

45 72 31 28

■ Circle the correct number.

① 2 tens, 3 ones

| 15 | 23 | 32 |

④ 4 hundreds, 1 tens, 7 ones

| 407 | 471 | 417 |

② 6 tens, 8 ones

| 16 | 86 | 68 |

⑤ 9 hundreds, 3 tens, 1 ones

| 931 | 913 | 319 |

③ 5 tens

| 50 | 5 | 55 |

⑥ 2 hundreds, 4 ones

| 24 | 204 | 240 |

Skip Counting

Usually when we count, we count every number. But when we skip-count, we skip over certain numbers. For example, when we skip-count by 5, we skip up by five every time we count.

■ Skip-count by 5 to draw a line from the start to the goal.

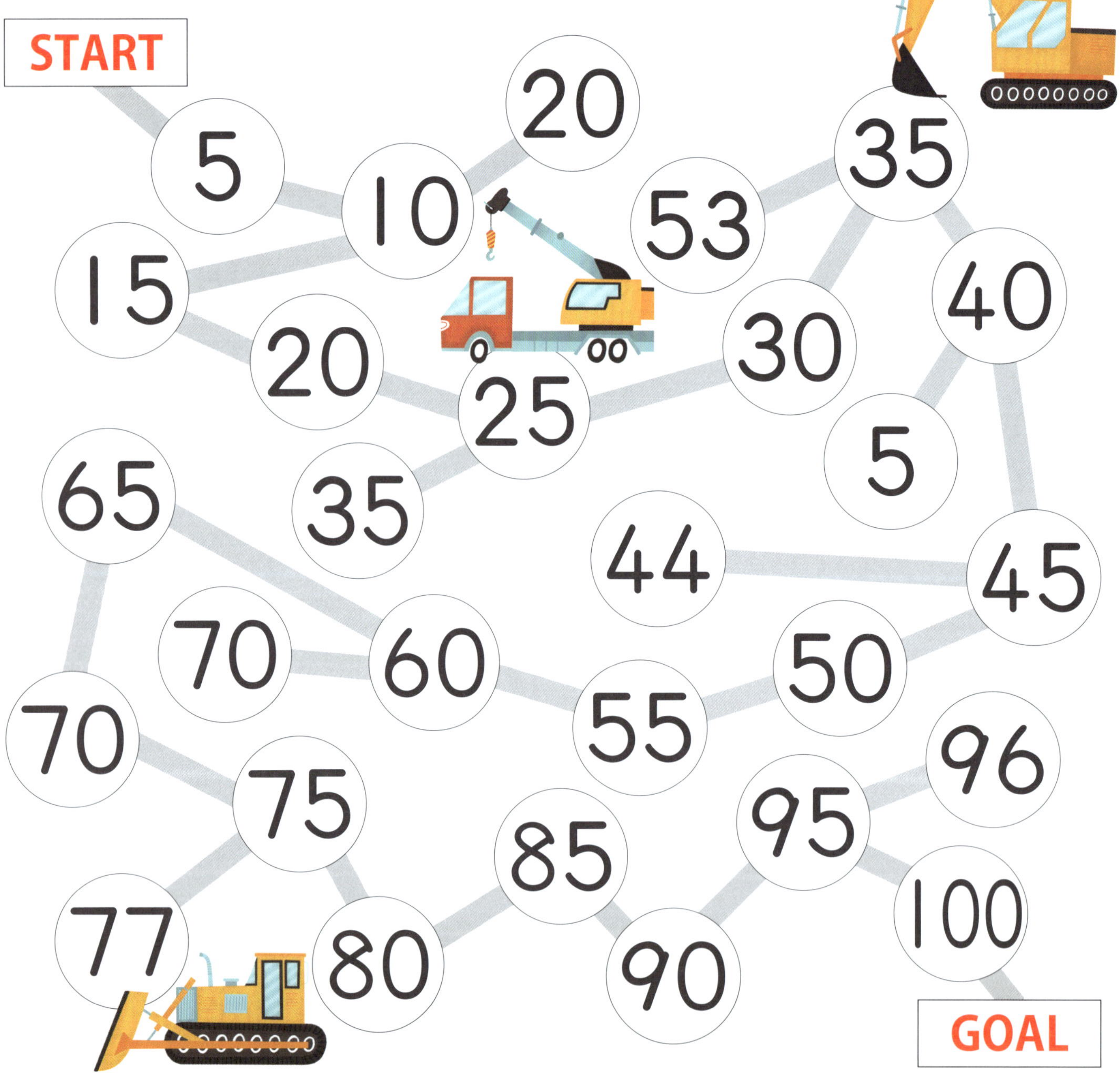

START

5
20
35
10
53
15
40
20
30
25
5
65
35
44
45
70
60
50
70
55
96
75
95
85
77
80
90
100

GOAL

■ Skip-count by 10 to fill in the missing numbers.

SKIP COUNTING

10	20	30	40	50	60	70	80	90	100
110	120	130			150	160	170	180	190	200
210	220	230	240	250	260		280	290	300
	320	330	340	350	360	370	380	390	400
410	420		440	450	460	470	480	490	500
510	520	530	540		560	570	580	590	600
610	620	630	640	650	660	670	680	690	
710	720	730	740	750	760	770		790	800
810		830	840	850	860	870	880	890	900
910	920	930	940	950	960	970	980		1000

Skip Counting / Words to Numbers

■ Draw a line from the start to the goal by skip-counting by hundreds.

START

100	200	201	330	404
120	300	202	909	990
450	400	700	800	900
505	500	600	760	1000

GOAL

■ Circle the correct number.

1. twenty-seven   27   70   207

2. fifty-two   25   52   152

3. nineteen   9   19   90

4. twelve   12   20   21

5. one hundred thirty-four   104   134   341

6. six hundred sixty   66   606   660

Greater Than or Less Than

KEY POINTS

Greater Than	Less Than	Equal To
>	<	=
20 > 10	35 < 36	77 = 77

■ Write a check mark (✓) if the statement is correct. Write an ✗ if the statement is incorrect.

1 25<26

2 80>90

3 101=111

4 473>437

5 599<600

6 456>546

■ Write >, <, or = in the box.

1. 17 ☐ 27

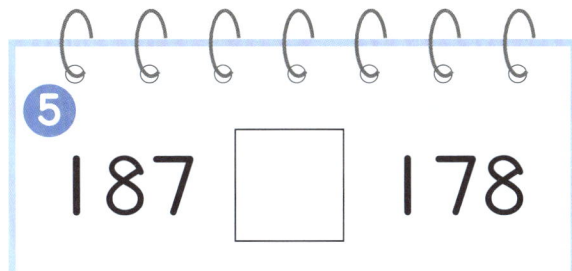

5. 187 ☐ 178

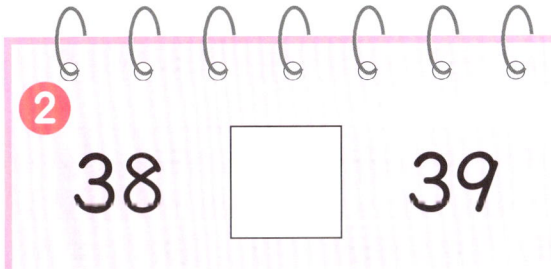

2. 38 ☐ 39

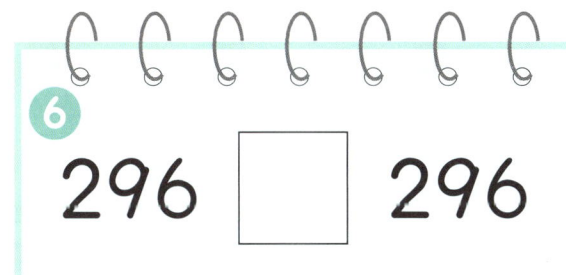

6. 296 ☐ 296

3. 55 ☐ 53

7. 343 ☐ 339

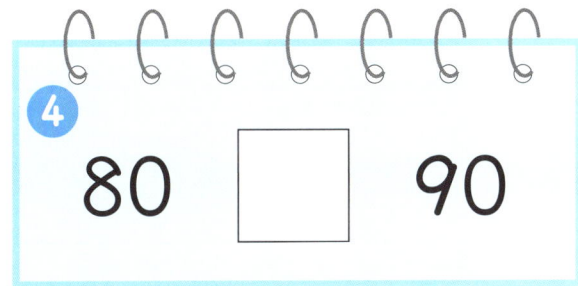

4. 80 ☐ 90

8. 606 ☐ 660

Brain Break
Greater or Less Than Game

■ Make each statement true! Use the numbers in the boxes to make each
< , >, or = statement true.

1

| 1 | 2 | 3 | 3 |

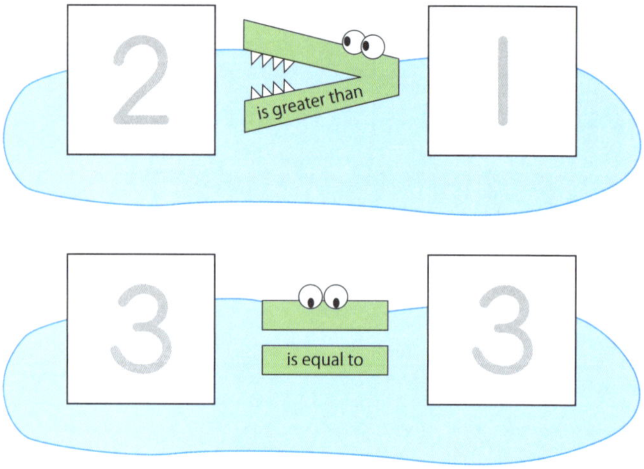

2 is greater than 1

3 is equal to 3

2

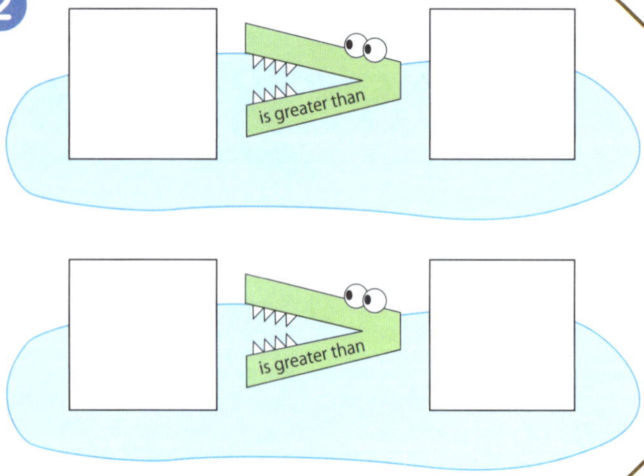

[ ] is greater than [ ]

[ ] is greater than [ ]

| 3 | 5 | 7 | 9 |

[ ] is less than [ ]

3

| 4 | 6 | 6 | 8 |

[ ] is greater than [ ]

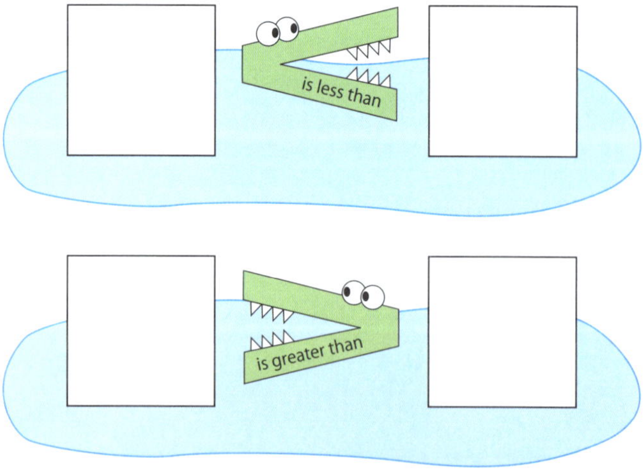

Maze Break!

■ Trace the path from start to finish!

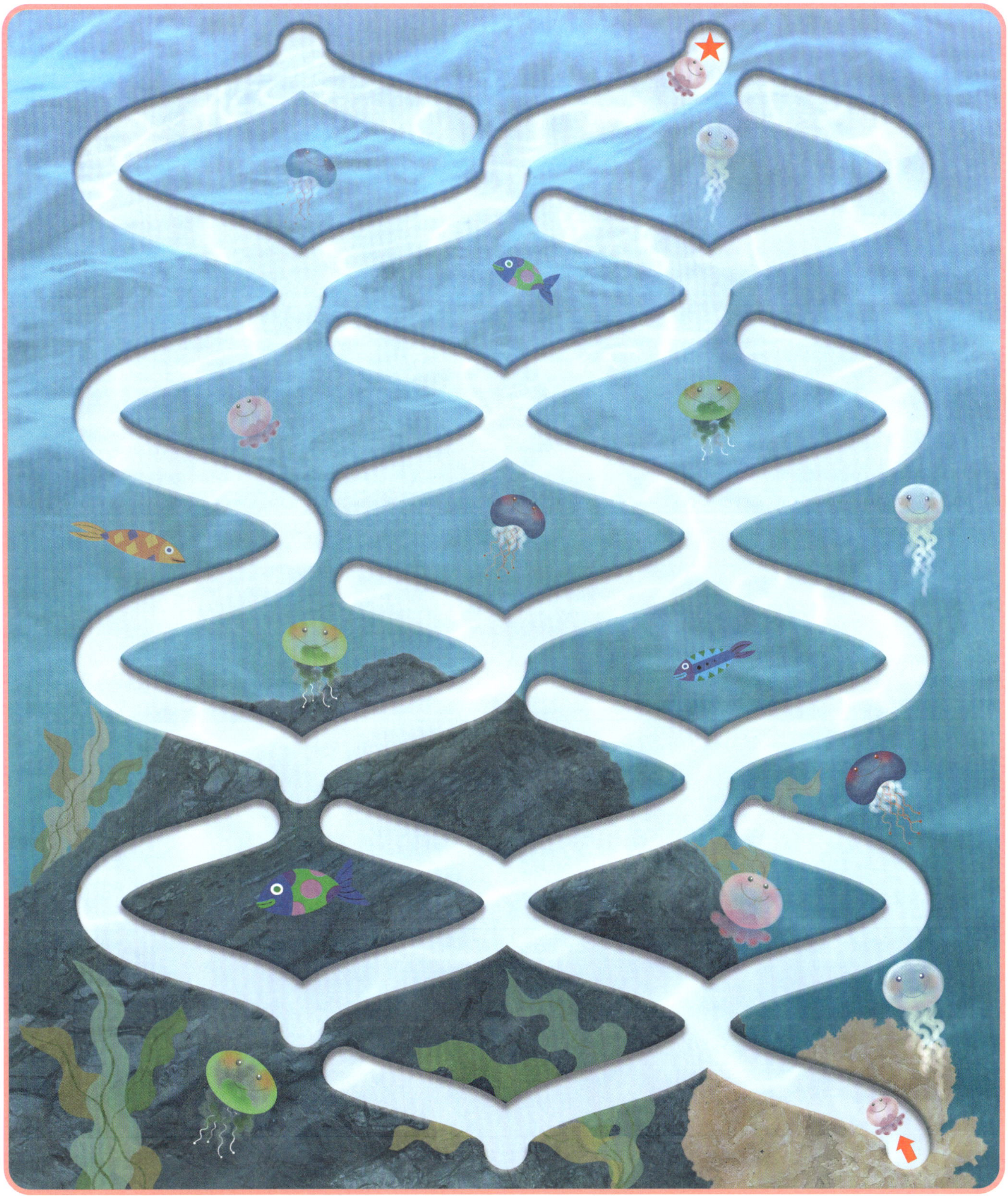

Plants as Living Things

KEY POINTS

Plants are living things that need food and water to grow. Plants make their food using the sun's rays. They take in sunlight through their leaves. Plants also take in water from the ground using their roots. They use water, sunlight, and carbon dioxide to make food. This is called photosynthesis.

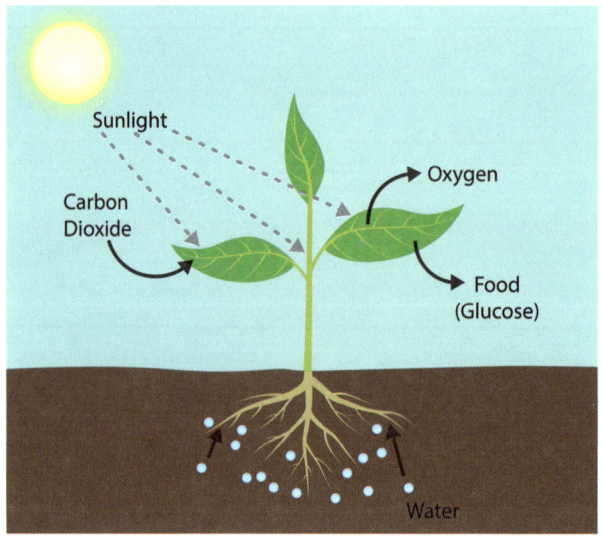

Sunlight

Carbon Dioxide

Oxygen

Food (Glucose)

Water

■ **Answer the questions.**

❶ How do plants make their food?

_____

❷ What is photosynthesis?

_____

■ Read the questions below and write a check (✓) if the answer is true or false.

① Plants need water to live.

True ☐   False ☐

② Plants need food to grow, just like humans.

True ☐   False ☐

③ Plants need sunlight to make their food.

True ☐   False ☐

④ Plants use their flowers to take in water.

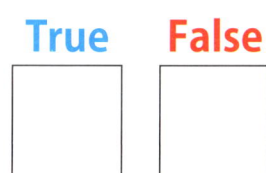

True ☐   False ☐

Plant Diversity

Plants grow in different habitats. A habitat is a place where plants or animals live. Plants have traits that help them get food and water in different habitats. These traits are called adaptations.

Plants that grow in hot, dry habitats have roots that grow near the surface of the soil to help them take in rainwater. Other plants live in cold, dry habitats. They don't lose their leaves in cold weather and can live off the food stored in them.

■ Answer the questions.

❶ What is an adaptation?

_____

❷ What are some examples of plant adaptations?

_____

■ **Read the facts and match the plant to its habitat.**

The desert is a dry area that does not get a lot of rain. Plants here have shallow roots that spread out and grow near the surface of the soil. This helps them collect more rainwater.

Seaweed

The rainforest has a hot climate with heavy rains. Plants here have waxy leaves with pointed tips to help extra water roll off. Too much water would cause the leaves to rot.

Oak Tree

The temperate forest has four seasons and bad winters. Trees here have thick bark to protect them against the cold. They also have broad leaves that capture a lot of sunlight to help them make food.

Monstera

Plants can grow in bodies of water like oceans or lakes. Some plants don't grow roots because they take in water through their stems and leaves. They also produce seeds that float.

Cactus

Plants reproduce, or make new plants, in a number of ways. Most plants have seeds that will become new plants if they find a good place to grow. There are different ways a seed might be carried to a new place where they can grow.

Some seeds—like the helicopter shaped seeds from a maple tree—just fall to the ground. The shape of the seed helps carry it a little further from the parent tree.

Plants like oak trees and apple trees have their seeds protected by nuts and fruits, which animals eat. When the animal poops out the seeds in a new place, more trees canl grow.

Some seeds are spiky and stick to an animal's fur. When an animal goes to a different place, it carries the seed far away from the mother plant and gives it a better chance to grow.

Plants like dandelions grow lightweight seeds that can be carried away by the wind. They land far away from the mother plant and have more room to grow.

■ Match the seeds to the way they find a new place to grow.

Carried by the wind

By sticking to an animal's fur

Falling from the parent plant

Eaten and disposed of by animals

Pollination and Pollinators

KEY POINTS

Pollen is a powder found inside the flowers of plants. Animals, like insects, move pollen from one plant to another. An animal that moves pollen from one plant to another is called a pollinator. The process of moving pollen from one plant to another is called pollination.

Insects, like bees, are the main pollinators of plants. Bees fly from flower to flower collecting food. Pollen sticks to them and they carry it to the next flower. This helps the new flower reproduce.

Animals, like hummingbirds, also help pollinate plants while looking for food. Pollen sticks to their wings and falls off at the next flower they visit.

■ Answer the questions.

❶ What is pollination?

_____

❷ Name two examples of pollinators.

_____

■ Write 1 through 5 under each picture to show how pollination happens.

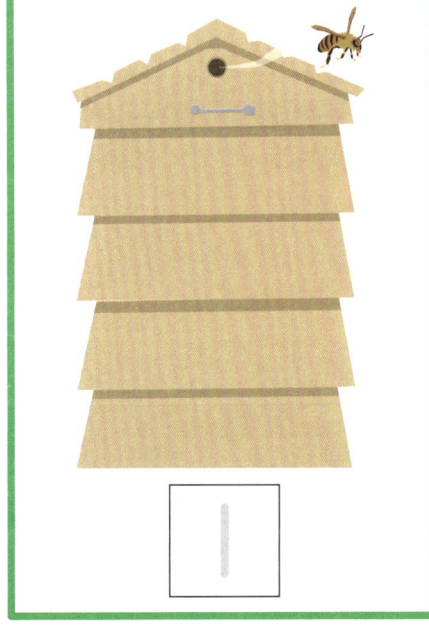

Brain Break
Science Journal 1

Humans can help pollinate plants too!

Design a device to help humans pollinate flowers by hand!

■ Draw a new plant! Give it adaptions like you learned about in this section. What kind of habitat would it grow in? How would it reproduce?

Native Americans

Native Americans are the indigenous peoples of the United States. Indigenous people are the first people to live in an area. Native Americans live throughout North and South America. In the United States, there are many Native Americans throughout the mainland, as well as in Alaska and Hawaii.

Today, Native Americans from all different tribes live all throughout the US. Some live on reservations, which are government assigned land. Others live near where their tribes traditionally lived. Many Native Americans are still working to reclaim their ancestors' lands throughout the US.

■ Answer the questions.

❶ Who are the indigenous people of the United States?

❷ What parts of the United States have Native American tribes?

■ Fill in the blanks to complete the statements.

Word Box

Native Americans   North

South   people

❶ Who? ➡ [   ] are the indigenous peoples

of the United States.

❷ What ? ➡ The original [   ] to live in a

land are called indigenous.

❸ Where ? ➡ Native Americans live throughout [   ]

and [   ] America.

KEY POINTS

There are many different Native American tribes. Tribes are groups with their own culture. They originally lived in different regions, and they have different traditions based on where they are from. For example, the Plains people lived in the middle of the country and were made up of tribes such as the Comanche and Arapaho. In the Southeast lived tribes such as the Cherokee and the Seminole.

Some smaller tribes were part of a bigger tribe or nation. There were hundreds of tribes throughout the United States. Today, members of these tribes live in different areas than their ancestors, but still practice and teach about their culture and beliefs.

■ Answer the questions.

❶ Where did the Comanche and Arapaho tribes traditionally live?

_____

❷ What tribes traditionally lived in the Southeast United States?

_____

■ Use the map to answer the questions about where the Native American tribes traditionally lived.

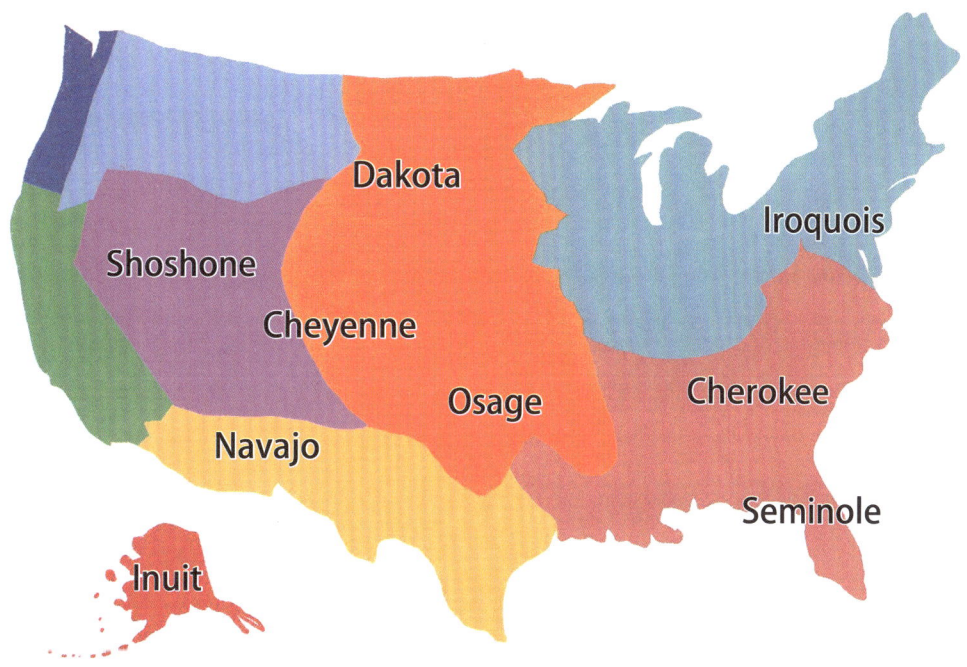

1 Where did the Cherokee tribes live?

2 Where did the Iroquois tribes live?

3 In what area would you find the Cheyenne tribes?

4 In what area would you find the Inuit tribes?

Native American Tribes 2

Native American tribes used the materials in their area to build their society. Because of this, different tribes traditionally ate different foods, built different types of homes, and had different clothing.

Navajo

The Navajo tribe is one of the largest tribes of American Indians. They lived in the Southwest of the United States. A Navajo house was called a hogan. A hogan was a domed-shaped house with a wood frame and walls made out of clay. The Navajo were farmers who grew three main crops corn, beans, and squash.

Sioux

The Sioux Nation is a large group of Native American tribes that lived in the Great Plains. Many Sioux tribes were nomadic people who moved from place-to-place following buffalo herds. Much of their lifestyle was based around hunting buffalo. The Sioux lived in teepees made from long wooden poles and covered with buffalo hides.

Iroquois

The Iroquois people live in the northeast of the US and in parts of Canada. The French named them the Iroquois, but they called themselves the Haudenosaunee which means People of the Longhouse, after the homes they lived in. Iroquois clothing was made from tanned deerskin.

Seminole

The Seminole people lived in present day Florida. They used canoes to travel the waterways. Some Seminoles made their homes in log cabins or raised platforms in swampy areas. They wore loose lightweight clothes and glass beaded jewelry.

■ Answer the questions using the Key Points.

❶ Where did the Navajo tribes live?

❷ What animal was important to the Sioux tribes?

❸ Which tribe called themselves "People of the Longhouse"?

❹ Which tribe mainly used canoes for travel?

❺ Which tribe lived in hogans?

Famous Native Americans

KEY POINTS

There are many Native Americans who had a great impact on American culture.

Sacagawea was a Shoshone woman who assisted explorers Lewis and Clark as an interpreter and guide on their exploration of the western United States.

Sitting Bull was a famous leader of the Lakota Sioux Plain Indians. He led a group of Native Americans in a famous battle called the Battle of Little Big Horn that was fought against General Custer. Under Sitting Bull's leadership the tribes were able to defeat Custer's forces.

Maria Tallchief was the first Native American to become a prima ballerina. She is part of the Osage tribe and work hard to become one of the greatest dancers in the word. When she retired from dancing she founded the Chicago City Ballet company.

Jim Thorpe was an Olympic and professional athlete. He is known as one of the greatest athletes in the world. He participated in the 1912 Olympics and took home two gold medals in Track and Field events. He also played professional baseball and football in the United States.

■ Match the person to the fact.

● ●

She led Lewis and Clark on an expedition across the western United States.

● ●

He won two Olympic gold medals in Track and Field.

● ●

She was the first Native American prima ballerina.

● ●

He led the Sioux people in battle against General Custer.

Brain Break
Word Search

■ Circle the words in the Word Search.

Apache	Cherokee	Inuit	Iroquois
Navajo	Seminole	Sioux	Cree

C	W	S	Q	A	S	C
H	T	E	V	C	T	Q
E	H	M	Y	R	Y	I
R	J	I	T	E	I	R
O	K	N	B	E	R	Y
K	X	O	W	H	O	U
E	C	L	A	G	Q	I
E	O	E	P	W	U	O
N	A	V	A	J	O	K
V	M	P	C	X	I	L
B	K	O	H	W	S	P
N	L	I	E	Q	G	R
I	N	U	I	T	S	V
A	R	L	M	E	A	C
E	S	I	O	U	X	B

Mindfulness Break!

Gratitude is feeling thankful for the people and things in your life.

■ Draw or write something you are grateful for on each piece of the wheel.

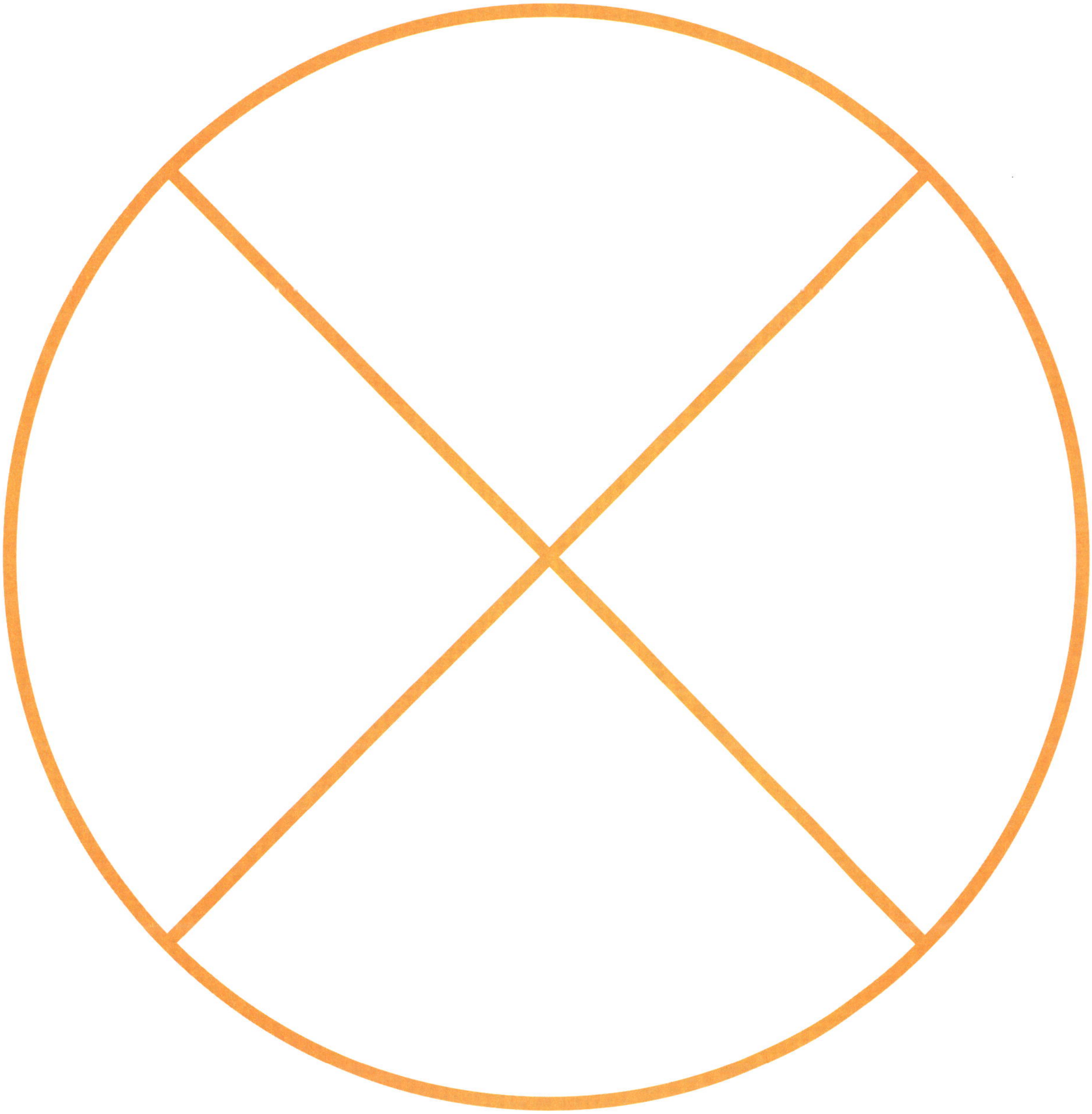

Inventions

■ Draw a line from the arrow (↓) to the star (★). Each time you reach a picture, follow the sign that correctly names the invention.

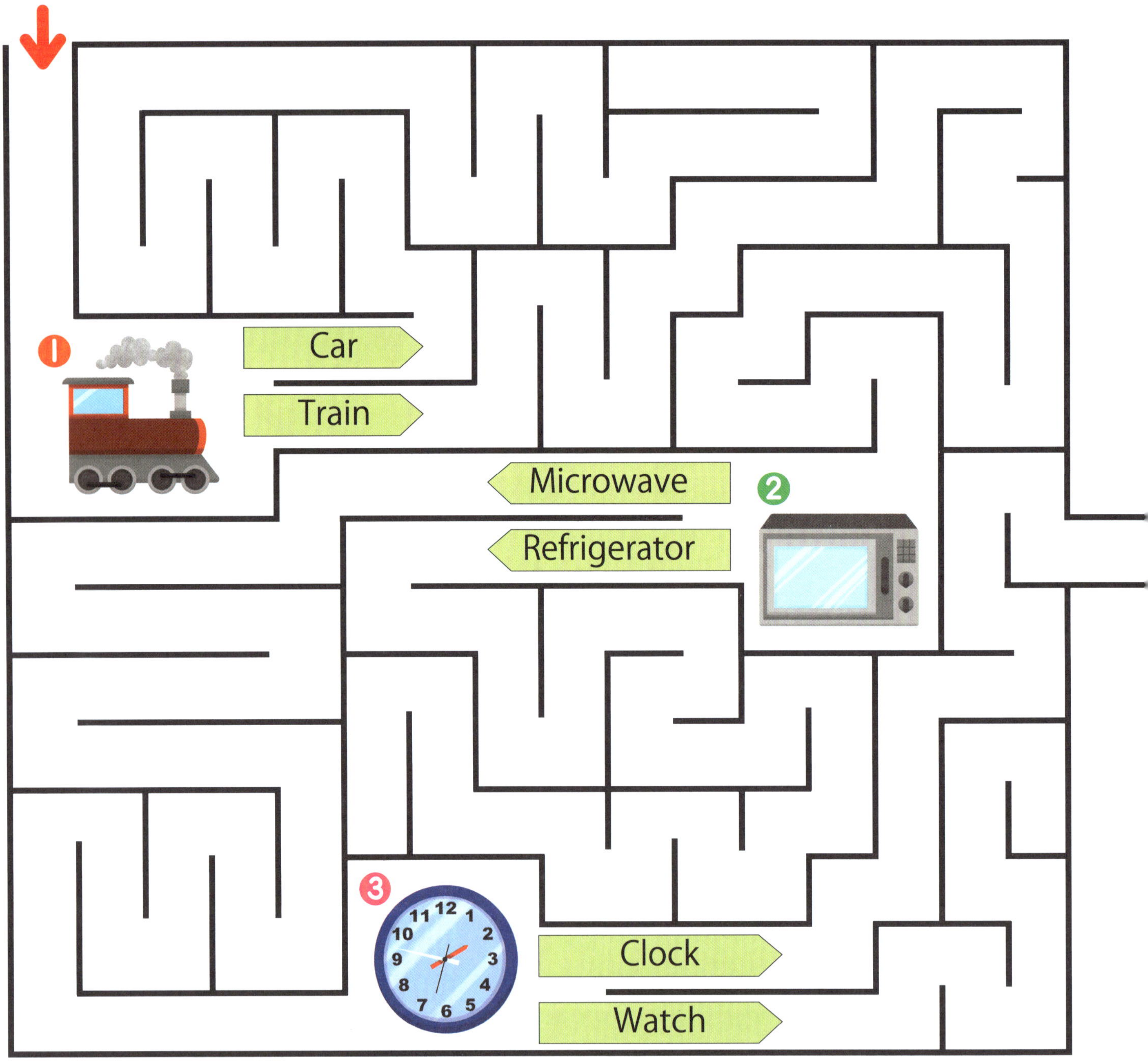

1 Car / Train

2 Microwave / Refrigerator

3 Clock / Watch

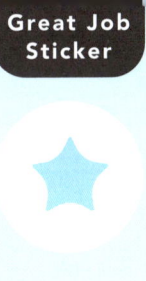

Date

Great Job Sticker

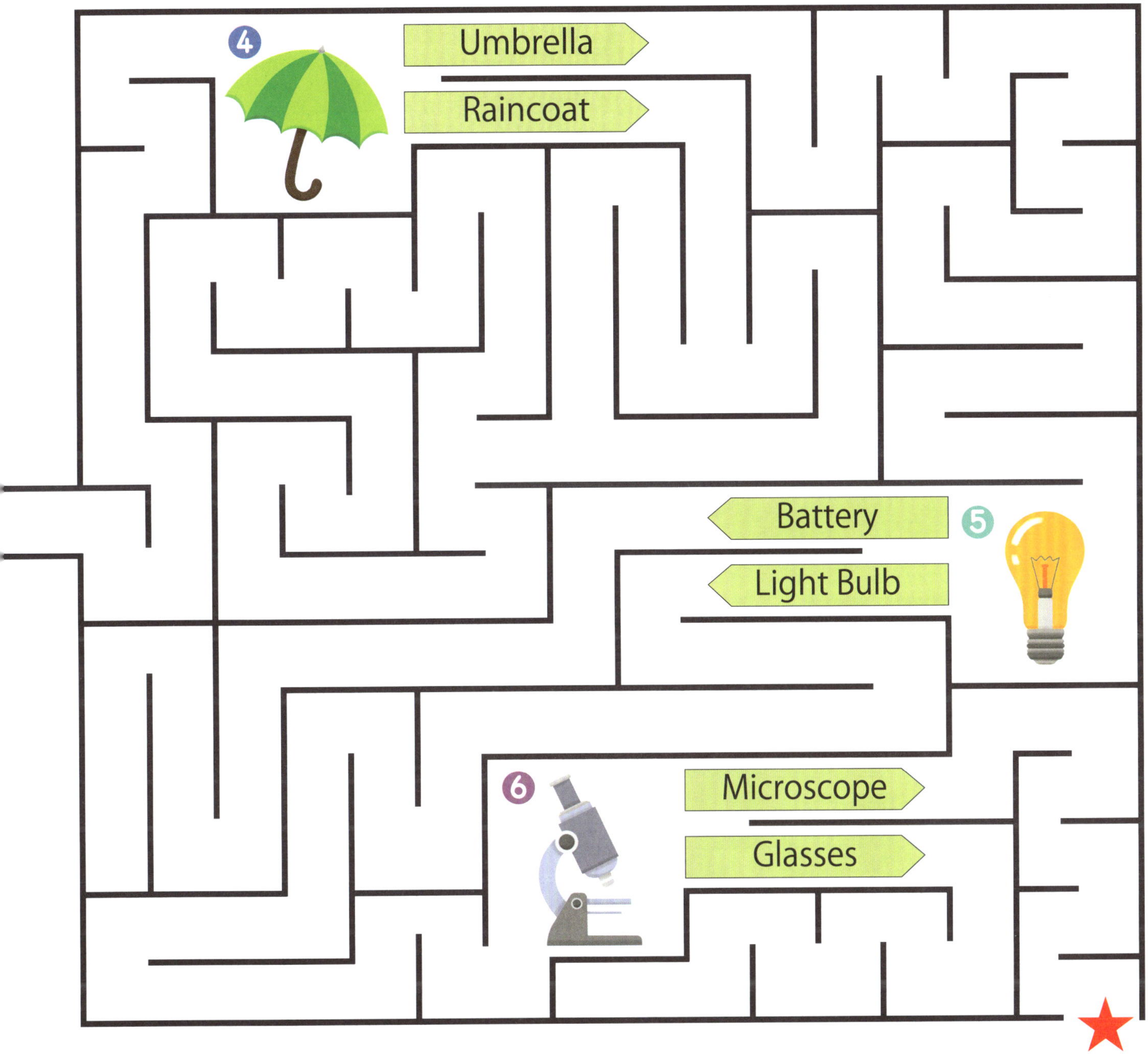
4
Umbrella
Raincoat
Battery
5
Light Bulb
6
Microscope
Glasses

Computers

■ Draw a line from the arrow (↓) to the star (★) in this order: screen, keyboard, mouse, speaker.

Date

Great Job Sticker

KEY POINTS

Did you know that there are many forms of computers? A computer is a device that stores and processes the information you put into it.

Can you identify the different types of computers below?

■ Draw a line from each kind of computer to its name.

1 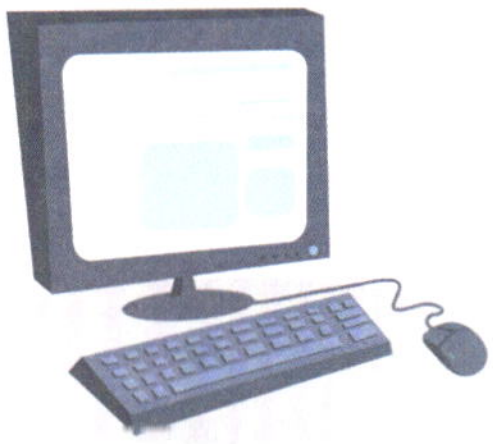	●	● Tablet
2 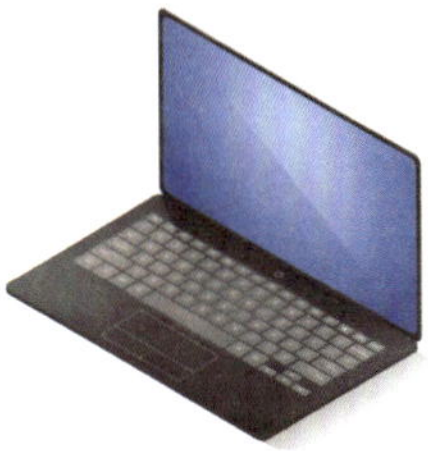	●	● Smartwatch
3	●	● Laptop
4 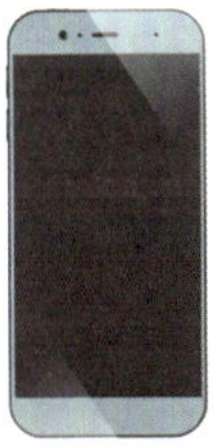	●	● Smartphone
5 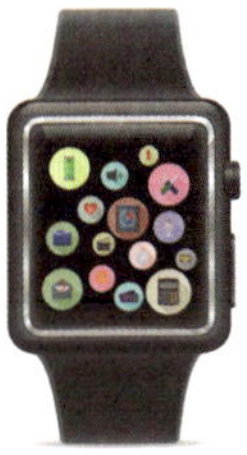	●	● Desktop Computer

Keyboard Skills

■ The top keyboard is a normal keyboard. Look at the bottom keyboard and circle the five keys that are not in the right place.

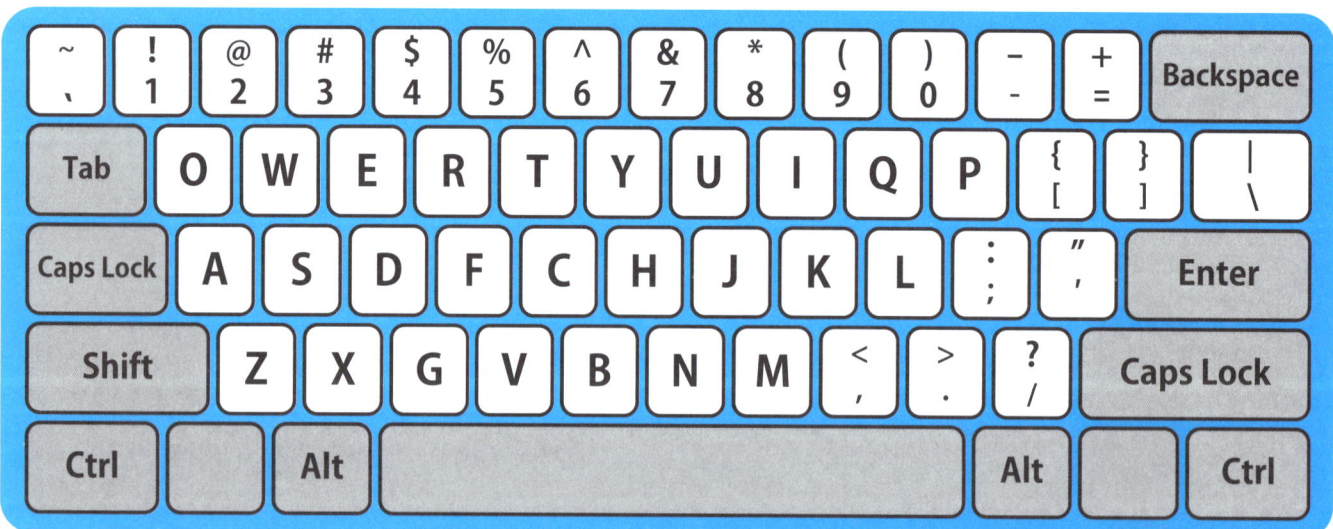

■ **Match the answers. Use the top keyboard on the previous page for help.**

The key on the right side of [T] ● ● [Tab]

The key on the left side of [J] ● ● [Shift]

The key on the right side of [M] ● ● [< ,]

The key on the left side of [Q] ● ● [Y]

The key below [Enter] ● ● [H]

Secret Code

■ Look at the table below. Each letter can be written by using a red number and green shape. For example, L is ● l. Use this information to read the secret codes below.

	●	○	◎	★	☆
1	L	T	C	O	M
2	G	I	K	A	E

①

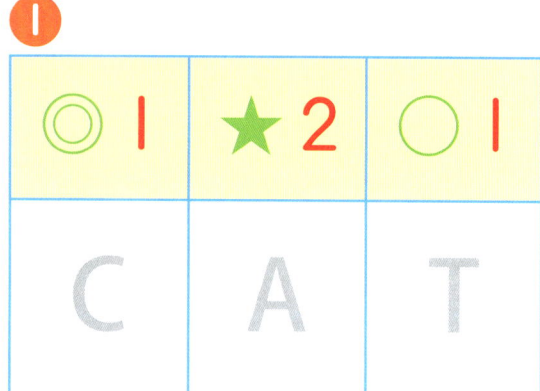

C A T

③

②

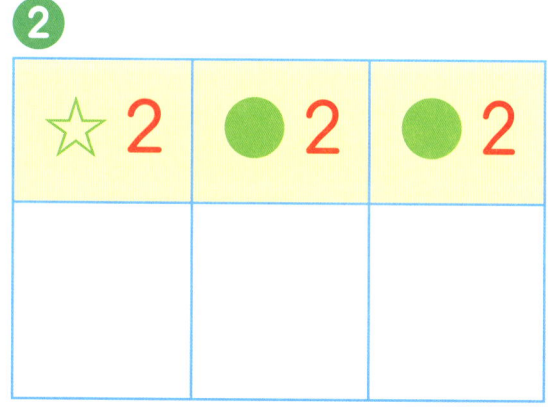

④

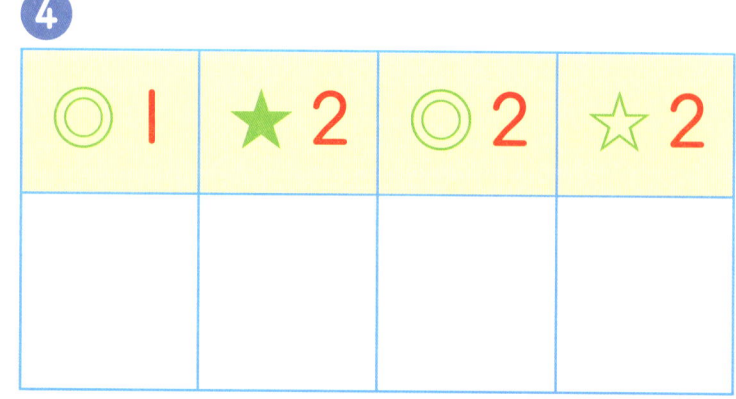

■ Use the table below to read the secret codes. Write the answer in each box.

	0	00	5	55	9	99
I	j	b	s	u	m	n
II	s	l	e	a	k	c
III	d	i	w	o	t	v

1

0 I	55 I	00 III	99 II	5 II

2

9 III	5 II	99 I	99 I	00 III	5 I

3

99 I	55 III	9 III	5 II	00 I	55 III	55 III	9 II

Physical Education Break!

It's important to move your body and exercise!
Try this fun activity below for a study break!

■ Get a coin and flip it. If it lands on heads, do that activity.
If it lands on tails, do the activity from the tails column.

 HEADS	 TAILS
1. 5 jumping jacks 	5 squats 
2. 10 arm circles 	10 toe touches 
3. 30 seconds run in place 	30 seconds march in place 

Unit **2** Table of Contents

Use this page to keep track of your progress throughout the book. Place a check mark in the box when you have completed a section.

Conventions of Language

KEY POINTS

When you write a holiday or place name, use a capital letter at the beginning of the word.

Halloween

Fourth of **J**uly

Memorial **D**ay

California

Texas

Florida

■ Circle the letters below that should be capitalized. Also, add commas after the greeting and closing.

Hi Nate ,

I can't wait for halloween this year.

I am planning to dress up as a ghost.

My aunt will be visiting from ohio.

Your friend ,

Mindy

■ Read the letter below. Add the two missing punctuation marks, and circle the three letters that should be capitalized.

Dear Aunt Tina

Today is thanksgiving, and I don't have school! This afternoon, my family will drive to chicago to visit my cousins. I am looking forward to playing with henry. Well, that's it for now! I hope you are doing well.

Love

Shanae

KEY POINTS

We can deepen our understandings of words by thinking about our own experiences. For example, when you see the word spicy, think about a food you have eaten that was spicy.

■ Match the noun with the adjective that best describes it.

Fire ●　　　● **Salty**

Ocean ●　　　● **Cold**

Ice cube ●　　　● **Smoky**

Orange ●　　　● **Juicy**

■ Name something from your own life that is described by each adjective.

Noisy

Scary

Bumpy

Sour

Dark

Fuzzy

Comfortable

Smelly

Some words have similar, but slightly different meanings.
Let's look at an example: toss, throw, hurl

She _____ the baseball.
She tossed the baseball.
She threw the baseball.
She hurled the baseball.

All of these sentences have the same basic meaning.
But changing the verb changes the sentence slightly.

She tossed the baseball. ➡ Toss is the most casual of the three verbs.

She threw the baseball. ➡ A throw usually takes a little more effort.

She hurled the baseball. ➡ To hurl sounds a little angry.

■ Follow the directions below to illustrate the difference between write, scribble, and sign.

❶ Write your name on the line:

_____

❷ Scribble your name on the line:

_____

❸ Sign your name on the line:

_____

■ Write a sentence using each of the words below:

Word Study 3

KEY POINTS

When you read a sentence that has an unknown word, sometimes you can find clues to help figure out the meaning. Look at the other words around it. Sometimes they give you information that can help you figure out the word.

Example: That <u>horse</u> is so <u>small</u>! I think she is <u>still</u> a foal.

You may not know what a foal is, but from these two sentences, you know that it is a type of horse, that it is small, and that it won't be a foal forever. That is enough clues to guess that it is a baby horse!

■ Read the sentences and match the red words to their meanings.

After you eat an apple, you can discard the core in the garbage can.	shake
I see my reflection in the mirror.	thow away
When my dog hears someone at the door, she trembles with fear.	an image that is shown back

■ Use the underlined words to determine the meaning of the words in red.

Last week, my family went to the Grand Canyon. It was amazing! We stood at the <u>top</u> and could see all the way <u>down</u> to the <u>bottom</u>. It was <u>rocky</u> and <u>dusty</u>.
There was a park ranger named Theresa. She <u>works</u> there, and she <u>told us all about</u> the area. She also gave us <u>safety tips</u>. The Grand Canyon is in a desert, so it's important to drink a lot of <u>water</u> while you are there. You should also make sure you don't get too <u>hot</u>.

Canyon ➜

park ranger ➜

desert ➜

Brain Break
Vocab Word Search

hurled	threw	tossed	desert
canyon	discard	reflection	

T	L	S	R	E	V	P	R	R	C
O	V	N	S	T	H	R	E	W	P
S	C	D	X	U	U	U	F	U	X
S	D	E	Z	R	R	Y	L	P	C
E	W	S	F	L	L	O	E	O	A
D	I	E	T	R	E	L	C	L	N
R	J	R	Y	Y	D	K	T	M	Y
S	U	T	U	Z	R	L	I	I	O
T	H	P	R	Y	N	M	O	H	N
X	G	B	T	U	A	N	N	O	E
D	I	S	C	A	R	D	M	S	Q

■ Use your finger to trace the path.
  Take a deep breath in at each circle and exhale out at each square.

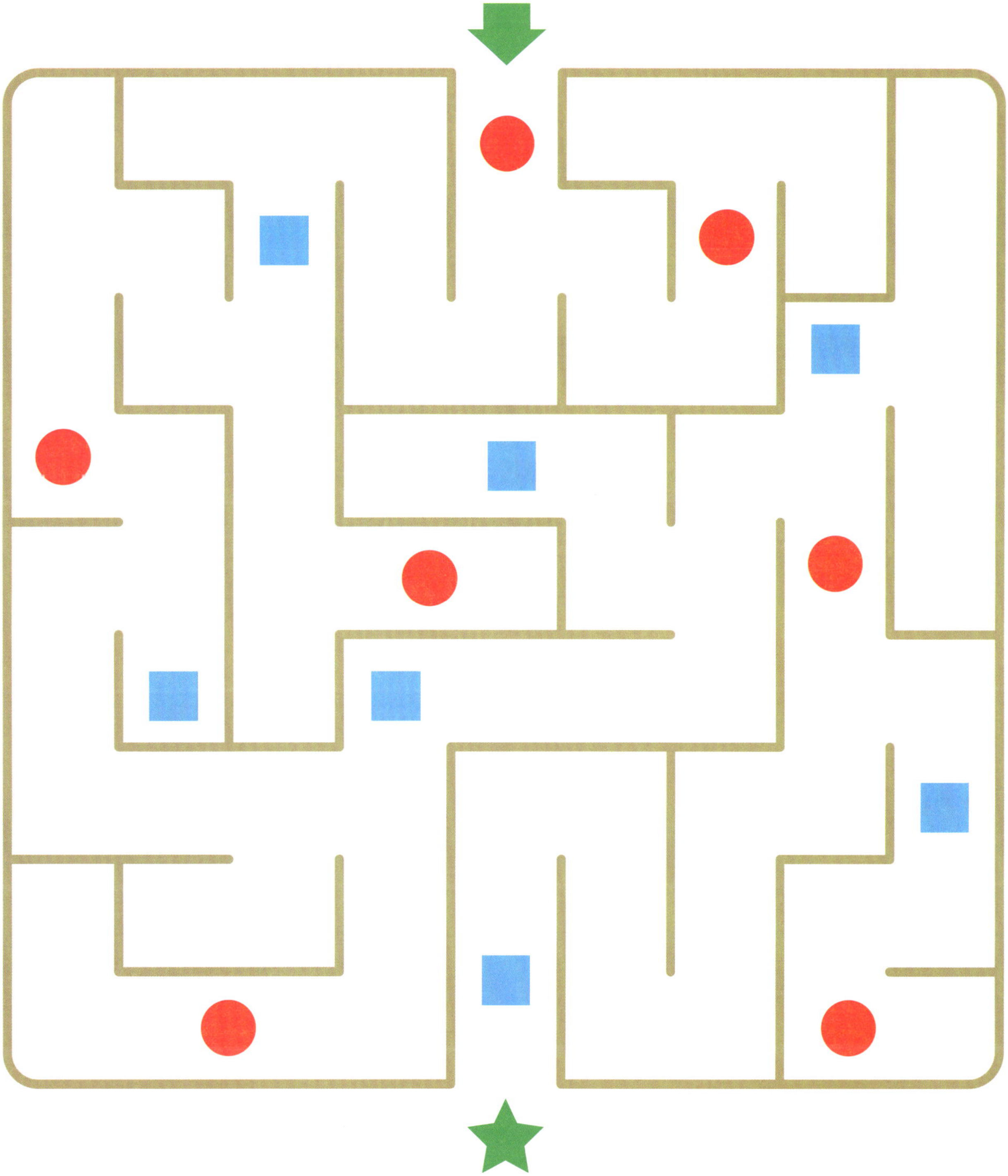

Five W Questions

KEY POINTS

When we read, we can ask ourselves questions to make sure we understand the text. There are five questions that start with *W* that can help: Who, What, When, Where, Why?

These questions ask: Who was in the story? What happened? When did it happen? Where did it happen? Why did it happen?

■ Read the story below. Then a̶ he five W questions.

Once, long ago, a̶ ̶med Cinderella lived in a small town w̶ ̶r family. She wanted to go to the ball. ̶he didn't have a dress to wear! Her family wouldn't help. So her friends had to make her a dress instead.

Who _____

What _____

When _____

Where _____

Why _____

■ Read the story below. Then answer the five W questions.

It was finally spring and Aleysha was ready. This year she was going to win the science fair! She made her poster and brought it into school. When she got to school, she felt nervous. There were a lot of other great projects! But when everyone was done presenting, the teacher called her name. "Aleysha, you are the winner of this year's science fair!"

Who _____

What _____

When _____

Where _____

Why _____

Main Idea

The main idea is what a story is all about. Some stories have a central message. That is the thing that the author most wants you to understand.

■ Read the story. Then circle the central message.

Reilly really wanted to see an owl. He could hear them outside when he was in the house. But when he came running outside, they were gone. "You're scaring them," his mom said. "You have to be patient and wait for them to come out." Reilly stood outside with his mother. They waited and waited. Finally, he looked up and saw an owl overhead. It was beautiful!

Owls come out at night time.

Sometimes you have to be patient to get what you want.

Reilly's mom is strict.

Stacey was new to Pine Ridge Elementary School. She had just moved with her family two weeks ago. Stacey was nervous. At her old school, she loved to play basketball with her friends. But she didn't know anyone at her new school. Her mom told her, "Just be yourself." At lunchtime, Stacey saw a group of kids playing basketball. "Can I join you?" she asked. "Absolutely! You're welcome to play any time," they said.

Central message:

_____

_____

_____

_____

Story Elements

The characters, or people in a story, have all sorts of things happen to them. These are events. You can learn a lot about a character by seeing how they react to different events.

■ Read the story and choose the correct answer.

Will went looking for Frank. He wanted to play baseball with him. But then he saw Frank was already playing baseball with their friend Lila. Will wondered, "Why didn't Frank wait for me?"

How did Will feel at the end?

☐ Excited to play with Frank

☐ Sad that Frank was playing with someone else

☐ Angry that he couldn't find Frank

■ Read the story and write the correct answer.

> Viviana didn't want to teach her sister, Lola, how to play piano. She wanted to play by herself. But her mom told her she had to. "She's young. And she wants to be just like you!" she said. Viviana's friends told her not to. "Just play by yourself," they said. But Viviana decided to give it a try. Lola looked so excited.

How do you think Viviana feels at the end of the story?

_____

_____

_____

_____

_____

Drama

A play is a live performance where actors act out a story for an audience. Most plays have multiple characters, or people in the play.

■ Read the dialogue below out loud. Use a different voice for each character or ask another person to read with you. When you're done, draw a picture that shows how you imagine each character.

> **Alice:** I need to get a present for my mom. But I'm not sure what to get.
>
> **Dan:** I can help you! What does she like?
>
> **Alice:** Hmm, let's see. She likes to read. She loves to bake. And her favorite food is pizza.
>
> **Dan:** Ok, let's take a look.
>
> **Alice:** I hope you have something. Her birthday is tomorrow!
>
> **Dan:** Do you think your mom would like a cookbook that teaches you how to bake pizza?
>
> **Alice:** Oh, that's perfect! You saved the day!

Alice

Dan

■ Read the dialogue out loud. Then write three things you notice about each character.

> **Maria:** Hooray! You're here! I was worried no one else would come.
> **Corey:** I'm here! I wouldn't miss it. This movie club is going to be so fun.
> **Maria:** Let's pick our movie. I like scary movies. How about you?
> **Corey:** No way! I get too scared. I like funny movies.
> **Maria:** What if it's just a little scary?
> **Corey:** I'll never be able to fall asleep!
> **Maria:** Ok, fine. Funny it is. But then I get to pick the snack!

Maria

Corey

Brain Break
Tongue Twisters

■ Read the tongue twisters out loud. How fast can you say them?

> Rubber baby buggy bumpers.

> Peter Piper picked a peck of pickled peppers.

> She sells seashells by the sea shore. The sea shells that she sells are sea shells, I'm sure!

> Fuzzy Wuzzy was a bear. Fuzzy Wuzzy had no hair. Fuzzy Wuzzy wasn't fuzzy, was he?

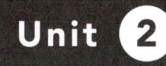

Mindfulness Break!

Be in the present moment. Write what you see, hear, feel, and smell right now.

■ Write a response for each sentence.

❶ Right now I see...

❷ Right now I hear...

❸ Right now I feel...

❹ Right now I smell...

2-Digit Addition 1

■ Add.

1
$$12 + 3 = 15$$

2
$$36 + 2$$

3
$$24 + 15$$

4
$$40 + 27$$

5
$$89 + 10$$

6
$$51 + 36$$

■ Add. Then draw a line to the problem with the same answer.

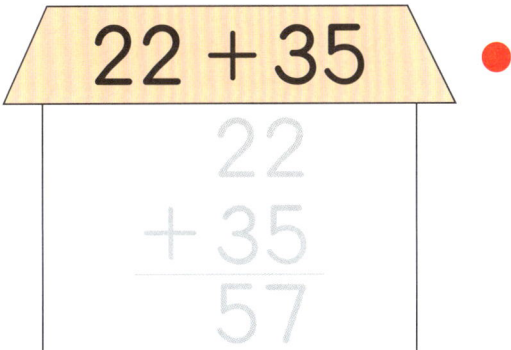

22 + 35

```
  22
+ 35
  57
```

21 + 43

```
+
```

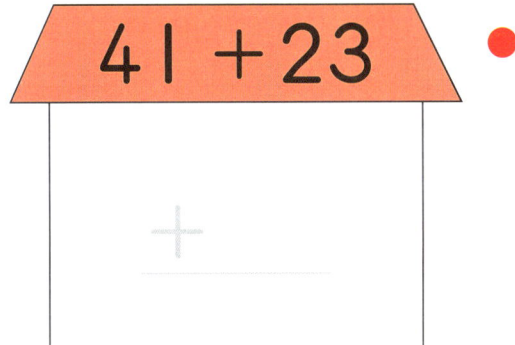

75 + 14

```
  75
+ 14
```

46 + 11

```
+
```

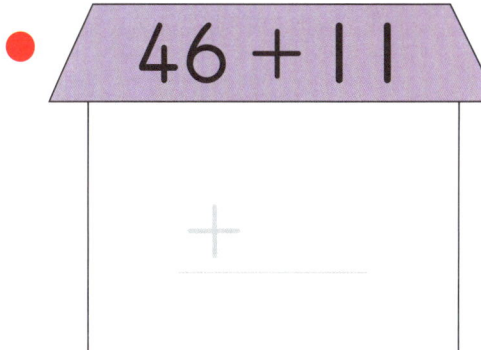

41 + 23

```
+
```

54 + 23

```
+
```

30 + 47

```
+
```

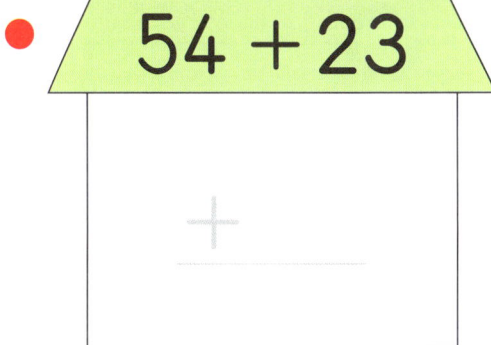

39 + 50

```
+
```

2-Digit Addition 2

■ Add.

1
```
  1
  16
+  7
  23
```

2
```
  42
+  9
```

3
```
  28
+ 14
```

4
```
  55
+ 26
```

5
```
  77
+ 43
```

6
```
  34
+ 68
```

■ Add. Then draw a line to the problem with the same answer.

46 + 29

```
  46
+ 29
```

●

●

86 + 38

```
+
```

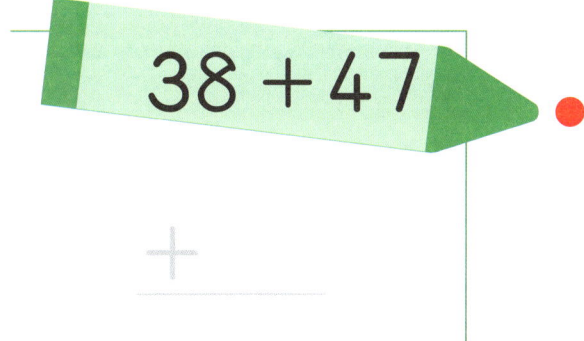

38 + 47 ●

```
+
```

●

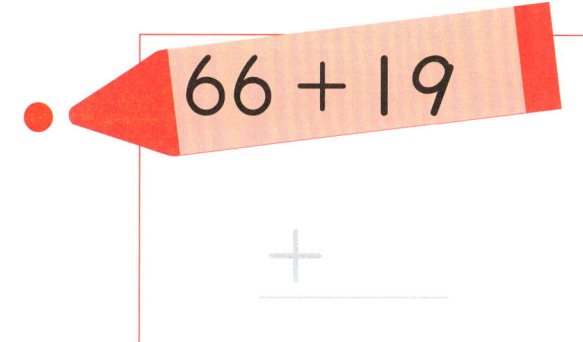

66 + 19

```
+
```

95 + 17 ●

```
+
```

● 38 + 37

```
+
```

59 + 65 ●

```
+
```

● 43 + 69

```
+
```

Adding Three Numbers

■ Write a check mark (✔) by the larger answer.

$$\begin{array}{r} 13 \\ 44 \\ +22 \\ \hline \end{array}$$

☐

$$\begin{array}{r} 50 \\ 12 \\ +16 \\ \hline \end{array}$$

☐

$$\begin{array}{r} 15 \\ 17 \\ +26 \\ \hline \end{array}$$

☐

$$\begin{array}{r} 14 \\ 39 \\ +21 \\ \hline \end{array}$$

☐

$$\begin{array}{r} 38 \\ 43 \\ +19 \\ \hline \end{array}$$

☐

$$\begin{array}{r} 30 \\ 55 \\ +\ 5 \\ \hline \end{array}$$

☐

■ **Add. Then circle the three problems with the same answer.**

1
```
   32
 + 50
 ____
```

4
```
   45
 + 38
 ____
```

7
```
   24
   14
 + 31
 ____
```

2
```
   50
    7
 + 26
 ____
```

5
```
   23
 + 61
 ____
```

8
```
   49
 + 33
 ____
```

3
```
   57
 + 67
 ____
```

6
```
   42
   40
 + 11
 ____
```

9
```
   61
 + 22
 ____
```

2-Digit Subtraction

■ Subtract.

1.
$$\begin{array}{r} 28 \\ -\,13 \\ \hline 15 \end{array}$$

2.
$$\begin{array}{r} 46 \\ -\,12 \\ \hline \end{array}$$

3.
$$\begin{array}{r} 17 \\ -\,5 \\ \hline \end{array}$$

4.
$$\begin{array}{r} 98 \\ -\,57 \\ \hline \end{array}$$

5.
$$\begin{array}{r} 68 \\ -\,26 \\ \hline \end{array}$$

6.
$$\begin{array}{r} 74 \\ -\,34 \\ \hline \end{array}$$

Date

Great Job
Sticker

■ Subtract. Then draw a line to the problem with the same answer.

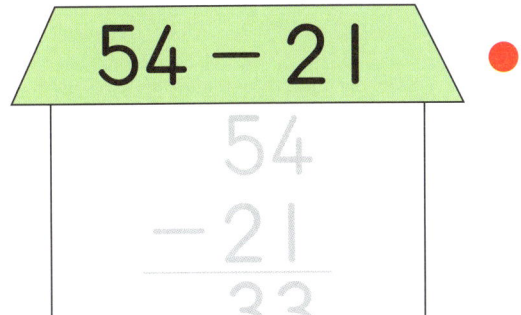

54 − 21

    54
  − 21
    33

● ●

44 − 21

38 − 15

    38
  − 15

● ●

28 − 4

74 − 42

● ●

65 − 33

97 − 73

● ●

86 − 53

3-Digit Subtraction

■ Subtract.

1.

$$\begin{array}{r} {}^{2}\cancel{3}{}^{12}\cancel{2} \\ -\ 13 \\ \hline 19 \end{array}$$

2.

$$\begin{array}{r} 45 \\ -\ 18 \\ \hline \end{array}$$

3.

$$\begin{array}{r} 84 \\ -\ 7 \\ \hline \end{array}$$

4.

$$\begin{array}{r} 90 \\ -\ 42 \\ \hline \end{array}$$

5.

$$\begin{array}{r} {}^{0}\cancel{1}\ {}^{1}1\ {}^{16}\cancel{6} \\ -\ \ 79 \\ \hline 47 \end{array}$$

6.

$$\begin{array}{r} 113 \\ -\ \ 35 \\ \hline \end{array}$$

■ Subtract. Then draw a line to the problem with the same answer.

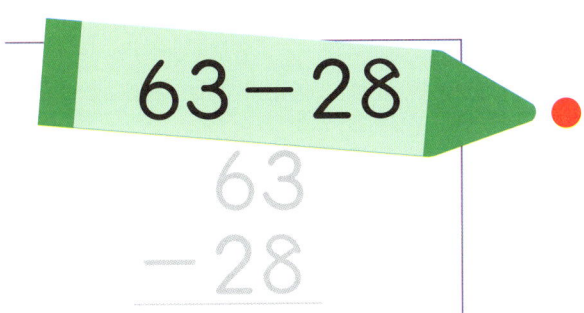

63 − 28

$$63$$
$$-28$$

82 − 37

141 − 54

113 − 46

122 − 35

76 − 9

134 − 89

51 − 16

Brain Break
Maze

■ Trace a path from the start to the goal, traveling through squares where the answer is 15.

START

8 + 7	15 − 9	5 + 15	15 + 3	15 − 5
7 + 8	6 + 9	15 + 5	18 − 15	15 − 10
15 − 7	9 + 6	20 − 5	18 − 3	10 + 5
15 − 8	15 − 6	20 − 15	3 + 15	5 + 10

GOAL

Maze Break!

■ Trace the path from start to finish!

Landforms

Earth's surface is covered in land and water. Landforms are natural features on the earth's surface like mountains, plateaus, canyons, and valleys.

■ **Answer the questions.**

❶ What is a landform?

❷ Name two examples of landforms.

■ Read the description and match the landforms.

A valley is a low area of land between hills or mountains.

A canyon is a deep valley with steep sides made by a water carving through rocks over a very long time.

A mountain is a big and tall landform that rises high above the land around it.

A plateau is a landform that rises above the land around it and has a flat top.

Water on Earth

KEY POINTS

About 70 percent of the earth's surface is covered in water. Oceans, lakes, ponds, rivers, and streams are examples of bodies of water. The earth's surface also has frozen water in the form of glaciers. Most lakes, rivers, and ponds have fresh water. Oceans have salt water.

■ Answer the questions.

1 How much of the earth's surface is covered in water?

_____

2 What are some examples of bodies on water?

_____

■ Label the bodies of water in the picture. Use the Word Box for help.

Word Box

glacier   pond   river   lake   ocean

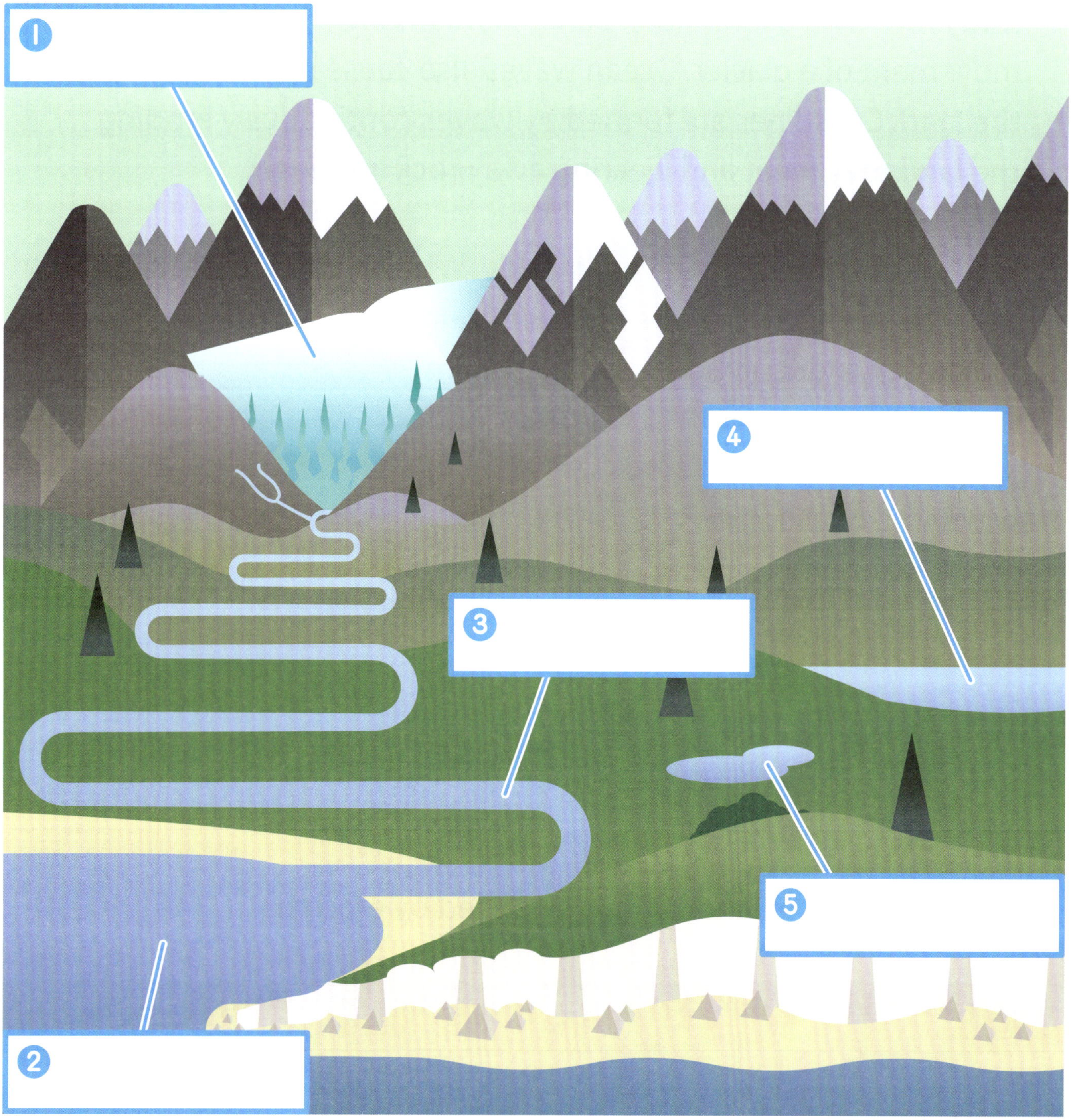

1.

2.

3.

4.

5.

Unit 2 Science

Erosion

KEY POINTS

Erosion is when wind, water, or ice slowly wear away rocks and soil, changing the land over time. Erosion helps form many of the earth's natural features. Canyons are made when water wears away rock over a long time. Some plateaus are shaped by the slow movement of a glacier. Ocean waves also cause major erosion to the land. Coastlines are formed by waves continuously eroding the land they meet and wearing away rock into sand.

Erosion can also happen very quickly. When wind and water wear away too much of the side of a mountain it can cause a landslide to happen suddenly.

■ Answer the questions.

❶ What is erosion?

_____

❷ What types of landforms are created by erosion?

_____

■ Look at the landforms. Write what type of erosion create them. Then answer if erosion happened quickly or slowly.

1

Coastline

Type of erosion:

water

Did erosion happen quickly or slowly?

2

Canyon

Type of erosion:

Did erosion happen quickly or slowly?

3

Plateau

Type of erosion:

Did erosion happen quickly or slowly?

KEY POINTS

Erosion is sometimes caused by natural forces like wind and water. It can also be caused by the actions of people. This type of erosion can be bad for the earth. Below are some solutions to help slow down bad erosion.

Hurricanes can wash away sand from beaches. People use barriers to help keep the sand on the beaches. They can also use tractors to add more sand to beaches where storms have washed it away.

People can make soil erosion worse. Too much farming can cause soil to erode faster. Less soil means fewer plants can grow. Then the animals who eat these plants have less food.

■ Read the questions below and check (✓) if the answer is true or false.

❶ Erosion is always a slow process.

True　False

❷ Hurricanes can cause beach erosion.

True　False

❸ The actions of people can make erosion worse.

True　False

❹ There is nothing people can do to slow down erosion.

True　False

Brain Break
Science Journal 2

Look around your town or state. What types of landforms are there? How many can you name? Draw your favorite in the box below.

Art Break!

■ Recall what you learned about landforms in this section. Make your own map using different landforms!

US Government

KEY POINTS

In the United States, there are three different levels of government: federal, state, and local. We vote to choose people in each level of government. This form of government is called a democracy. The federal government handles relationships between the US and other countries. It is also in charge of printing money and running the military. State governments are in charge of education, healthcare, and safety. Local governments provide services to their communities such as parks, police, and firefighters.

■ Answer the questions.

❶ What are the three levels of the United States government?

_____

❷ Which level of government handles relationships with other countries?

_____

❸ Which level of government provides communities with local parks?

_____

■ Write the services each level of government would provide.

Word Box

| local parks | fire stations | print money |

| military | schools | healthcare | police |

relationships with other countries

❶ Federal Government

❷ State Government

❸ Local Government

Government: Branches

The federal government is the national or country-wide level of government. In the United States, it is separated into three branches: the legislative branch, the judicial branch, and the executive branch. The three branches work together to make sure power is balanced in the government and that no branch is more powerful than the other. This creates a system of checks and balances.

The legislative branch is made up of two groups, the Senate and the House of Representatives. These two groups make up Congress. They are in charge of making laws for the country.

The judicial branch is made up of courts and judges. They are in charge of making sure people follow the laws.

The executive branch has several important powers, including approving or rejecting laws made by Congress and commanding the military. The president of the United States is in charge of this branch of government.

■ Read the questions below and check (✔) if the answer is true or false.

❶ There are three branches of the federal government.

True False

❷ The checks and balance system gives all the power to the executive branch.

True False

❸ The president works in the judicial branch.

True False

❹ The legislative branch is made up of two groups: the Senate and the House of Representatives.

True False

❺ The legislative branch makes the laws.

True False

Presidents

KEY POINTS

The head of the United States government is the president. The president of the US is a member of the executive branch. One of the main jobs of the president is to approve or reject laws from the Congress. The president also has a cabinet, or a group of people including the vice president, to help them make decisions about things that effect the country. As of 2024, the United States has had 45 presidents.

■ Answer the questions.

❶ Who is the head of the United States government?

_____

❷ What branch of government does the president belong to?

_____

❸ What is one of the president's main jobs?

_____

■ **Use the information below to answer questions about past presidents.**

George Washington was the first president of the United States. He is known for leading the Continental Army to victory over the British in the American Revolutionary War.

Abraham Lincoln was the 16th president of the United States. He is known for leading the country during the Civil War and pushing for the freedom of all enslaved people throughout the country.

Franklin D. Roosevelt was the 32nd President of the United States. He is best known for leading the US during the Great Depression and leading the Us through World War II. He also put the New Deal in place to improve people's lives during the Great Depression.

Barack Obama was the 44th President of the United States. He is most famous for being the first African-American president and for signing a law to make healthcare available to more people.

❶ Who was the first president of the United States?

❸ Which president led the country through the Great Depression?

❷ What is President Lincoln known for?

❹ What is President Obama most known for?

The United States has local governments as well as federal and state governments. Local government organizations include a county, a city, or a town government. The roles of these governments are different from state to state, but they are responsible for making and enforcing local laws. They are also in charge of public school funding, police and fire department funding, local courts, and local parks. They also collect tax money from the people who live in their area to help fund these organizations.

■ Answer the questions.

❶ What is the role of local government?

❷ What services do local governments provide?

■ **Match the service to the level of government in charge of it.**

Local

Federal

Create local parks

Approve new laws

Collect taxes

Fund public schools

Support police
officers and
firefighters

Brain Break
Crossword Puzzle

■ Use the clues to complete the crossword puzzle.

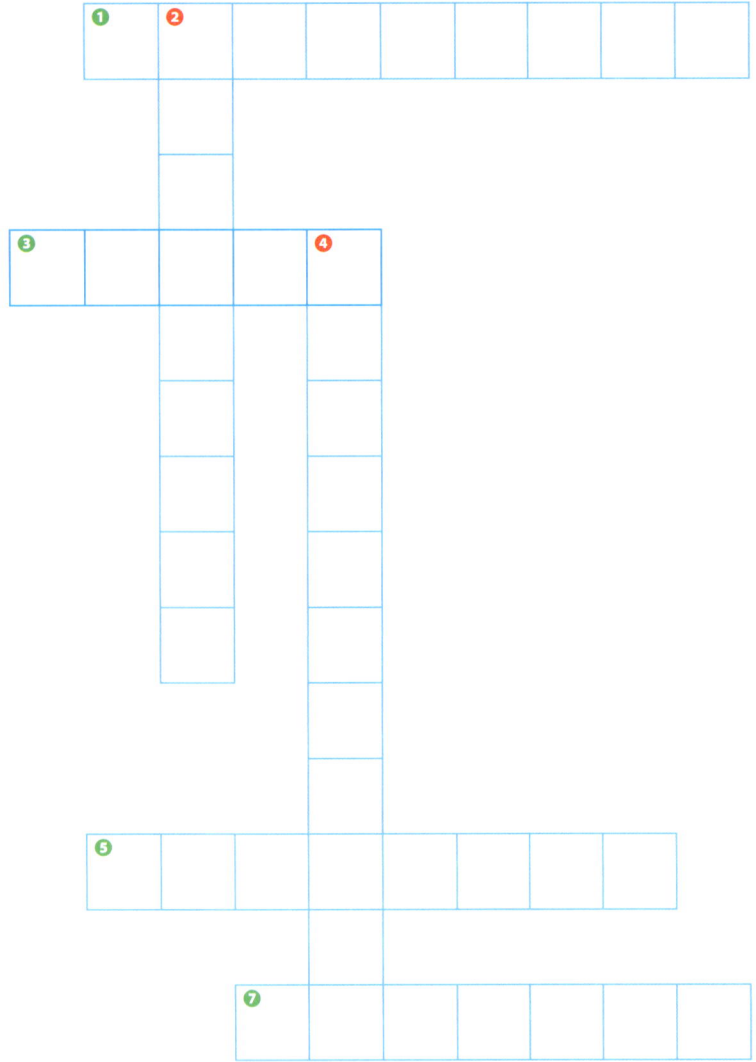

Across
❶ A government where officals are voted on by the people.

❸ The type of government found in a town or county.

❺ The branch of the US government in charge of the courts.

❼ A type of government that handles relationships between the US and other countries.

Down
❷ The branch of US government that the president is a part of.

❹ The branch of the US government in charge of making new laws.

■ Color the picture.

■ Write the correct arrow in the box for the car to go from start to goal.

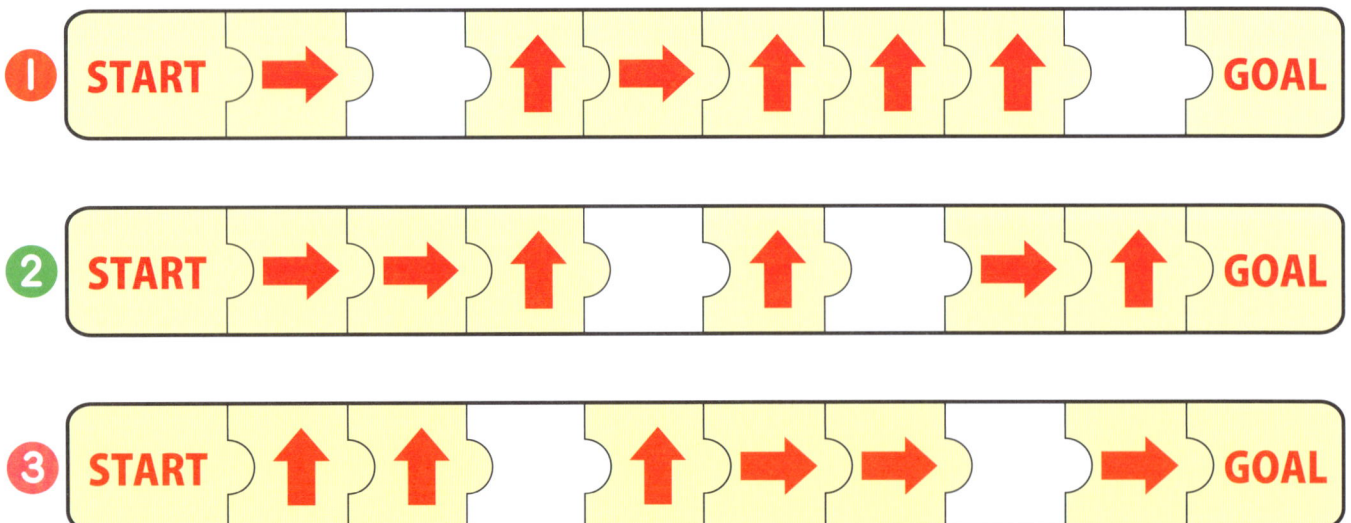

■ Which child is saying the correct sequence of the shapes? Write a check mark (✔) in the box.

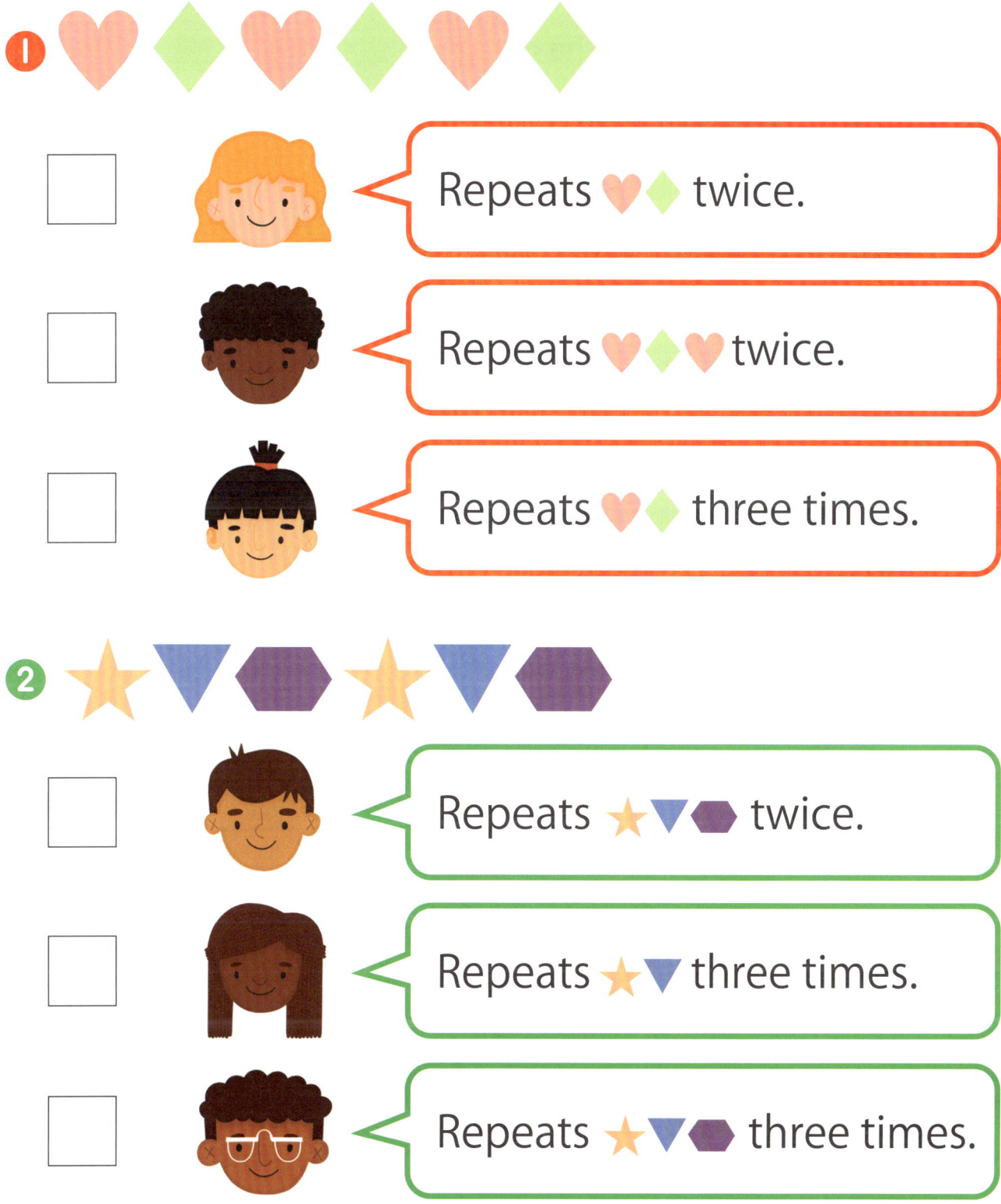

1

☐ Repeats ♥◆ twice.

☐ Repeats ♥◆♥ twice.

☐ Repeats ♥◆ three times.

2

☐ Repeats ★▼⬡ twice.

☐ Repeats ★▼ three times.

☐ Repeats ★▼⬡ three times.

■ The direction the robot will travel in depends on the signal at the fork in the road. It will go left at orange, right at green, and straight when both colors are on. Choose the correct place for the robot to arrive and write a check mark (✓) in the box.

1

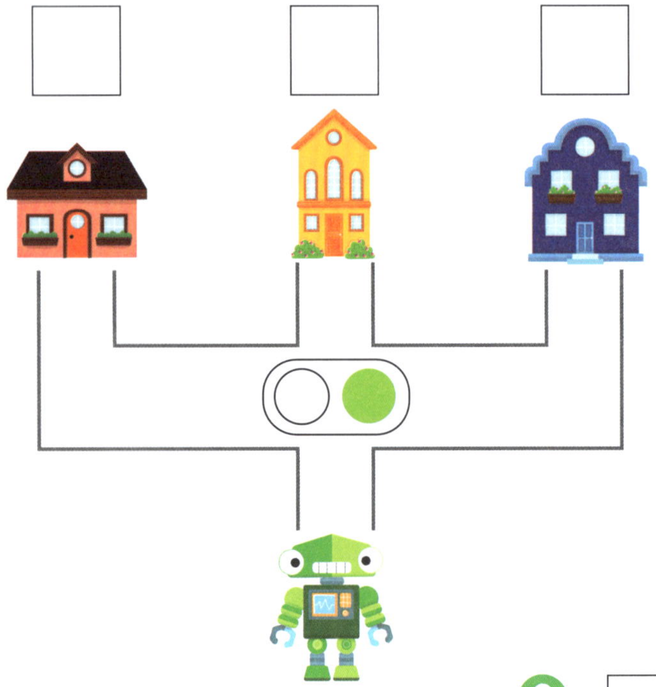

2

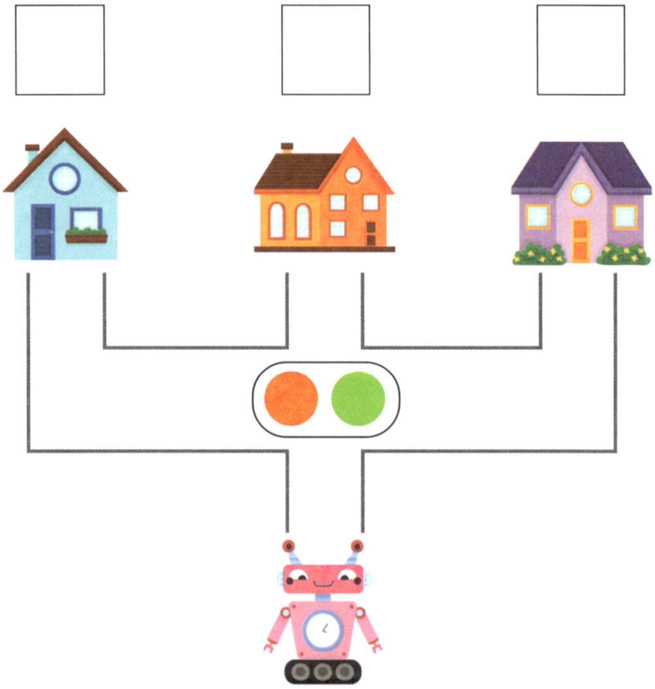

■ The direction the robot will travel in depends on the signal at the fork in the road. It will go left at orange, right at green, and straight when both colors are on. When each robot arrives at the following locations, choose the correct signal and write a check mark (✓) in the box.

1

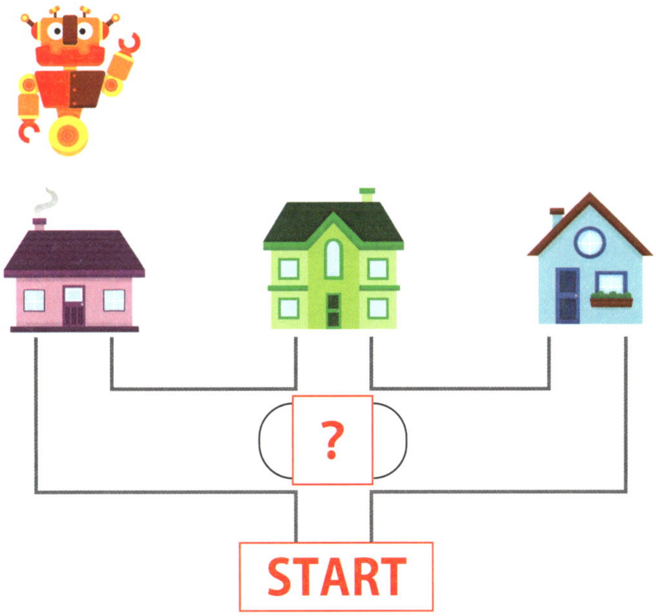

START

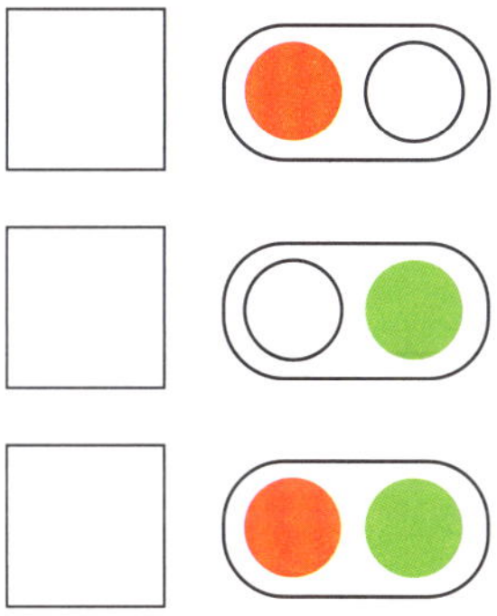

2

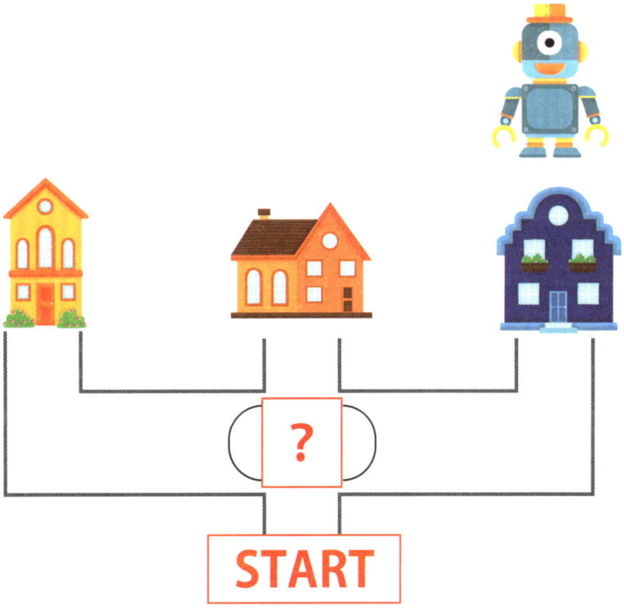

START

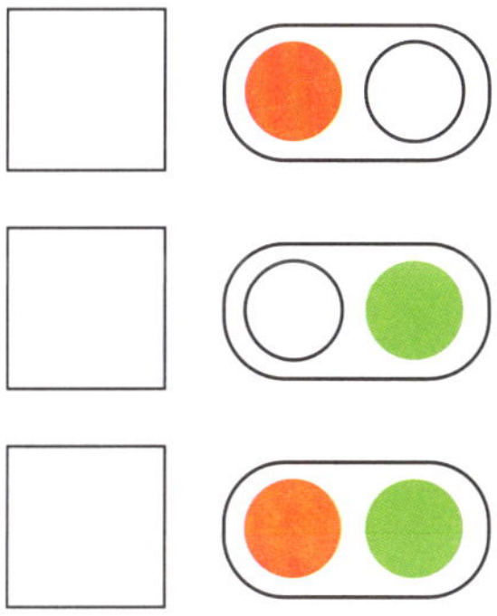

Coding 3

■ Look at the flowchart. Follow the commands below to find out where the robot turtle will end up. Write a check mark (✓) on the flag of the correct color.

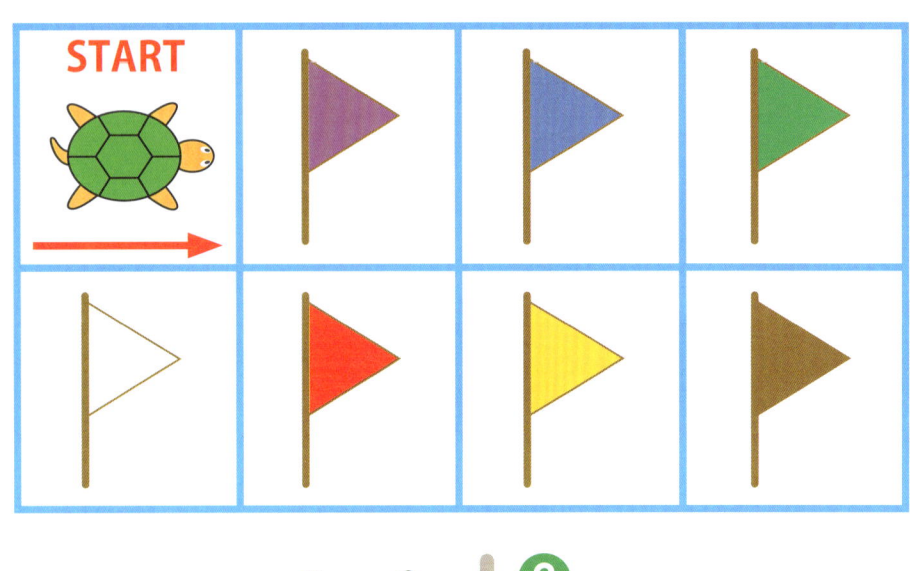

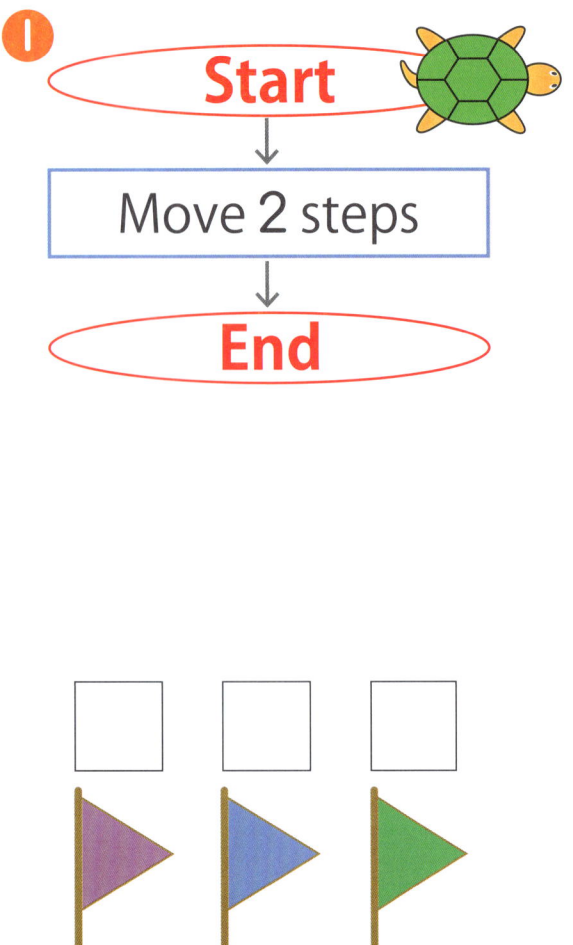

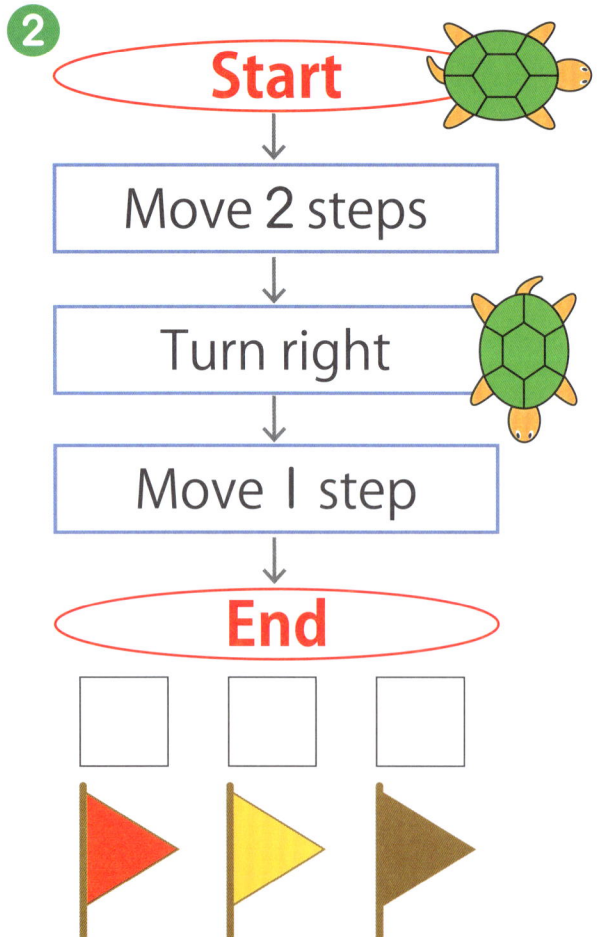

3

Start

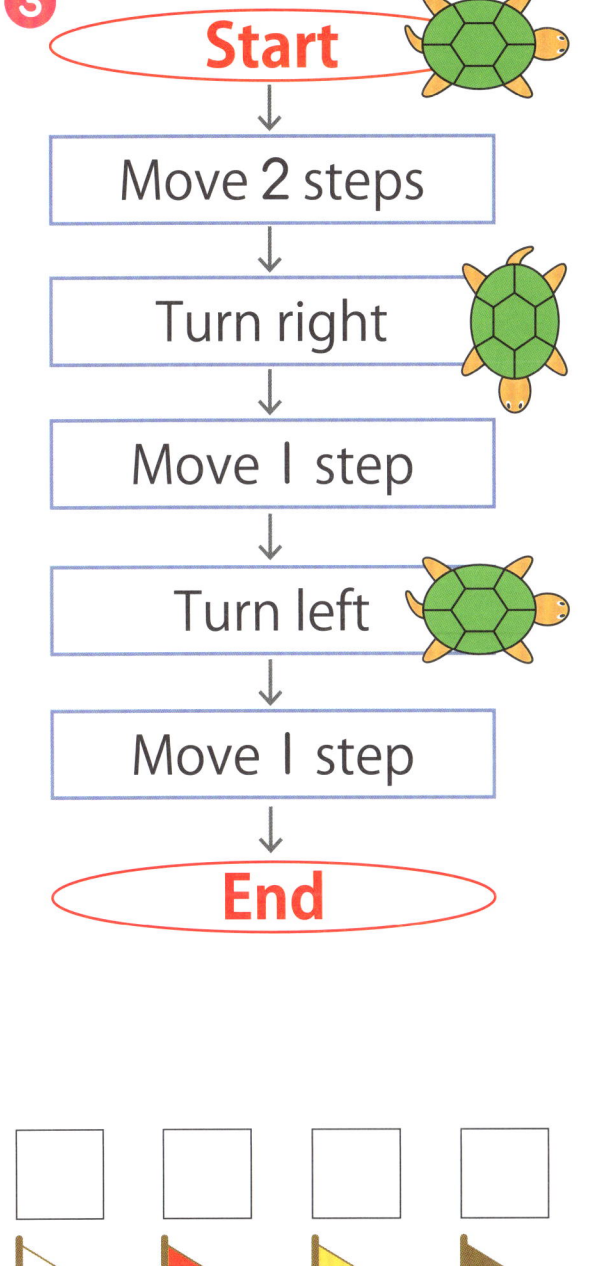

↓

Move 2 steps

↓

Turn right

↓

Move 1 step

↓

Turn left

↓

Move 1 step

↓

End

4

Start

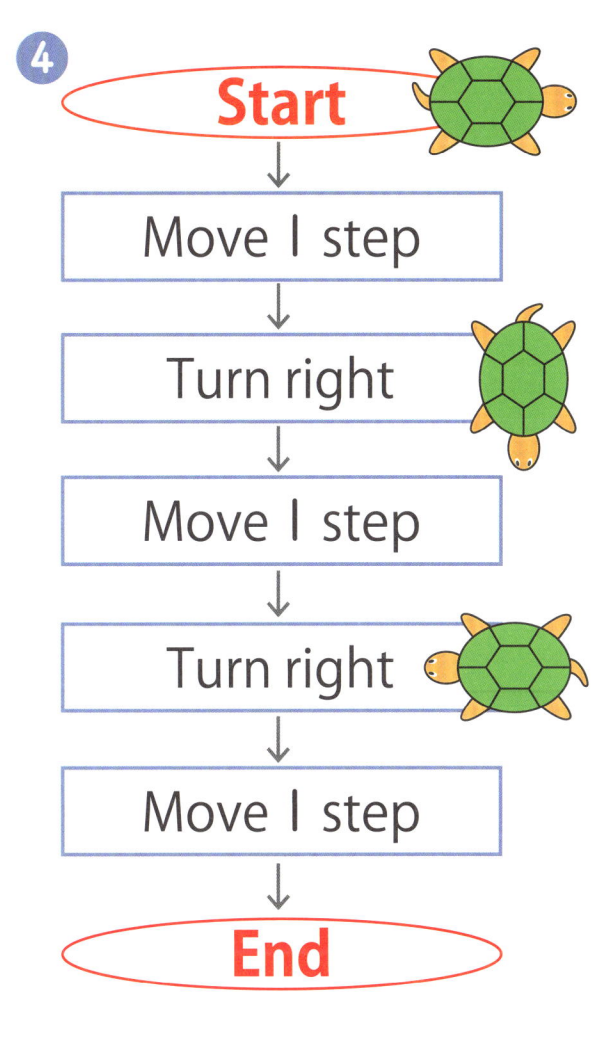

↓

Move 1 step

↓

Turn right

↓

Move 1 step

↓

Turn right

↓

Move 1 step

↓

End

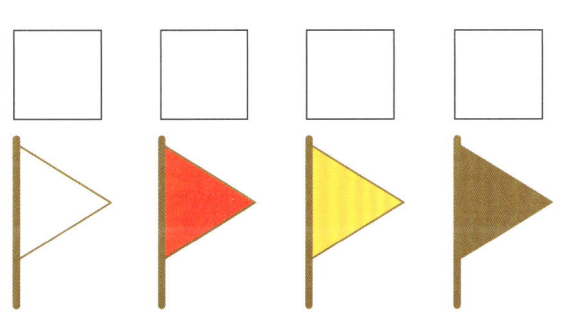

■ Using the flowchart, give the turtle robot the command to move from the start to the goal and pick up the apple along the way. In the flowchart on the next page, choose the correct command to fill in the blanks and write a check mark (✓) in the box for each.

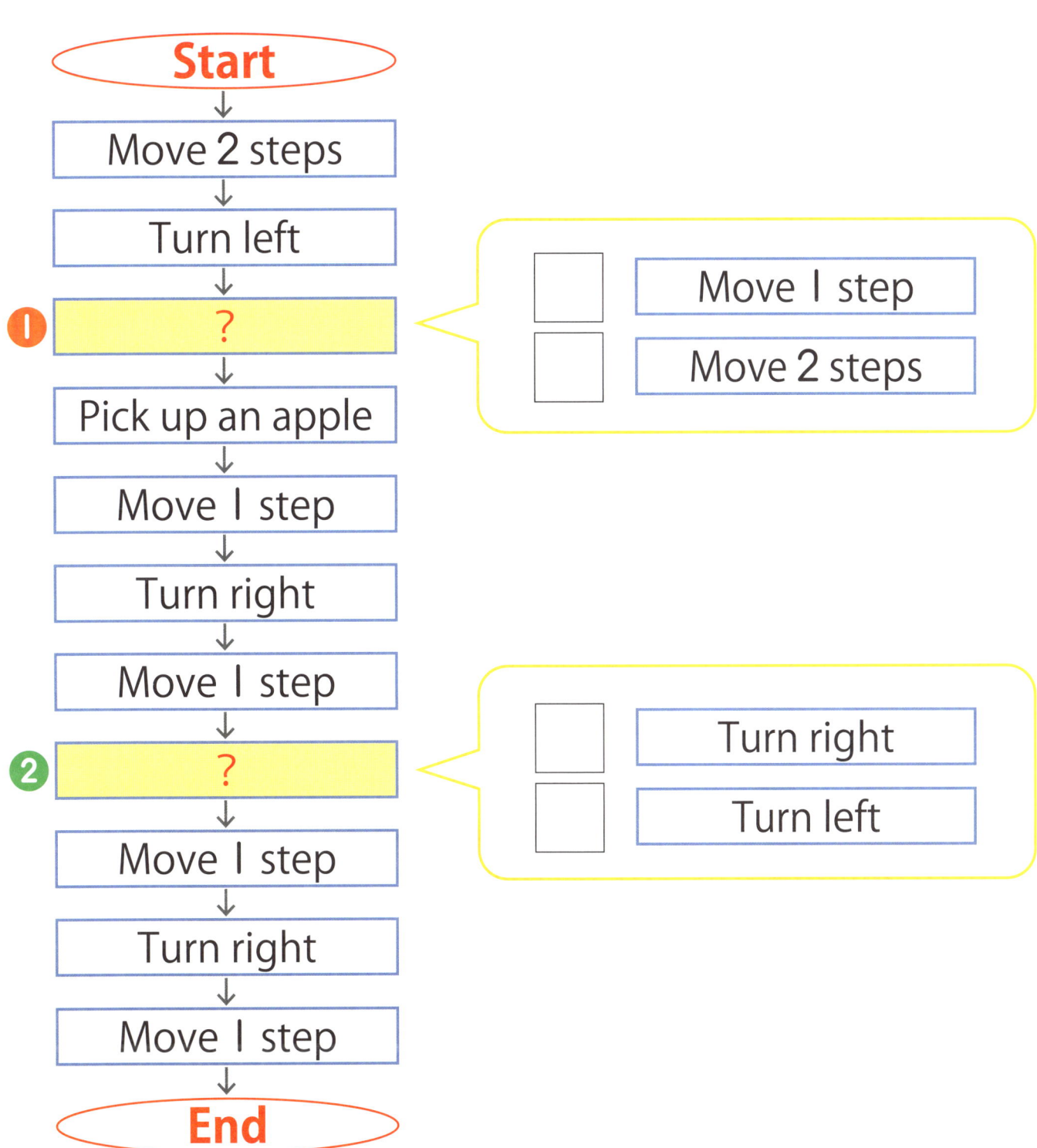

Start

↓

Move 2 steps

↓

Turn left

↓

1 ?

☐ Move 1 step

☐ Move 2 steps

↓

Pick up an apple

↓

Move 1 step

↓

Turn right

↓

Move 1 step

↓

2 ?

☐ Turn right

☐ Turn left

↓

Move 1 step

↓

Turn right

↓

Move 1 step

↓

End

It's important to move your body and exercise!
Try this fun activity below for a study break!

■ Follow the instructions to move like an animal!

Frog jumps!

Squat down and hop like a frog.

Elephant Stomps!

March in place, stomping your feet as hard as you can!

Flamingo Balance!

Try balancing as long as you can on one leg like a flamingo. Then try the other leg!

Crab Walk!

Sit down, place your palms on the ground behind you and lift your hips off the ground. Walk backwards like a crab!

Starfish Jumps

Jump up and down, spreading your arms wide like a starfish. Think of it like a jumping jack!

Did you try all five animal moves?

Unit **3** Table of Contents

Use this page to keep track of your progress throughout the book. Place a check mark in the box when you have completed a section.

■ You can use clues from the illustration and the passage to answer the question. Read the story. Then choose the correct answer.

> Marcus had a secret. It was his friend Luna's birthday, but he hadn't seen her yet. Luna wasn't expecting a birthday present. But she was going to be surprised when she saw Marcus!

What is Marcus's secret?

☐ **He knows it is Luna's birthday.**

☐ **He has a balloon for Luna.**

☐ **He saw Luna earlier.**

■ Read the story and look at the picture. Then choose the correct answer.

Sonya couldn't wait to get to school. Usually it took her ten minutes to get to school, but today it took her only two! She went into the building and there it was! The book fair was all set up.

How did Sonya get to school so quickly?

☐ **She was very excited.**

☐ **She ran the whole way.**

☐ **She rode her bicycle.**

Reading Comprehension Literature 2

■ Read the story and look at the picture. Then choose the correct answer.

Stefan was feeling a little lonely. He hadn't seen his friends in a few weeks. But he cheered himself up by taking a walk. He had the most beautiful view. And he was learning so much every day.

Why hasn't Stefan seen his friends in so long?

☐ He is in space.

☐ He is busy learning.

☐ He is feeling lonely.

■ Read the story and look at the picture. Then choose the correct answer.

"Oh no," said Glenn's mom. "Another shirt ruined." Glenn looked at the shirt. It had burn marks on one side and it smelled like smoke. "Sorry, Mom," said Glenn.

Why did Glenn ruin his shirt?

☐ **He didn't like it.**

☐ **He is a dragon.**

☐ **He tried to clean it.**

Reading Comprehension Literature 3

Stories have a beginning, middle, and end. Usually, the beginning introduces the situation. The action happens in the middle. And everything is solved at the end.

■ Circle the beginning of the story.
Underline the middle. Draw a box around the end.

Once upon a time, there was a girl who lived in the forest. She decided to bring her grandmother some muffins. But when she got to her grandmother's house, there was a wolf inside! Luckily, the girl was very brave. She saved her grandmother and threw the wolf out of the house. Then they ate their muffins in peace.

■ Reread the story about the girl who lived in the forest. Then choose the correct answer to each question.

❶ How does the beginning introduce the story?

☐ **It tells how the story ends.**

☐ **It shows the action of the story.**

☐ **It shows the main character and setting.**

❷ What happens in the middle?

☐ **The character is introduced.**

☐ **The setting is described.**

☐ **The action takes place.**

❸ What happens at the end?

☐ **There is a new character.**

☐ **The setting changes.**

☐ **Everything is solved.**

KEY POINTS

Some types of stories teach something. Fables are stories that have a lesson. They often have animals as characters. Myths are old stories that sometimes teach a lesson, or explain something about the world.

■ Read the fable. Then answer the question.

There once was a boy who loved to play tricks. One day, he decided to yell, "Wolf!" Everyone came to help him. But there was no wolf. He did it again the next day. Everyone came to help again. And then he did it again the third day. When everyone came to help, they were angry that he had tricked them again. The very next day, the boy saw a wolf and was very afraid. He yelled, "Wolf!" But no one came to help him. They didn't believe his cries.

What is the lesson? Choose the correct answer.

☐ Don't shout loudly and annoy others.

☐ If you lie, people won't believe you when it is an emergency.

☐ You shouldn't be somewhere where there are wolves.

■ Read the myth. Then answer the question.

Arachne was very good at weaving fabric. But she was also very proud. She said that she could weave even better than the gods. One goddess heard her and became very angry. She challenged Arachne to a contest. Arachne continued to brag and insult the gods. At the end, she the goddess turned Arachne into a spider!

Write the lesson you learned from this myth:

Brain Break
Your Favorite Story

■ Draw what happens in the beginning, middle, and end of your favorite story.

Beginning

Middle

End

Mindfulness Break!

■ Fill in the boxes using the prompts. It's important to try and keep a positive mindset when things don't go our way! Use the chart below to practice changing your mindset about what happened.

Situation: You did not make the team or club you tried out for...

❶ What happened?

❷ Why did it happen?

❸ Can I change the outcome?

❹ If yes: how?

❺ If no: then what's next?

❻ How does it make me feel?

Story Events

KEY POINTS

Stories have events, or things that happen. Most stories have several events. The order of events is important. When you are writing a story, it's important to make sure each event is clear.

■ Place the events below in order.

☐ I decided to make a sandwich.

☐ I saw that we were out of bread.

☐ I was feeling hungry.

☐ I asked my mom if we could go to the store to get bread.

■ Imagine that you are writing a story about your day. Write four events in your day. They can be real or made-up.

❶

❷

❸

❹

Writing with Details

KEY POINTS

Details help make a story feel real for the reader. You can include details about actions, thoughts, or feelings.

Actions: He walked slowly down the road.

Thoughts: He wondered how far away the house was.

Feelings: He felt relieved when he recognized the house.

■ Look at the illustration. Write three details that you see.

❶

❷

❸

■ Look back at the events you wrote that happened to you today.
Write four details to add to the story.

❶

❷

❸

❹

Temporal Words

Temporal words are words that show time. They can help the reader understand the order that the events happen in.

Here are some temporal words: *First*, *next*, *then*, *after*, *before*, *during*.

■ Fill in the blank with a temporal word.

❶ ☐ we went to the movie.

❷ ☐ we had dinner.

❸ ☐ dinner, we ate dessert.

❹ ☐ the movie, we ate popcorn.

■ Fill in the blanks with temporal words to complete the story.

I had a great day today! ☐ I got up

and had breakfast. ☐ I went for a

walk with my mom. ☐ I read my book.

☐ it was time for lunch. I had soup!

☐ , I called my grandma to wish her a

happy birthday.

143

Closure

KEY POINTS

Usually stories end with something that gives the reader closure. It could be a happy ending, or maybe a thoughtful ending.

■ Choose the sentence that would make the best ending for the story below.

Over the summer, we visited my aunt and uncle in New Mexico. It was my first time going, and I didn't know what to expect. I surprised by how hot it was! I also saw a lot of cactus. It felt very different.

☐ I ate ice cream to cool off.

☐ But once I saw my family, I felt right at home.

☐ I also saw a rabbit with very long ears.

■ Look back at the events and details you wrote about your day. Use what you wrote to create a story about what happened to you. Make sure to include temporal words and an ending.

Brain Break
What is Happening in the Picture?

■ What is happening in the picture? Write your own words for each character.

Mindfulness Break!

■ Write a letter to someone in your family and say something nice that they did for you.

_____

_____

_____

_____

_____

_____

_____

Length 1

■ How long is each bar? Answer in inches.

1

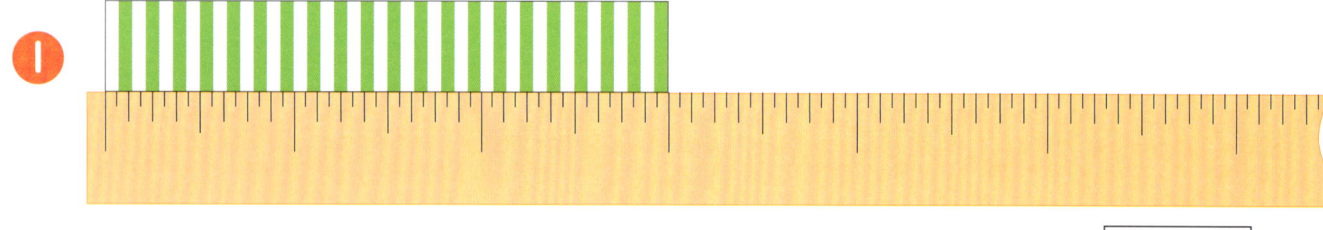

3 in.

2

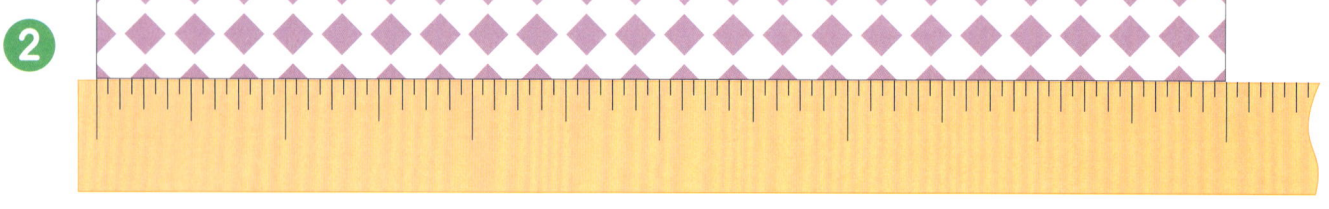

in.

3

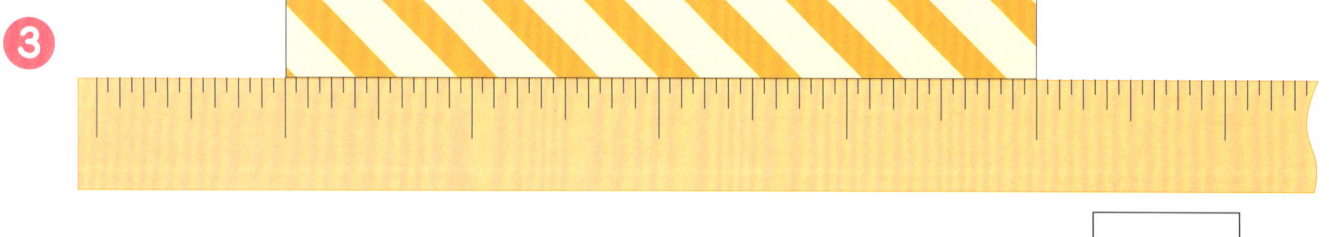

in.

4

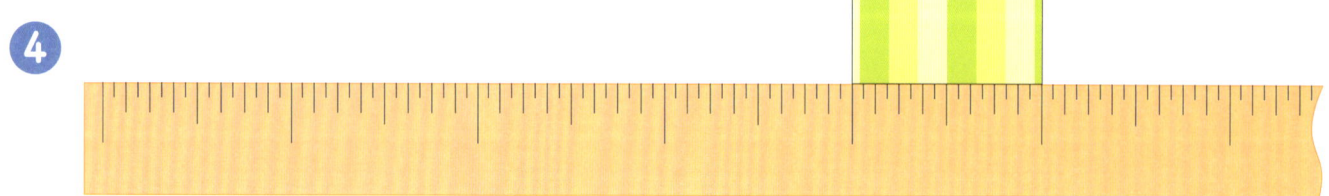

in.

■ **Answer the following questions.**

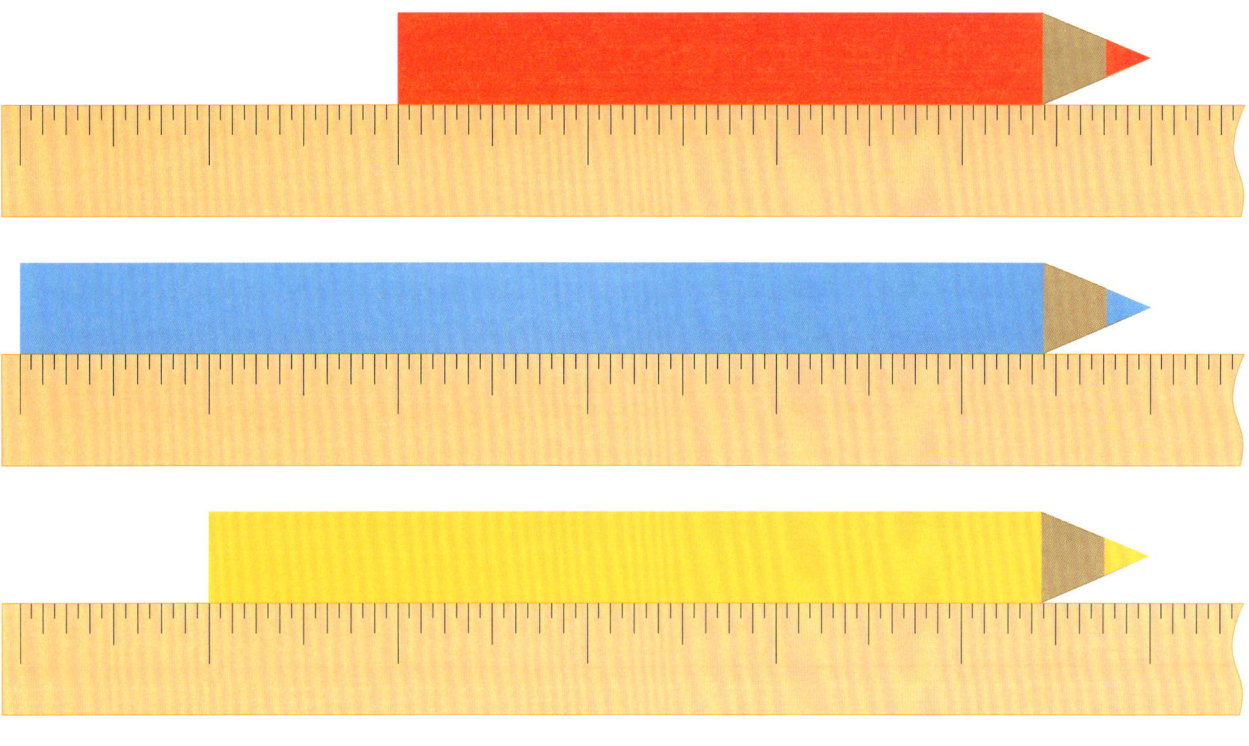

❶ How long is each colored pencil?

red ☐ in.   blue ☐ in.   yellow ☐ in.

❷ Which is longer, the red or the blue pencil?

The ☐ pencil is ☐ in. longer.

❸ Which is longer, the blue or the yellow pencil?

The ☐ pencil is ☐ in. longer.

❹ Which is longer, the red or the yellow pencil?

The ☐ pencil is ☐ in. longer.

Length 2

12 inches (in.) = 1 foot (ft.)

■ Write the appropriate number in each box.

1 1 ft. 3 in. = 15 in.

2 1 ft. 8 in. = ☐ in.

3 2 ft. = ☐ in.

4 2 ft. 2 in. = ☐ in.

5 14 in. = 1 ft. 2 in.

6 17 in. = ☐ ft. ☐ in.

7 21 in. = ☐ ft. ☐ in.

8 25 in. = ☐ ft. ☐ in.

■ Circle the answer that gives the best estimate.

①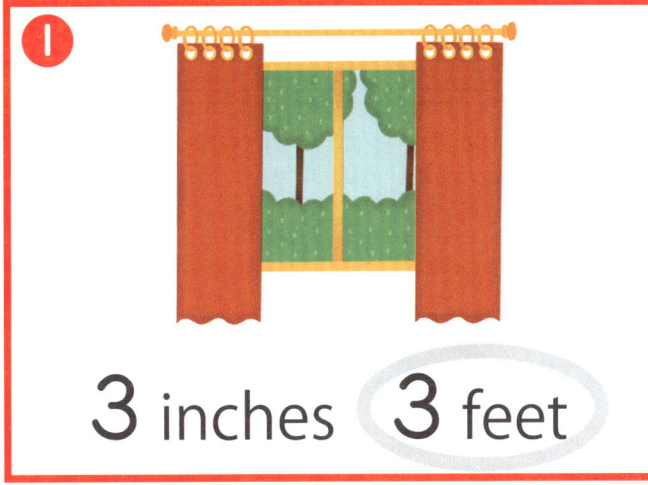

3 inches (3 feet)

②

5 inches 5 feet

③

10 inches 10 feet

④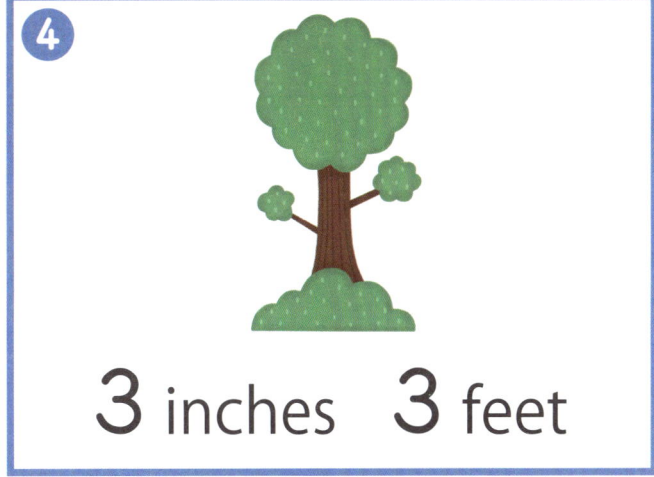

3 inches 3 feet

⑤

20 inches 20 feet

⑥

6 inches 6 feet

Weight

■ **Read the weight on each scale and write it below.**

1

 2 lb.

4

lb.

2

 lb.

5

lb.

3

lb.

6

 lb.

■ Which is the heaviest bag? Write a check mark (✓) in the box.

Telling Time 1

KEY POINTS

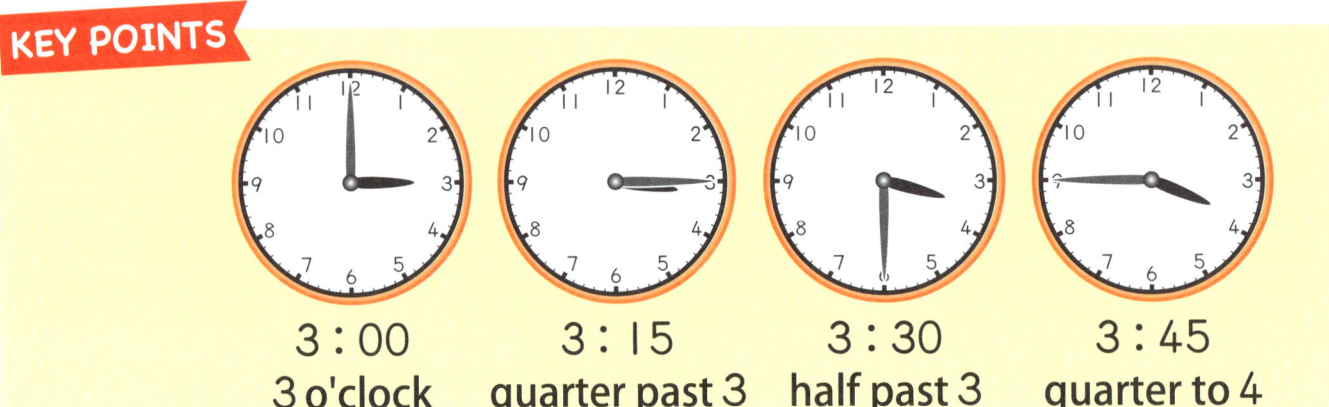

3 : 00	3 : 15	3 : 30	3 : 45
3 o'clock	quarter past 3	half past 3	quarter to 4

■ Draw a line to the same time.

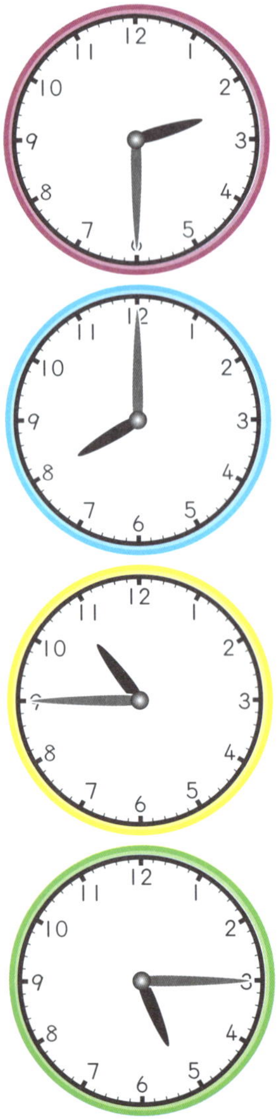

8 : 00

5 : 15

2 : 30

10 : 45

■ Draw the hand on each clock to show the time.

7 : 00

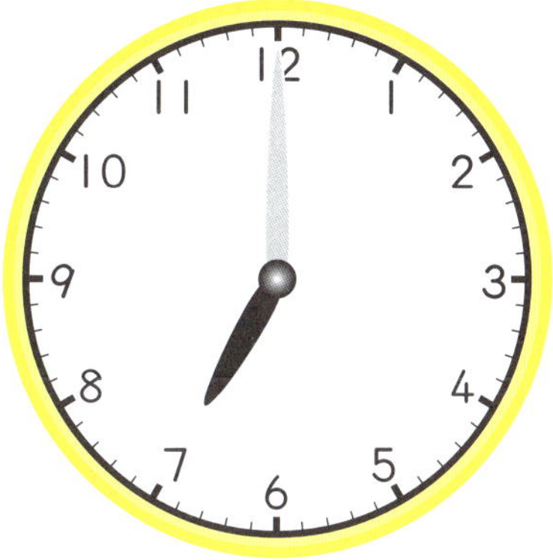

1 : 45

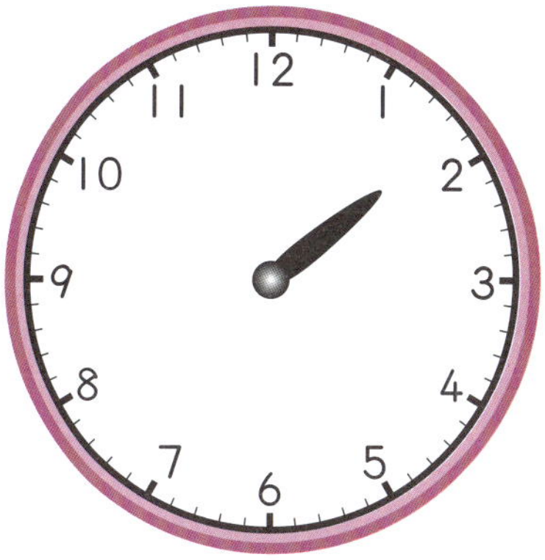

4 : 00

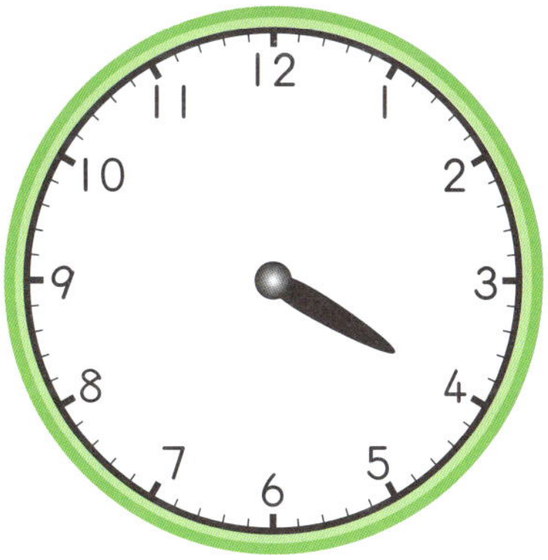

5 : 15

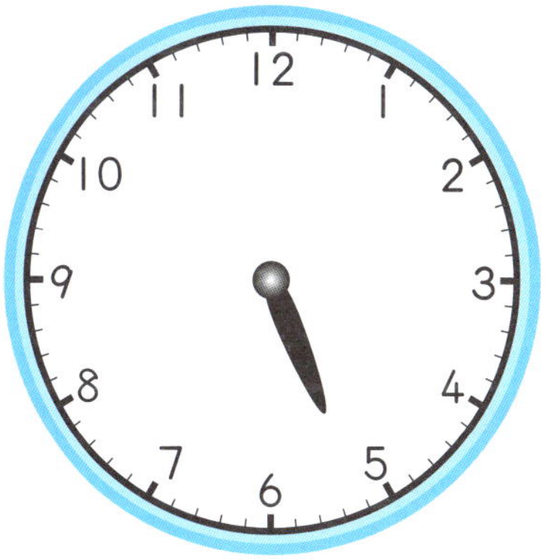

11 : 30

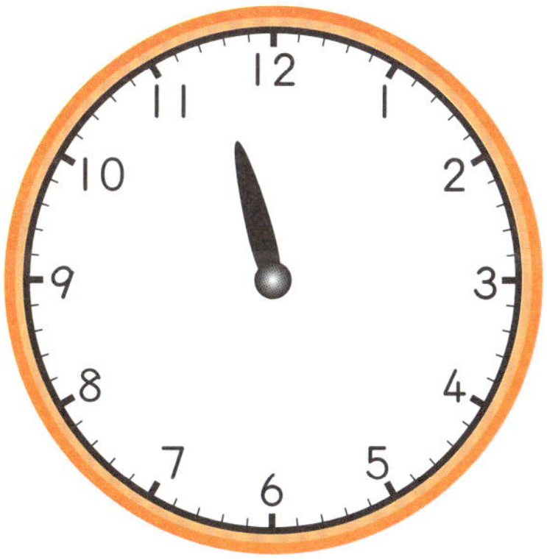

9 : 45

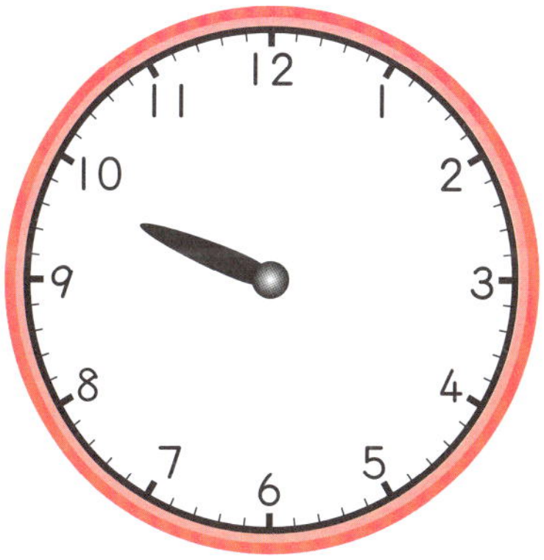

Telling Time 2

■ **Write the time inside each clock below.**

1

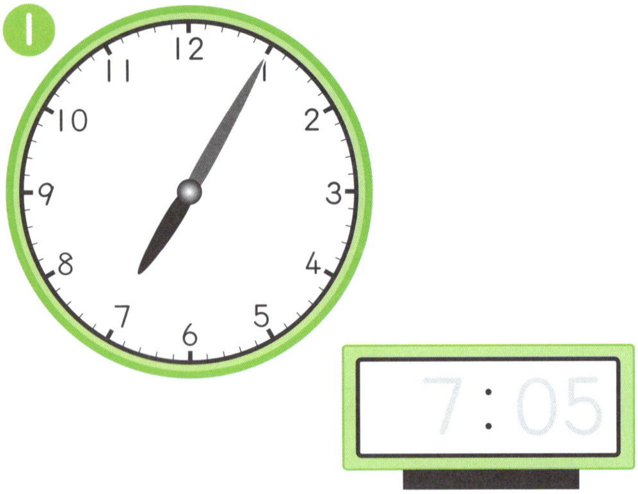

7 : 05

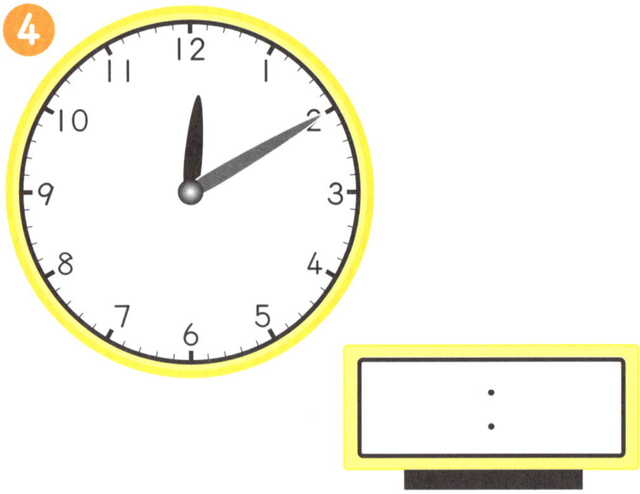

2

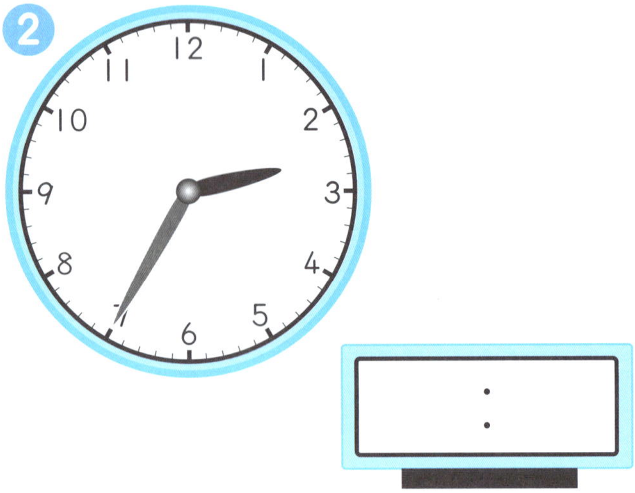

:

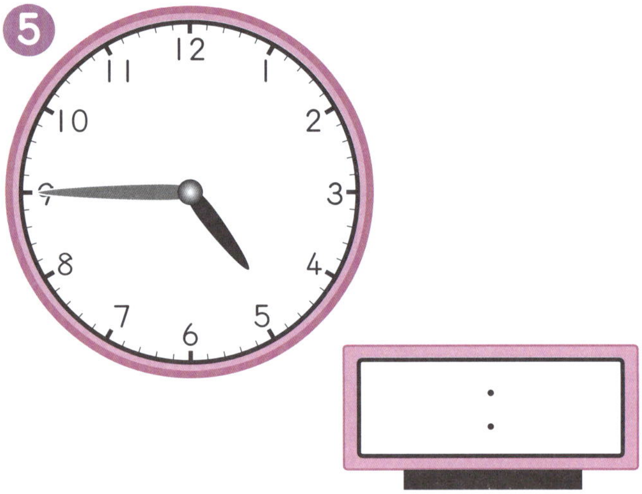

3

:

4

:

5

:

6

:

■ Trace a path where each clock moves forward 5 minutes.

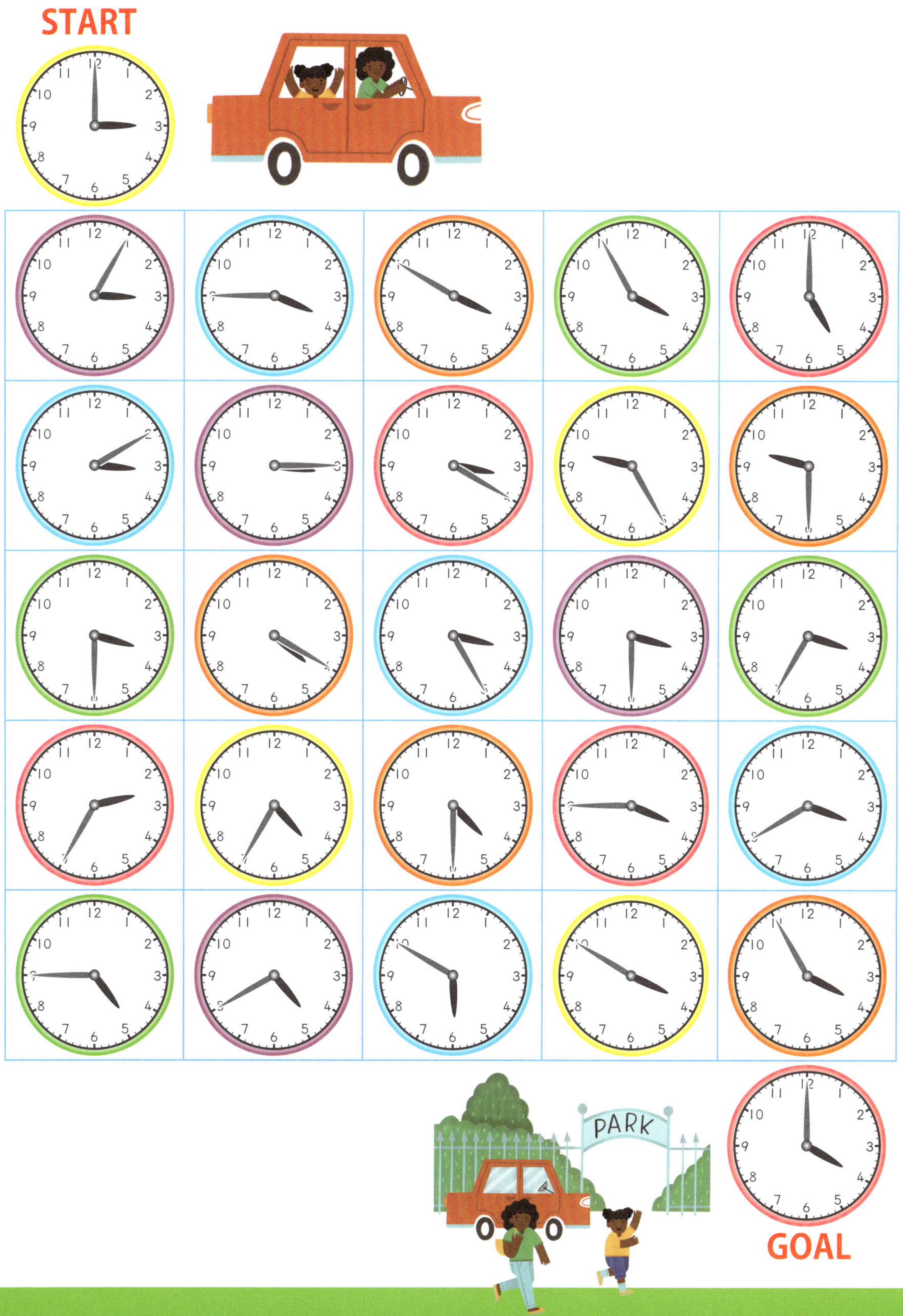

START

GOAL

PARK

Brain Break
Measurement Tools

■ Draw a line to match each object with the correct tool for measurement.

What is the width of the clip? ●

● Tape measure

What is the temperature of the room? ●

● 12-inch ruler

What is the length around the box? ●

● Measuring cup

How much orange juice is in the bottle? ●

● Thermometer

Maze Break!

■ Trace the path from start to finish!

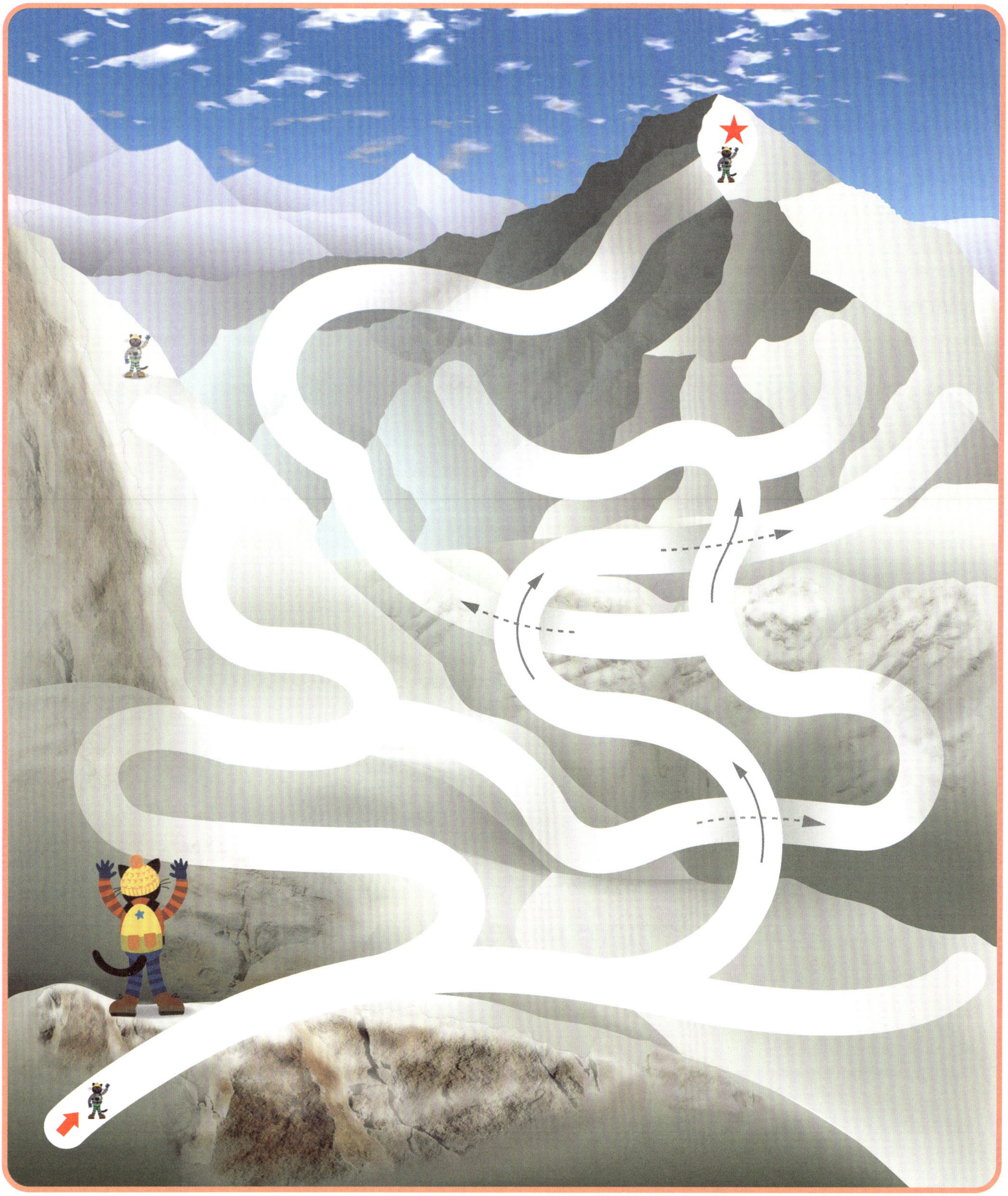

Weather

Weather is the state of the atmosphere, or the air around the earth. There are many types of weather such as sunshine, rain, snow, wind, and storms. The type of weather you experience each day is affected by many things like the temperature, season, and where you are.

Most of the time weather like wind and rain are mild. But sometimes, weather can be severe like a thunderstorm or a hurricane, with very strong winds and rains.

■ Answer the questions.

❶ What is weather?

_____

_____

❷ What are some examples of weather?

_____

_____

■ Read the questions below and check (✔) if the answer is true or false.

❶ Weather is the state of the earth's atmosphere.

True　　False
☐　　☐

❷ Rain is a type of weather.

True　　False
☐　　☐

❸ What season it is affects the type of weather.

True　　False
☐　　☐

❹ Hurricanes are an example of mild weather.

True　　False
☐　　☐

Severe Weather

KEY POINTS

Some weather can be dangerous. Severe weather like thunderstorms can have strong winds, heavy rain, hail, and even lightning. These conditions can cause damage to peoples' homes and property. It can be unsafe to go outside during this type of weather.

Another example of severe weather is a blizzard. A blizzard is a snowstorm with low temperatures, very strong winds, and large amounts of snow.

■ Answer the questions.

❶ What is severe weather?

❷ What are some examples of severe weather?

■ Use the picture to fill in the information.

Weather Event	① hurricane	④
What happens?	②	⑤
What should people do during this event?	③	⑥

Types of Natural Disasters

Natural disasters are severe weather events or other natural events that can be dangerous and cause damage to buildings.

Types of Natural Disasters

A tornado forms from very strong winds that spin around very fast. A tornado can be strong enough to rip trees from the ground and cause a lot of damage to buildings.

A hurricane is a severe storm with strong winds and heavy rain that forms over the ocean. A hurricane can cause flooding and destroy ships, buildings, and roads.

An earthquake happens when pieces of Earth's crust shift and move. Earthquakes can be small, or they can be very big and cause houses to fall down and roads to crack.

A flood happens when a lot of water rushes into an area due to heavy rain, melting snow, or a river overflowing.

A wildfire is a large, uncontrolled fire that spreads very fast through forest or grasslands. A wildfire is dangerous for people and animals.

■ Read the description and match the severe weather.

This event forms when very strong winds spin around very fast.

●   ●

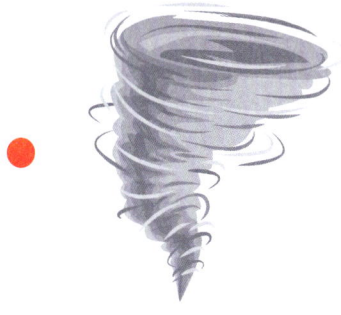

This event is a severe storm with strong winds and heavy rain. It forms over the ocean.

●   ●

This event happens when pieces of Earth's crust shift or move against each other.

●   ●

This event happens when a lot of water rushes into an area.

●   ●

This event is a large, uncontrolled fire that spreads very fast through forest or grasslands.

●   ●

Preparing for Natural Disasters

KEY POINTS

Natural disasters can cause a lot of damage and be dangerous for people and animals. Here are some ways people can prepare for natural disasters.

In some areas where floods happen a lot, people build flood barriers along rivers. These barriers help stop flood waters from damaging homes and businesses.

In places where hurricanes happen often, houses are built with hurricane shutters that go over their windows to help protect the inside of homes and businesses from the strong winds of a hurricane.

In areas where earthquakes happen often buildings have special bases to help support them. When the earthquake shakes the ground the building moves with it instead of staying rigid. This can help prevent damage to the building.

KEY POINTS

In case of a natural disaster, families can make an "Emergency Kit." Emergency kits should have water, food, flashlights, safety gear, and other items that might be helpful.

■ Pick a natural disaster and create an emergency kit. Choose from some of the items below.

Canned Food	Bottled Water	Flashlight	Batteries
Radio	Phone charger	First Aid Kit	

My Emergency Kit:

Brain Break
Science Journal 3

How can I protect my home from a natural disaster? Create a plan to keep your home safe. What can you build? What can you do to prepare?

My plan...

Art Break!

■ Not all weather is severe. It is safe to go out in every day rain. Design your own umbrella to keep you dry!

What is Culture?

KEY POINTS

Culture is the shared way of life of a society, or group of people. Many different things make up a society's culture. These include food, language, clothing, music, arts, customs, beliefs, and religion.

■ Answer the questions.

❶ What is culture?

_____

_____

❷ What are some things that make up a culture?

_____

_____

■ Write an example of each for your own culture. Then pick a new culture to learn about. Answer the questions for the new culture.

	My Culture	New Culture
The Culture		
A food		
A Celebration/ Holiday		
A belief		
A type of music		
A type of clothing		
A language		

US Holidays – Presidents' Day

KEY POINTS

Many cultures have special dates where they celebrate historical events or important people. In the United States, there are several holidays that celebrate important historic events. One example is Presidents' Day. Presidents' Day honors past presidents and their contributions to the government and society of the United States. It takes place in Feburary around the dates of George Washington and Abraham Lincoln's birthdays.

■ Answer the questions.

❶ When does Presidents' Day take place?

_____

_____

❷ Why do we celebrate Presidents' Day?

_____

_____

■ Match the presidents.

George Washington

Abraham Lincoln

Franklin D. Roosevelt

Thomas Jefferson

President from 1861-1865
This US president is best known for leading the country during the Civil War and Signing the Emancipation Proclamation to free all enslaved people in the US.

President from 1933-1945
This US president is best known for signing the New Deal, which created many services for people in the United States during the Great Depression. He also led the country during World War II.

President from 1789-1797
This US president is best known for leading the Continental Army during the American Revolutionary War and for becoming the first President of the United States.

President from 1801-1809
This US president is best known for writing the Declaration of Independence, which declared the United States a free country separate from England. He is also one of the founding fathers.

US Holidays – The Fourth of July

KEY POINTS

Another US holiday is the Fourth of July or Independence Day. This holiday celebrates the signing of the Declaration of Independence, which said that the US was its own country and would no longer be ruled by the British. The Fourth of July is a federal holiday, which means most people have the day off from work or school to celebrate with their families and friends. There are a lot of ways people celebrate the Fourth of July. Some people have barbecues, watch fireworks, or attend parades. Many Americans display US flags and wear red, white, and blue to honor the United States.

Happy 4th of July!

■ Answer the questions.

❶ What is the Fourth of July?

_____

❷ How do Americans celebrate it?

_____

■ Read the questions below and check (✓) if the answer is true or false.

❶ The Fourth of July celebrates the signing of the Declaration of Independence.

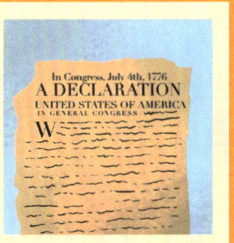

True False
☐ ☐

❷ The Fourth of July celebrates the day the United States joined Great Britain.

True False
☐ ☐

❸ People celebrate the Fourth of July by going sledding and building snowmen of George Washington.

True False
☐ ☐

❹ People watch fireworks on the Fourth of July.

True False
☐ ☐

❺ The Fourth of July is also called Independence Day.

True False
☐ ☐

Another US holiday is Juneteenth, which celebrates the end of slavery in the United States. President Abraham Lincoln signed the Emancipation Proclamation in 1863, which said that all enslaved people should be freed. But it took until June 19, 1865 for the last  enslaved people in Texas to be freed. The name Juneteenth was created by combining the words June and nineteenth. The day  is also called Emancipation Day or Freedom Day. People celebrate by getting together with their families, attending parades, ceremonies, and prayer services. It is a time when Americans celebrate Black culture in the United States.

■ Answer the questions.

❶ What is Juneteenth?

_____

❷ How do people celebrate it?

_____

■ Fill in the blanks using the Key Points to complete the sentences.

What? ➡ **Juneteenth celebrates the end of**

[   ] **in the United States.**

Who ? ➡ [   ] **celebrate Juneteenth.**

When ? ➡ **Juneteenth is celebrated on** [   ] .

Why ? ➡ **Although President Abraham Lincoln signed the**

[   ]

in 1863, it took until June 19th 1865 for all enslaved

people in the United States to be free.

Brain Break
Crossword Puzzle

■ Use the clues to complete the crossword puzzle.

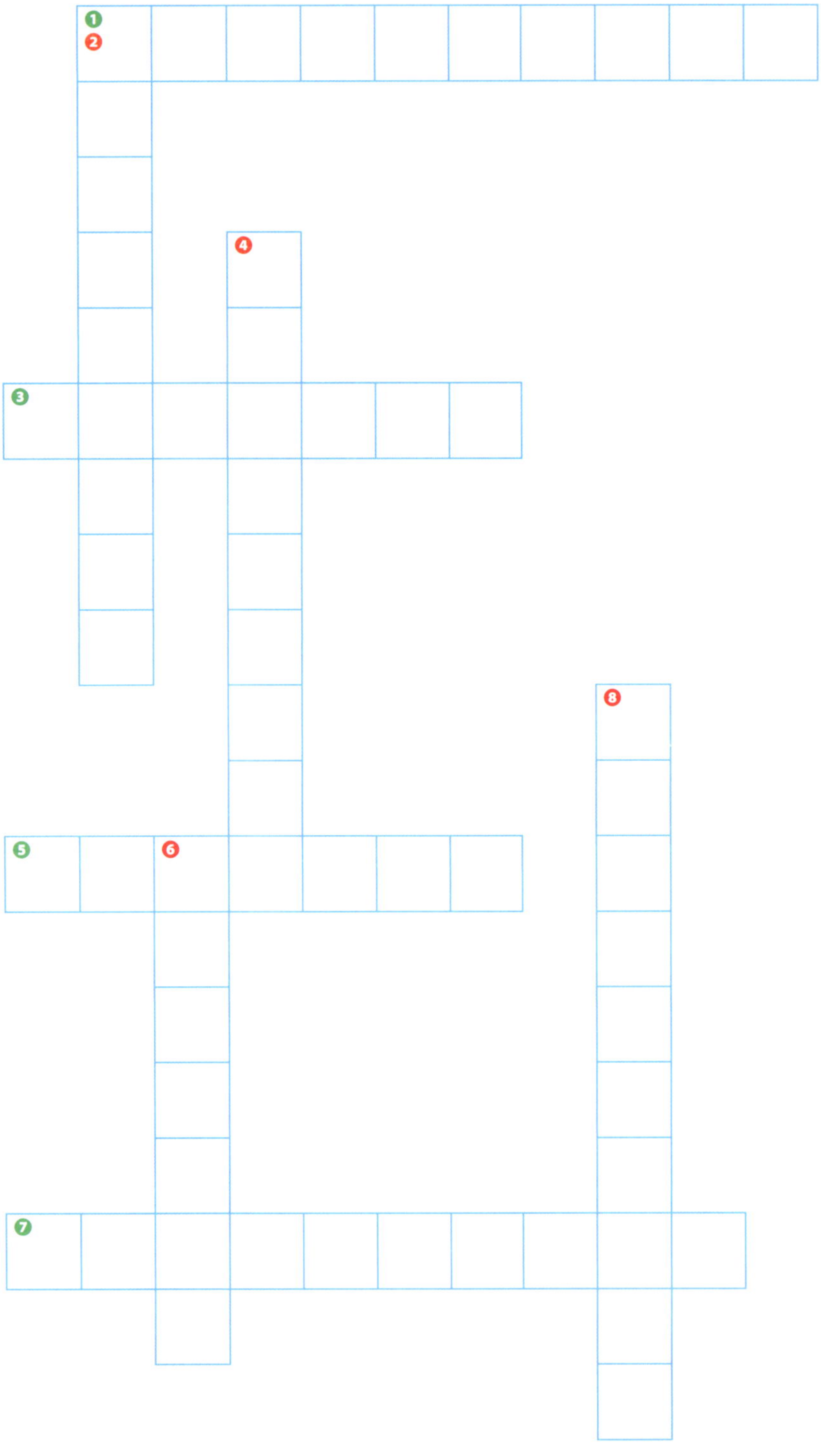

Across

1 A holiday that celebrates the end of slavery in the US.

3 The state of being free to act, think, and speak without consequences.

5 The shared way of life of a group of people.

7 A holiday that celebrates the adoption of the Declaration of Independence in the US.

Down

2 The US President known for writing the Declaration of Independence.

4 The leader of the United States.

6 The US president who led the country during the Civil War.

8 The first President of the United States.

■ **Choose an emotion to illustrate and answer the questions.**

❶ **Choose an emotion and draw a moment when you felt this way.**

❷ **How can you be mindful of the emotion you picked?**

Counting Money 1

100¢ = $1
100 cents equals 1 dollar

■ Count the coins. Which wallet adds up to $1.00?
Write a check mark (✔) in the box.

☐

☐

☐

☐

KEY POINTS

Front   Back

$ 1 (1 **dollar**)

$ 1	→ $ 1.00
$ 1 and 1¢	→ $ 1.01
$ 1 and 10¢	→ $ 1.10

■ Draw a line from each amount to the item it can buy.

 ●   ●  $2.03

 ●   ●  $2.25

 ●   ●  $1.15

Counting Money 2

■ Is there enough money to buy each item? Write check mark (✓) by correct answer.

1

$1.99

Yes

No

2

$2.93

Yes

No

3

$1.23

Yes

No

4

$2.48

Yes

No

■ Choose all the wallets that contain the money needed to purchase the items on the left and write a check mark (✔) in the box.

1

$5.30

☐ ☐

☐ ☐

2

$4.85

☐

☐ ☐

Change

■ How much change will you get back after paying? Write the number in the screen of each cash register.

1

$1.99

You have

Change
$0.01

2

$3.30

You have

Change
$0.

3

$4.67

You have

Change
$0.

4

$6.15

You have

Change
$0.

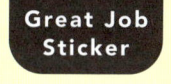

■ **What did each person buy? Choose one answer from the word box.**

Hamburger	French Fries	Ice Cream	Salad
$3.49	80¢	$2.35	$2.25

1 James paid

The change was 20¢.

He bought

_____.

2 Hannah paid

The change was 5¢.

She bought

_____.

3 Owen paid

The change was 65¢.

He bought

_____.

Finance Vocabulary

KEY POINTS

To spend is to use money to buy something.

To earn is to receive money as payment for work that you do.

Cost is the price or amount you pay for something.

Income is money you get for working a job or performing a task.

To save is to not spend money because of a goal or another reason.

Charity is when you donate money, goods or services to an organization.

A budget is a plan you make to help spend or save money wisely.

Needs are important things that we need in order to live.

Wants are things we would like to have.
But we don't really need them in order to live.

■ **Which finance word does the following sentence describe? Choose one from the word box and write it down.**

Spend / Earn / Save / Charity / Budget

❶ You carefully plan how you will spend your money.

❷ You buy a new pencil case.

❸ You decide to use your money to help another person.

❹ Your job pays you twenty dollars.

❺ You want to buy a new bike, but you don't have enough money. You decide to stop spending money on another things until you have enough to buy a bike.

**It's important to move your body and exercise!
Try this fun activity below for a study break!**

■ Look at the images and read the text below. Try the yoga poses!

Mountain Pose

Stand up straight with your feet apart and your arms out to the side with palms facing foward. Imagine being strong and unmovable like a mountain.

Butterfly Pose

Sit on your behind with your back straight. Bend your legs and place the bottom of your feet together.

Tree Pose

Stand on one leg. Bend the knee of the leg you are not standing on, place the bottom of your foot on the inside of your leg, and then balance.

Frog Pose

Squat down with your knees apart and your arms resting between your knees. Touch your hands to the ground. Hold.

Unit 4 Table of Contents

Use this page to keep track of your progress throughout the book. Place a check mark in the box when you have completed a section.

Just like with stories, we can ask ourselves the 5 W questions to make sure we understand the text: Who, What, When, Where, and Why?

These questions ask: Who was in the story? What happened? When did it happen? Where did it happen? Why did it happen?

■ Read the text below. Then answer the five W questions.

Martin Luther King, Jr. was an important leader. In the 1950s and 1960s, he fought against unfair treatment of Black people in the United States. He believed that everyone should have equal rights.

Who _____

What _____

When _____

Where _____

Why _____

■ Read the text below. Then answer the five W questions.

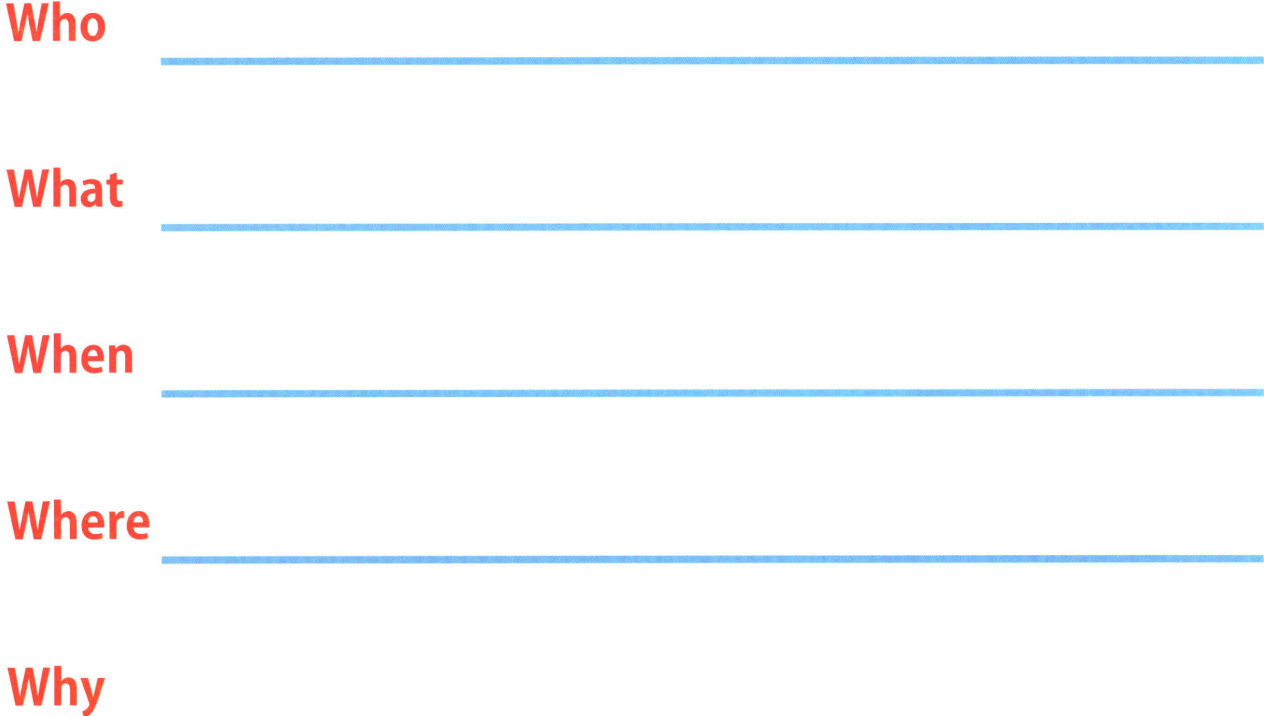

Amelia Earhart was a great American pilot. In 1932, she became the first woman to fly across the Atlantic Ocean by herself. She loved to fly, and she was determined to prove that women were just as talented as men.

Who _____

What _____

When _____

Where _____

Why _____

Informational texts have a main topic. The main topic is what the text is mainly about.

■ Read the text below. Then choose the main topic.

Have you ever looked up in the sky and seen a rainbow? You might be wondering how they are made. Rainbows look like bright stripes of color. But actually, they are made of droplets of water in the air that shine light back at us. The light forms a rainbow.

☐ **What rainbows look like**

☐ **How rainbows are made**

☐ **Why rainbows are beautiful**

■ Read the text below. Then write the main topic.

You've probably seen a waterfall before, either in real life or in a photo. But did you know that there are many types of waterfalls? Some waterfalls pour down along a big rock. Some pour up and over a rock, and don't touch the rock as they fall. These are called pony tail waterfalls. Some waterfalls have one main stream, and some are made up of many streams of water. Then there is my favorite type of waterfall, the cascade. These waterfalls have many parts, almost like they are going down a flight of stairs.

Reading Comprehension 3

Some texts have steps to follow. It's important to pay attention to the order of the steps.

■ Read the text. Then answer the question.

How to make a pizza:
1 Prepare your dough. Knead it carefully.
2 Shape the dough into a flat circle.
3 Put tomato sauce on the dough.
4 Add cheese.
5 Bake the pizza in the oven.
6 Take it out carefully, slice it up, and eat it!

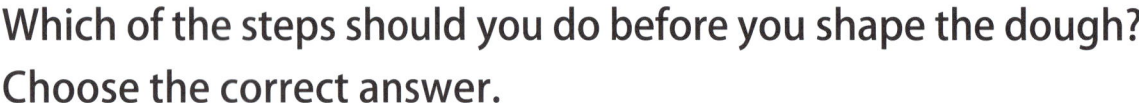

Which of the steps should you do before you shape the dough?
Choose the correct answer.

☐ **Put sauce on it.**

☐ **Knead the dough.**

☐ **Add cheese.**

Date

Great Job Sticker

Draw each step in order.

Popsicles please!

1. Pour fruit juice into a popsicle tray.
2. Add a few pieces of chopped fruit to each popsicle.
3. Place the sticks in.
4. Put the tray into the freezer and wait several hours.
5. Take them out and enjoy!

1

2

3

4

5

Reading Comprehension 4

If you see an unfamiliar word in a text, you can use context clues to help determine the meaning.

■ Read the story. Then answer the question.

If you're going for a walk in the woods, you might have some help finding your way. Some trails have markers, which are little colored patches painted or nailed into trees. Follow your markers, and you'll be on the trail the whole way. Sometimes hikers leave cairns to mark an interesting spot or a tricky turn. If you aren't paying attention, you might just think it's a pile of rocks! But it's actually another hiker trying to help you out.

❶ Circle words that help you understand what the red word means.

❷ What is a cairn? Choose the correct answer.

☐ A colored patch that shows the trail

☐ A map to help you know where you are

☐ A pile of rocks left by another hiker

■ Read the story. Then answer the question.

> Bats are amazing creatures.
> They are asleep during the day,
> and awake at night. They can't
> see well, so they use echolocation
> to get around. They make a
> sound and listen to see if it hits an
> object or not. Their hearing helps them know where
> everything is.

❶ Circle words that help you understand what the red word means.

❷ What does echolocation mean? Choose the correct answer.

☐ Not seeing well.

☐ Using sound to know where things are.

☐ Sleeping during the day.

Brain Break
Think of a Task

■ Think of a task you are good at. Write the steps below.

①

②

③

④

⑤

Think of a place that makes you feel happy. You can imagine you are there whenever you feel sad or upset.

■ Draw a place that makes you feel happy.

Introducing a Topic

KEY POINTS

Informational texts have topics. Main topics are what the text is mostly about. Informational texts usually start off with an introduction that tells the reader what the topic will be. It doesn't usually have details about the topic.

> **Topic: Dogs come in many shapes and sizes!**
> Humans have been raising dogs for many years, and now there are many breeds of dog. Some dogs can help hunt. Some dogs can be trained to help people. And of course, small dogs are best as lap dogs.

■ Choose the sentence that would make the best introduction for a text about squirrels.

☐ Some people see squirrels as pests, but they're a special animal.

☐ Squirrels hide acorns so that they can come back and eat them later.

☐ Newborn squirrels are only an inch long.

■ **Choose the best sentence to introduce the text.**

Most pandas live in China. They eat bamboo. There are not many pandas living in the wild. Most live in zoos or in parks where they are taken care of by humans.

☐ Pandas have black and white fur.

☐ Pandas are a very interesting animal.

☐ Pandas can climb trees.

Unit 4 Writing

Using Facts

KEY POINTS

When you are writing about a topic, you should include facts about it. You may also want to include a definition. This is important to do if you think your reader may not know the word.

> Did you know that the blue whale is the largest mammal, or warm-blooded animal? Blue whales can be almost one hundred feet long! That's the size of a school bus! Even though they are huge, they only eat tiny fish!

■ Write three facts you learned from the text above.

❶

❷

❸

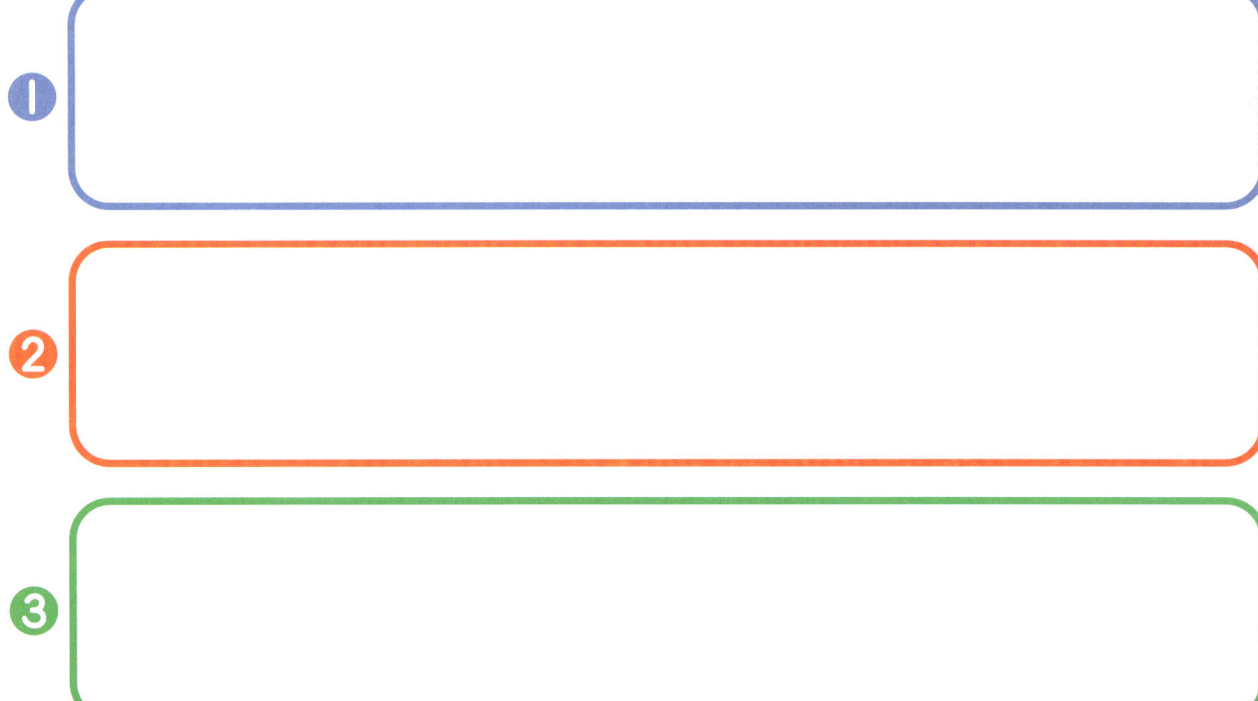

Date

Great Job Sticker

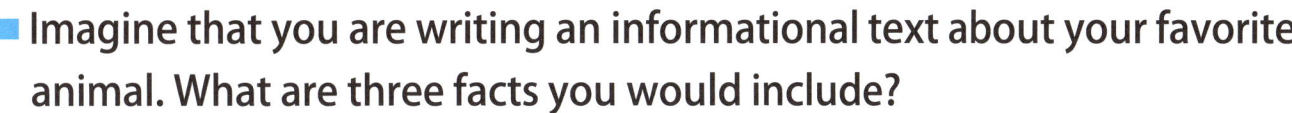

Imagine that you are writing an informational text about your favorite animal. What are three facts you would include?

1

2

3

Conclusions

Informational texts have conclusions that help tie everything together. Let's look at an example:

Dogs really are man's best friend! Many of them have been trained to help humans. Seeing eye dogs are dogs that help blind people get around safely. Guard dogs are dogs that keep humans safe by barking to let them know when someone comes to the house. And some dogs go to schools and hospitals to help people feel more confident.
It's amazing to see how many jobs dogs can do!

■ Write a conclusion for the info text below:

Cat communicate in all sorts of ways. When they meow, it usually means they want human attention. A hiss means "back off!" Purring usually means they are happy and comfortable.

Date

Great Job Sticker

Write three possible conclusions for an informational text about your favorite animal.

1

2

3

Putting It All Together

■ Write an informational text about your favorite animal.
Include an introduction, facts, and a conclusion.

■ Write an informational text about your favorite movie.
Include an introduction, facts, and a conclusion.

■ Circle the words in the Word Search.

introduction	conclusion	topic
facts	information	

R	S	F	H	G	R	F	Z	I	H	R
D	I	V	C	D	E	V	U	L	G	P
I	N	F	O	R	M	A	T	I	O	N
P	T	V	N	P	T	K	O	V	S	L
O	R	E	C	E	O	F	P	E	X	L
L	O	W	L	G	R	D	I	D	S	I
H	D	V	U	S	U	R	C	P	R	G
W	U	F	S	Z	Y	Z	O	E	V	S
B	C	Z	I	O	R	E	I	L	I	B
R	T	L	O	K	E	B	F	X	X	F
X	I	W	N	G	E	V	V	B	H	V
U	O	O	D	S	H	F	A	C	T	S
W	N	E	W	R	D	H	G	V	V	B
H	K	F	X	H	J	L	J	I	S	K
R	W	P	K	F	X	C	K	E	U	R

Unit 4

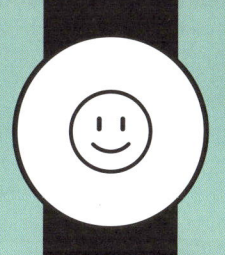

Mindfulness Break!

■ Read the emotion on each circle. Write or draw as many things as you can in each circle that make you feel each emotion.

❶ happy

❷ surprised

❸ excited

❹ calm

❺ scared

2D and 3D Shapes 1

■ Draw a line to match the shapes with their names.

 • • Pentagon

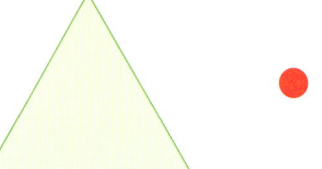 • • Square

 • • Trapezoid

 • • Triangle

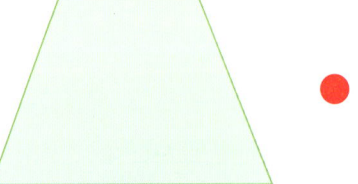 • • Circle

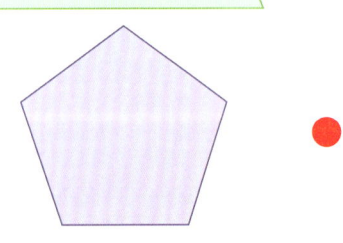 • • Hexagon

 • • Rectangle

KEY POINTS

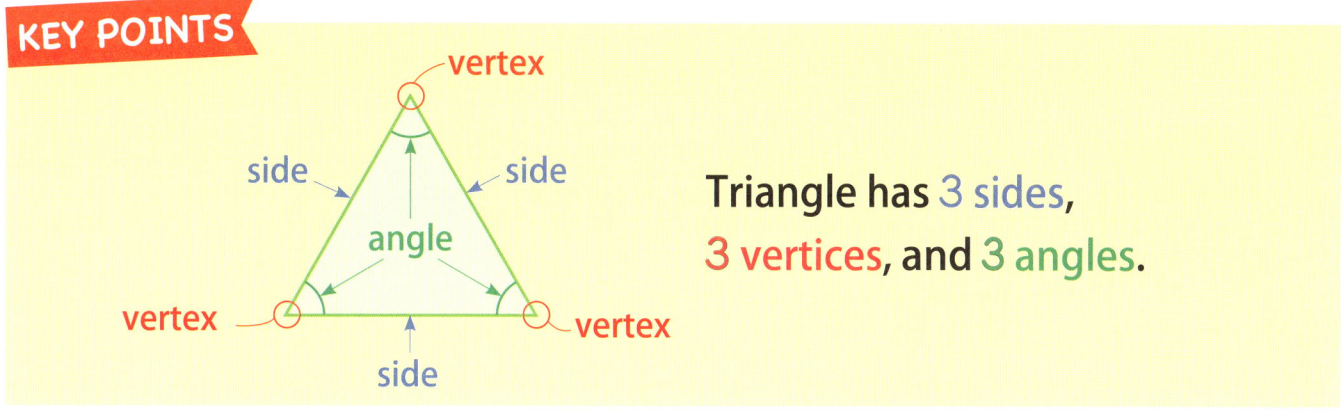

vertex

side   side

angle

vertex   vertex

side

Triangle has 3 sides,
3 vertices, and 3 angles.

■ Write a check mark (✔) under the shapes that have all of their sides
correctly shown with arrows.

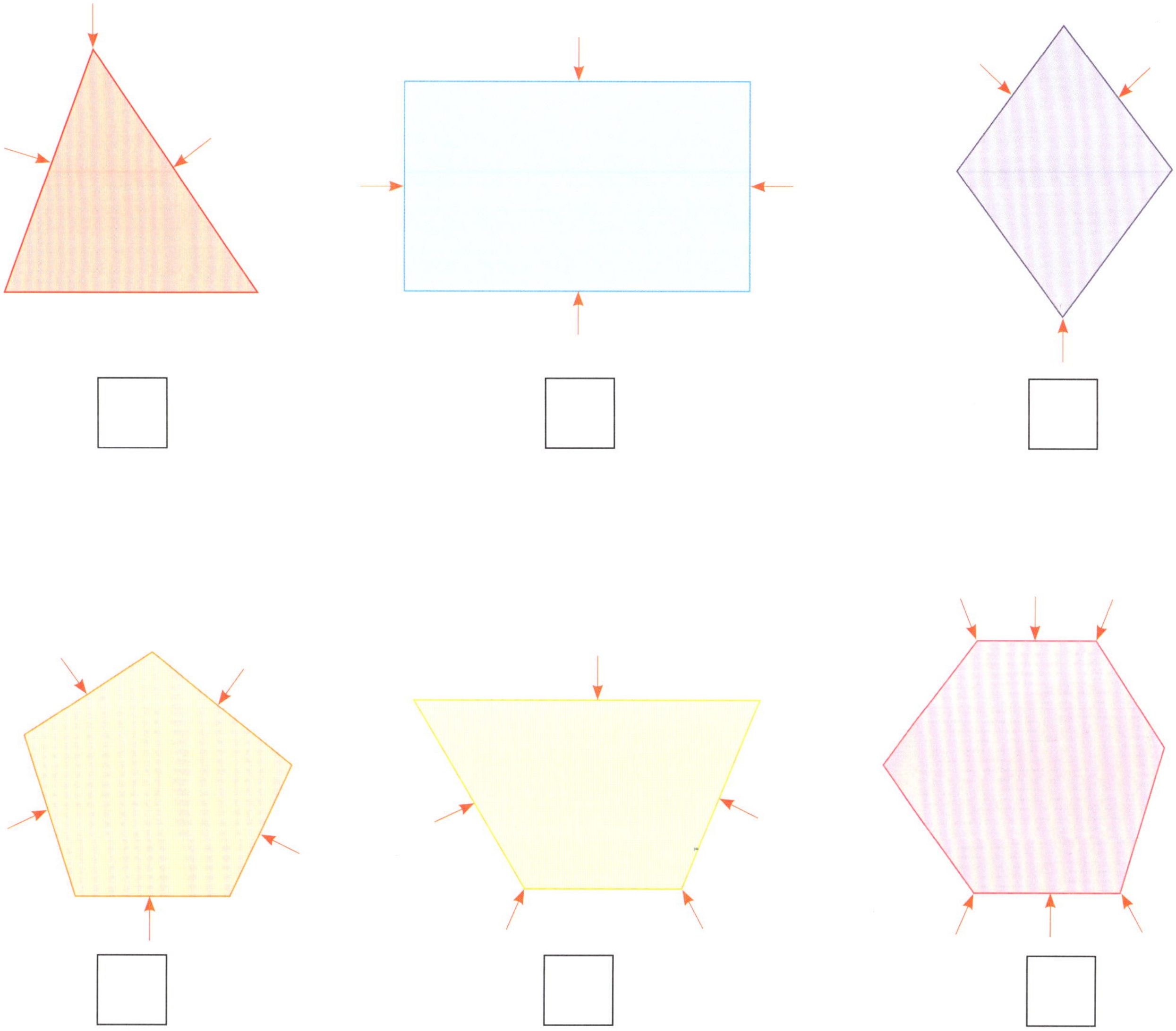

2D and 3D Shapes 2

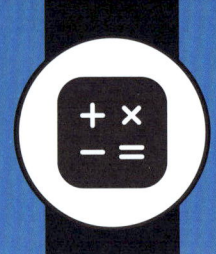

Write a check mark (✓) under the shape that matches the description.

1
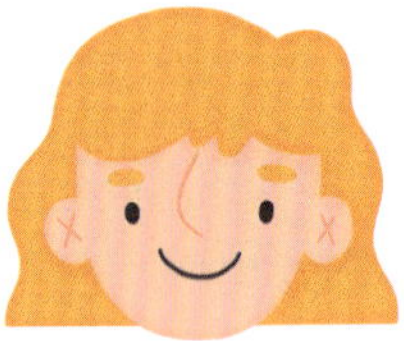

It has 4 sides and 4 angles.

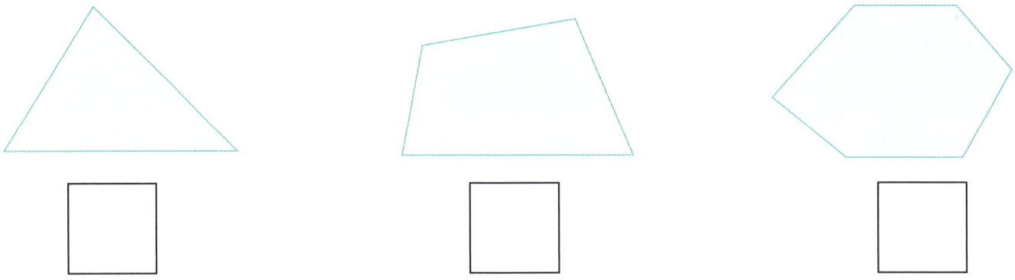

2
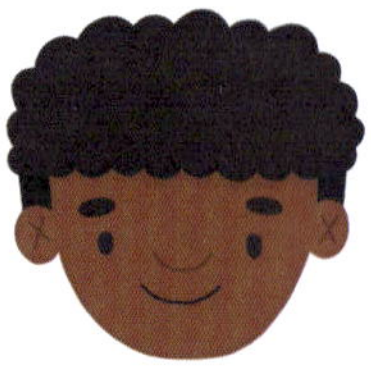

It has 6 sides and 6 angles.

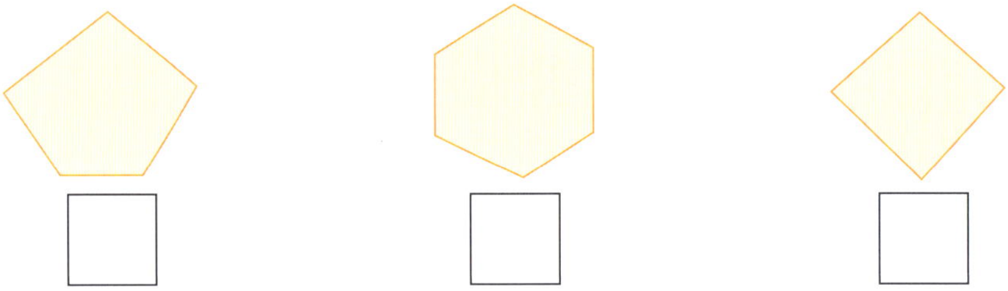

3
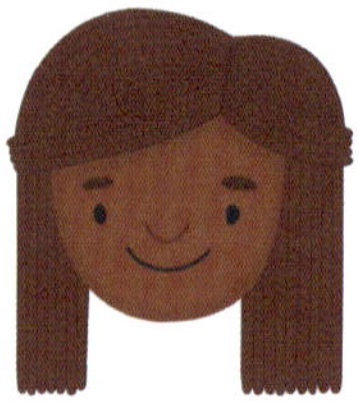

It has 4 equal sides.

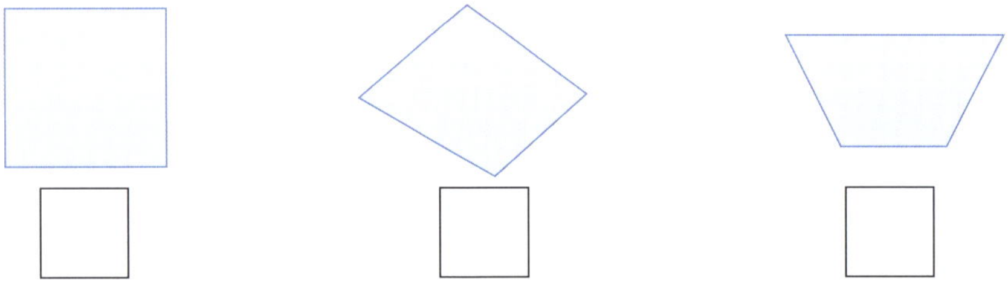

4
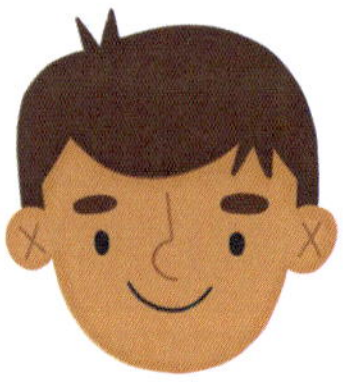

It has no angles.

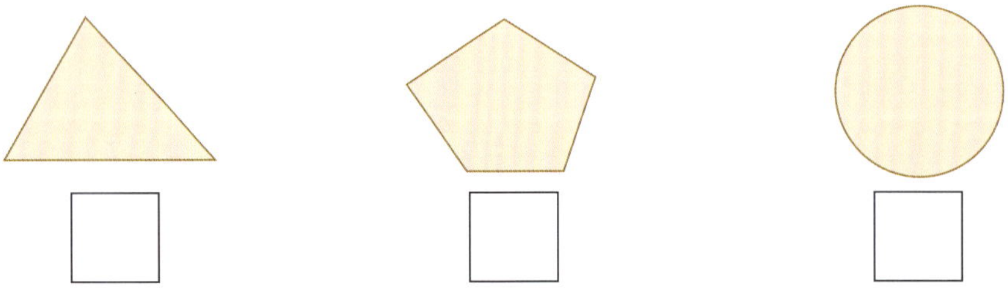

■ Draw a line to match the shapes to their name.

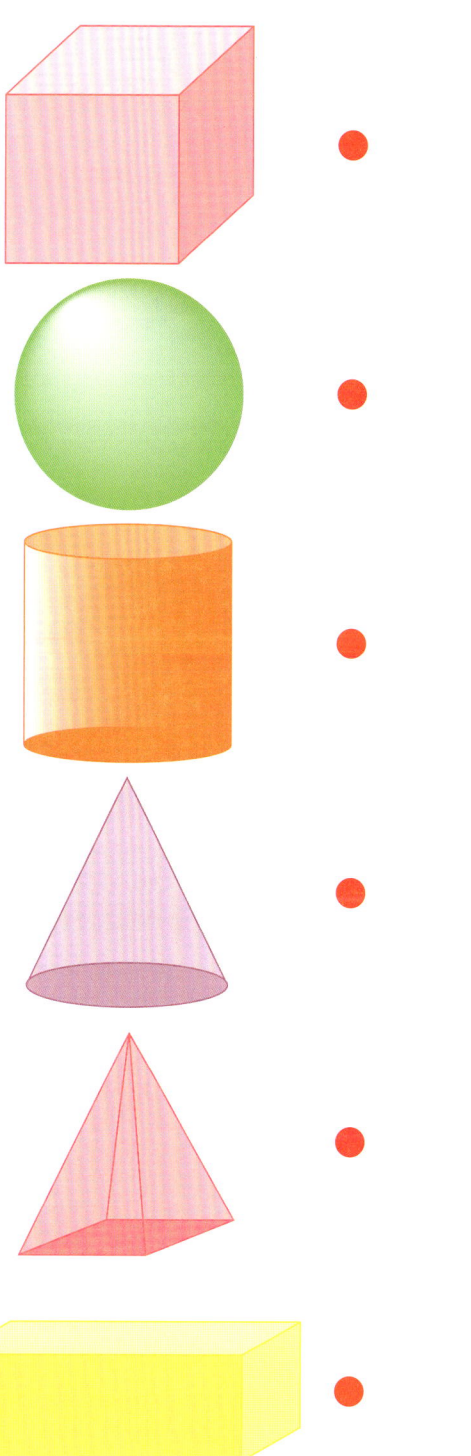

●   ● Cylinder

●   ● Pyramid

●   ● Sphere

●   ● Cube

●   ● Rectangular prism

●   ● Cone

2D and 3D Shapes 3

■ Circle all the 3D shapes.

■ Draw a line to match the 3D shapes to their 2D look alikes.

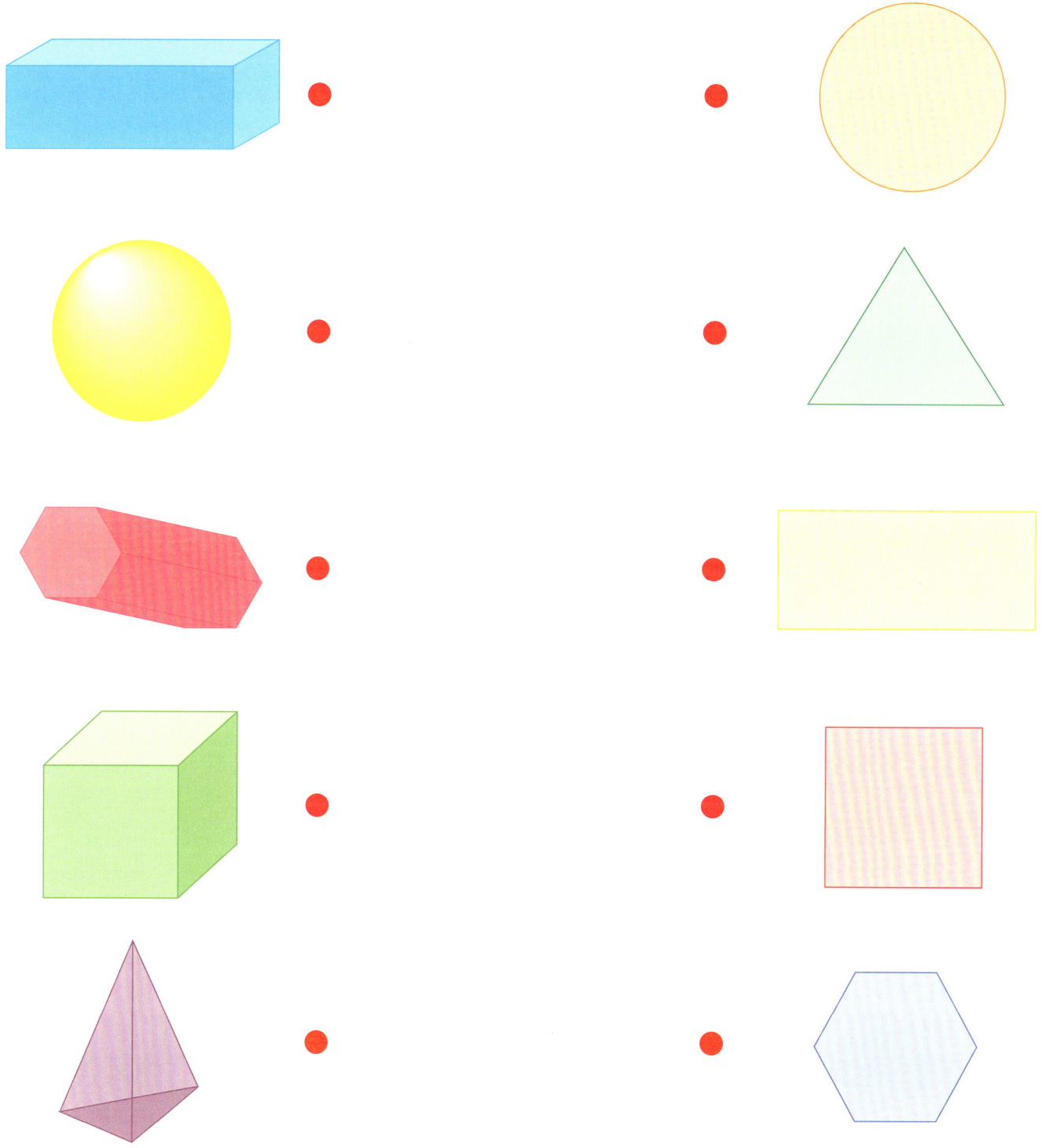

Dividing Shapes 1

■ Write a check mark (✓) in the box for each rectangle that is made of from equal blocks.

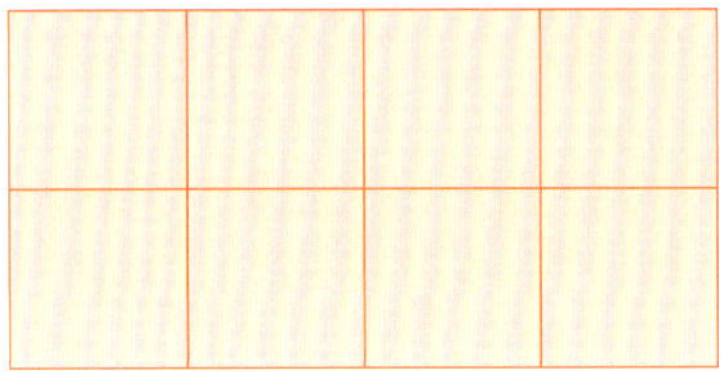

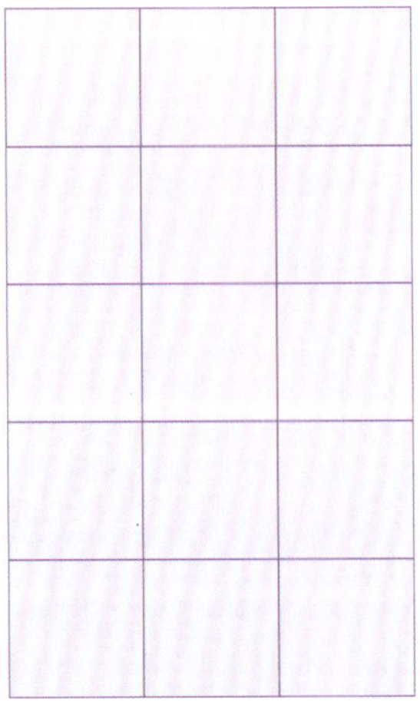

■ How many square blocks make each rectangle? Write the numbers in the box.

 squares

 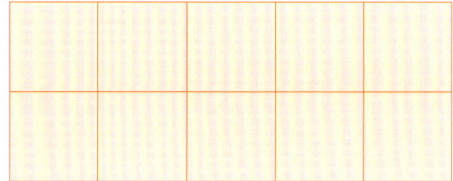

 squares

 squares

squares

Dividing Shapes 2

■ Circle the shapes that have been split into equal parts.

■ Write a check mark (✓) in the box to show how many parts each shape is divided into.

① ☐ Halves   ☐ Fourths

② ☐ Halves   ☐ Fourths

③ ☐ Thirds   ☐ Fourths

④ ☐ Halves   ☐ Thirds

⑤ ☐ Thirds   ☐ Fourths

Brain Break
What can you make?

■ Write a check mark (✓) in the box for the shape that can be made from the triangles.

1 → ☐ ☐ ☐

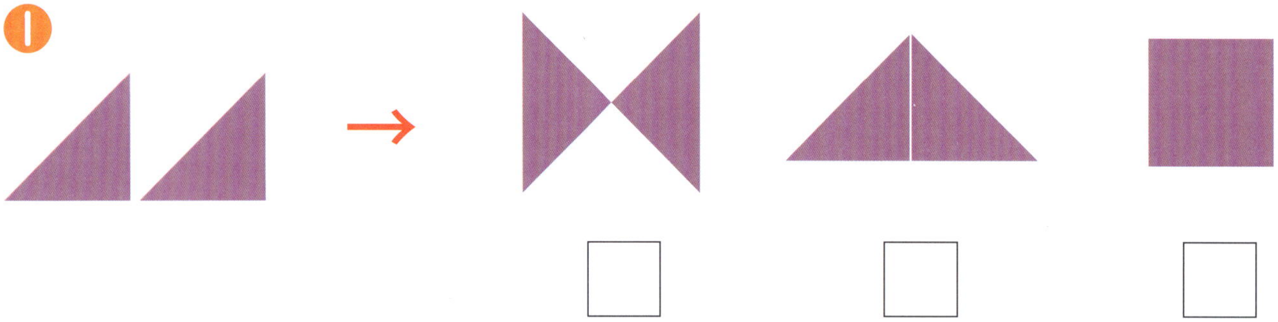

2 → ☐ ☐ ☐

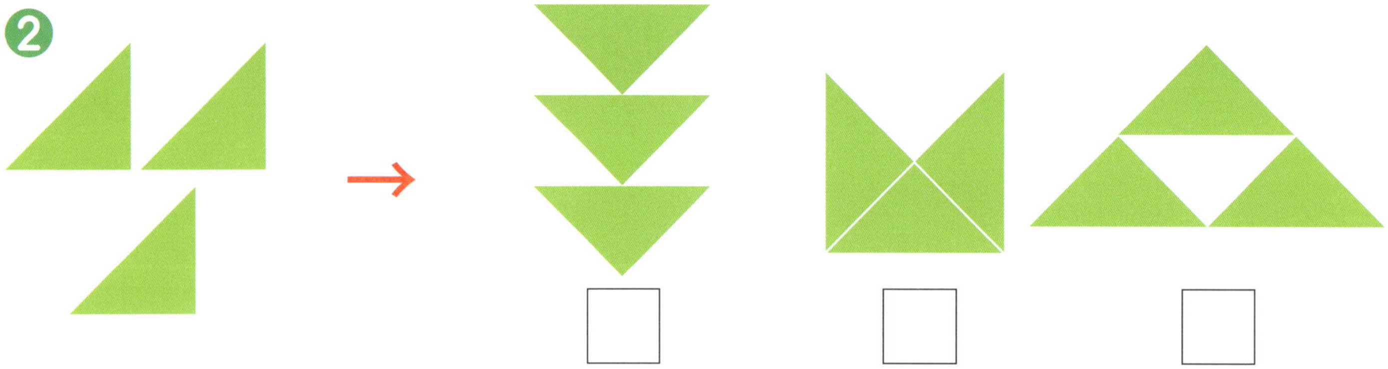

3 → ☐ ☐ ☐

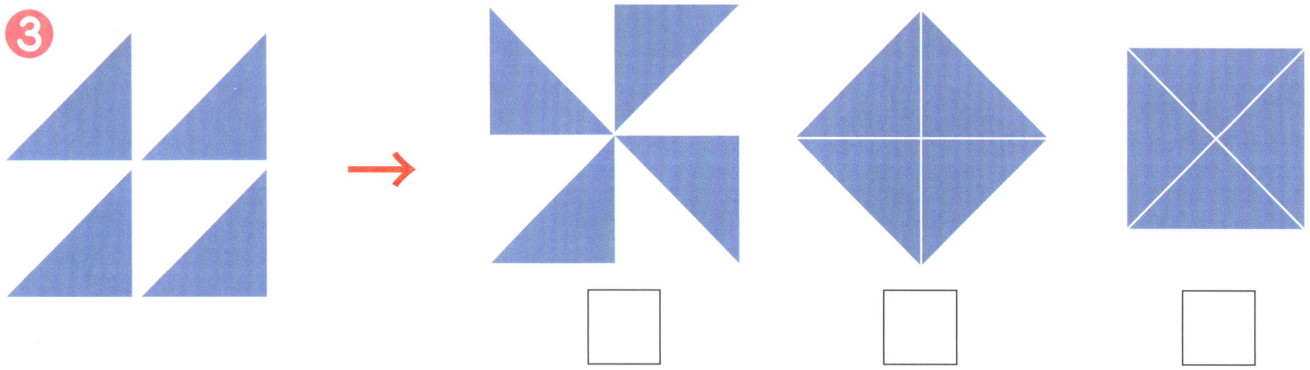

4 → ☐ ☐ ☐

Maze Break!

■ Trace the path from start to finish!

States of Matter

Matter is anything that takes up space and has weight. The three main states of matter are solids, liquids and gases. A solid keeps its shape, a liquid takes the shape of its container, and a gas expands to fill its container.

Solid	Liquid	Gas

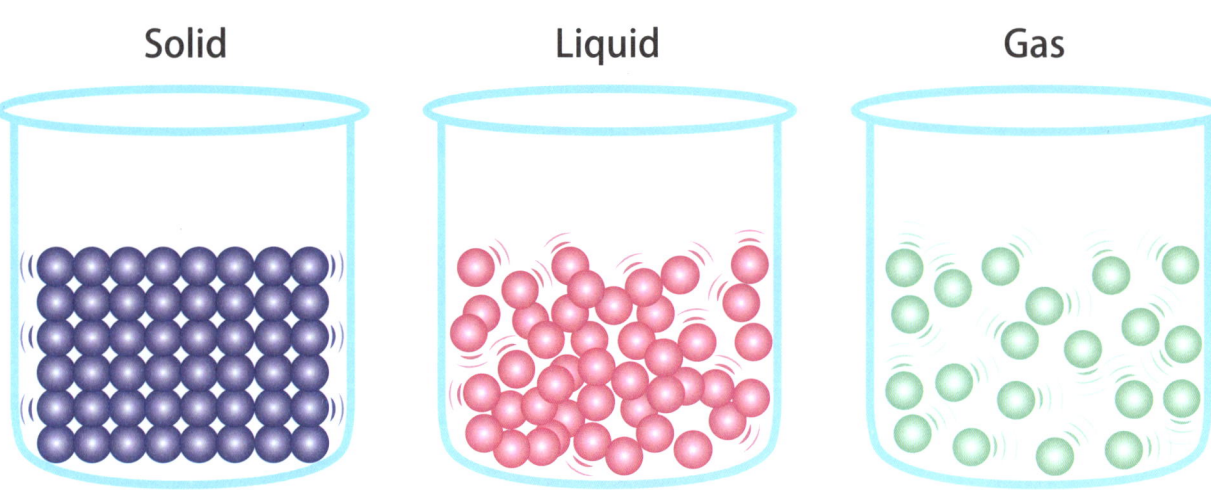

■ Answer the questions.

❶ What is matter?

_____

❷ What are the three states of matter?

_____

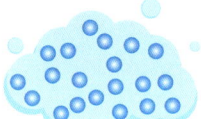
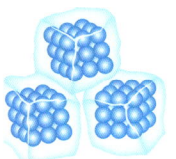
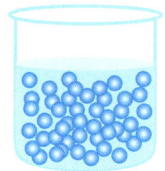

■ Read the questions below and check (✔) if the answer is true or false.

❶ Matter is anything that takes up space and has weight.

True   False

❷ There are three main states of matter: solid, liquid, and gas.

True   False

❸ A solid takes the shape of its container.

True   False

❹ A gas expands to fill its container.

True   False

❺ A liquid keeps its shape inside a container.

True   False

Properties of Matter

All matter is made of small units called molecules. These molecules are arranged differently in each state of matter.

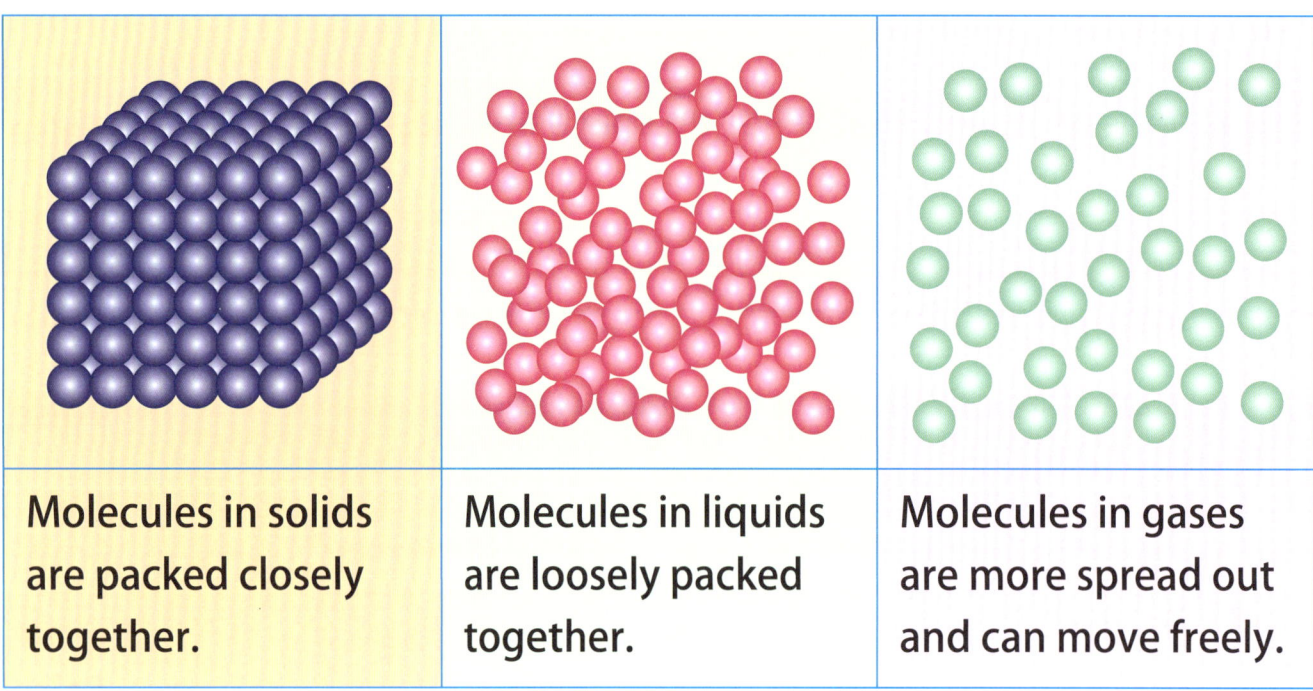

Molecules in solids are packed closely together.	Molecules in liquids are loosely packed together.	Molecules in gases are more spread out and can move freely.

■ Answer the questions.

❶ What is all matter made of?

_____

❷ How do the molecules in a liquid act?

_____

■ Draw what the molecules would look like in each object.

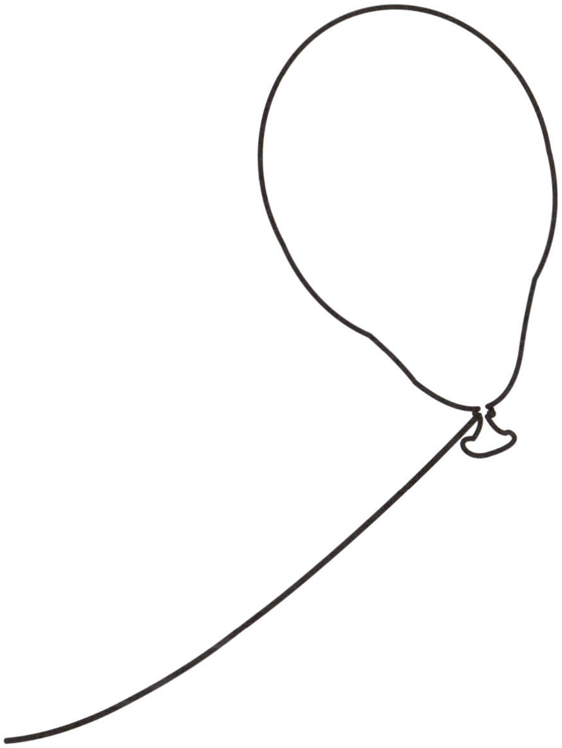

Changes in Matter

Matter can be heated or cooled. This changes it from one state of matter to another. When matter changes state, its molecules remain the same, but act differently. For example, when the solid matter of an ice cube melts into water, its molecules remain the same, but go from being solidly packed to loosely packed together.

■ Answer the questions.

❶ What happens when matter are when heated or cooled?

_____

❷ How do the molecules act when a solid turns into a liquid?

_____

■ Circle what happens to the object when it is heated or cooled.

Heated →

Cooled →

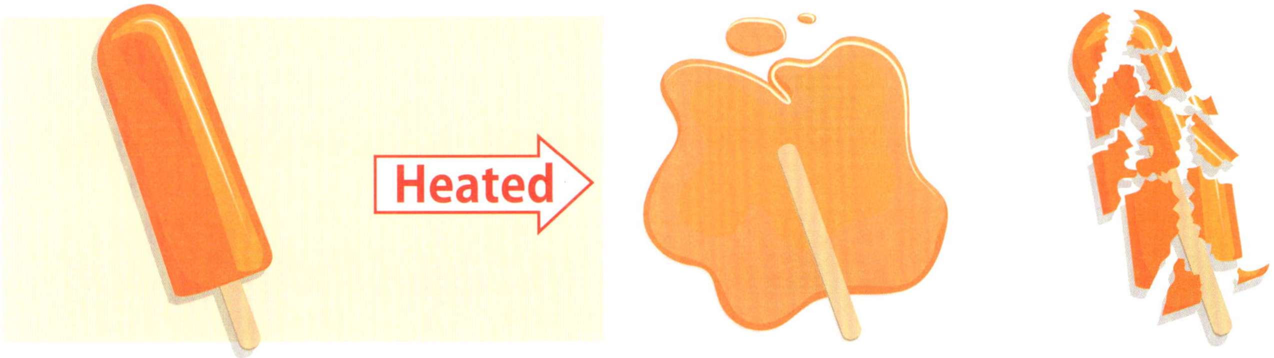

Heated →

Heated →

Reversable vs Non-reversable Changes

KEY POINTS

When matter is heated or cooled, it changes states. Sometimes matter can return to its previous state, like when water freezes into ice and then melts back into water. This is called a reversible change. When matter is heated or cooled but does not change back to its original state, it is called an irreversible change.

For example, when you cook an egg, it starts off as a liquid. When it's heated, it becomes a solid. This is an irreversible change because even after the egg cools down, it will not turn back into a liquid.

■ Answer the questions.

❶ What is a reversible change?

_____

❷ What is an irreversible change?

_____

■ Write an "R" for a reversible change and an "I" for an irreversible change.

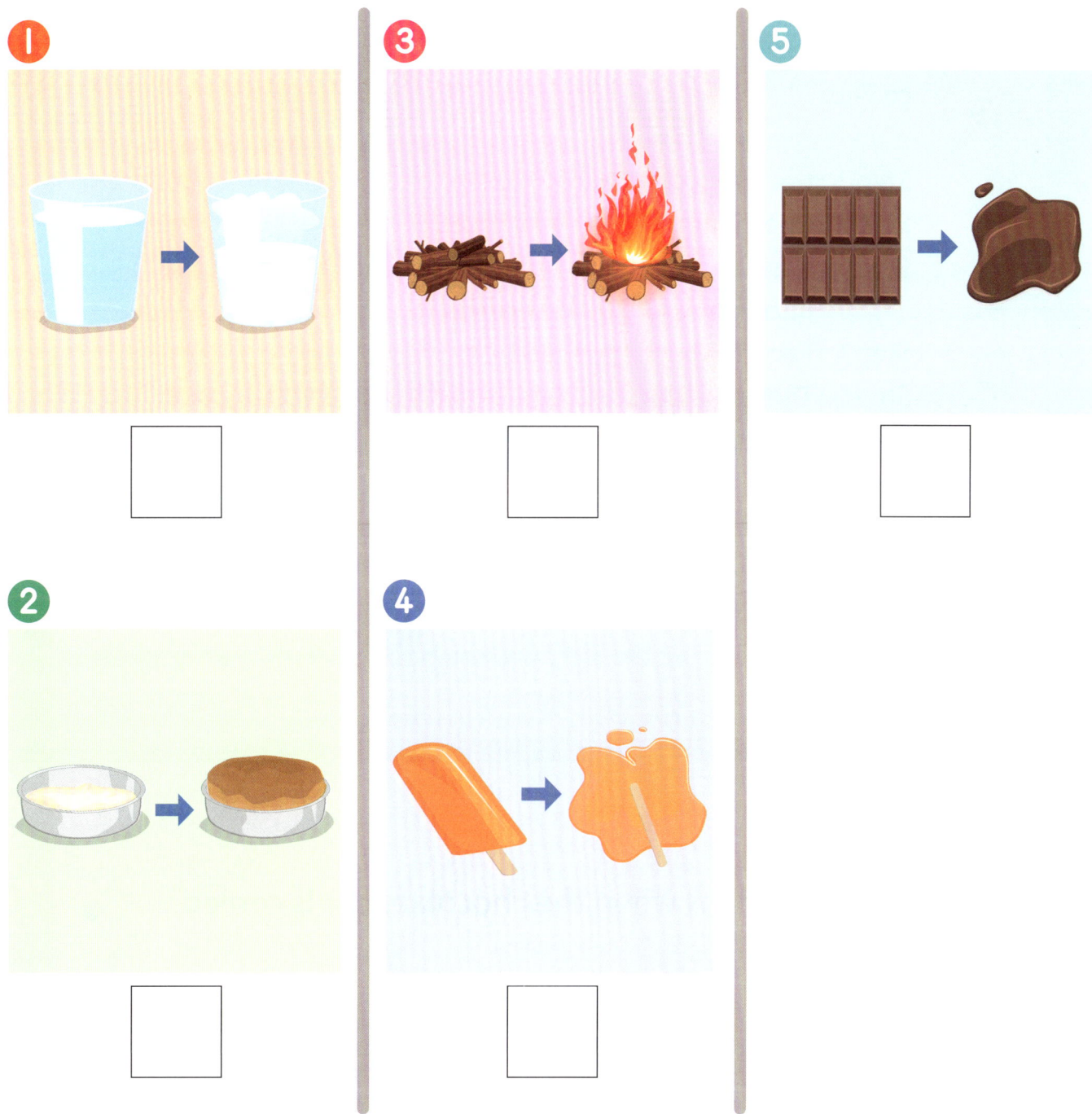

1

2

3

4

5

Brain Break
Science Journal 4

See what happens to a chocolate bar when it is heated and cooled.

Step 1 : Get a chocolate bar.
Step 2 : Open it and place it on a plate.
Step 3 : Have an adult help you heat the chocolate bar in the microwave for 30–45 seconds.
Step 4 : Record what happened to it.
Step 5 : Then take the chocolate bar and put it in the freezer.
Step 6 : Record what happened to it.

1. What happens when the chocolate bar is heated?

2. What happens when the chocolate bar is cooled?

Unit 4

Art Break!

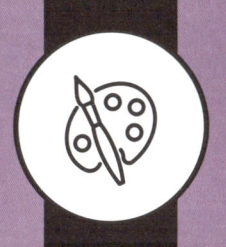

Look at the objects below. Draw what would happen to each when it was heated.

1

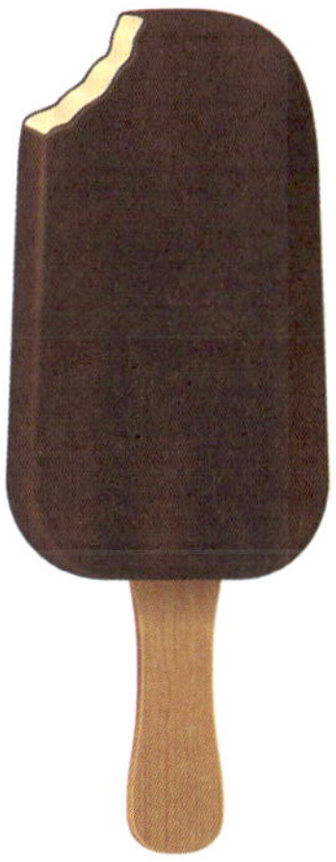

2

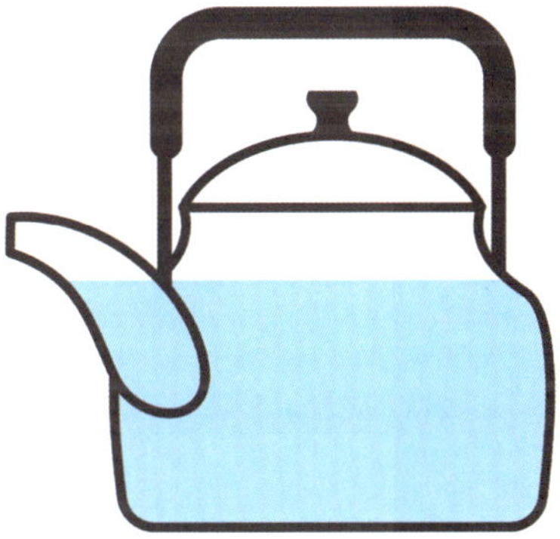

3

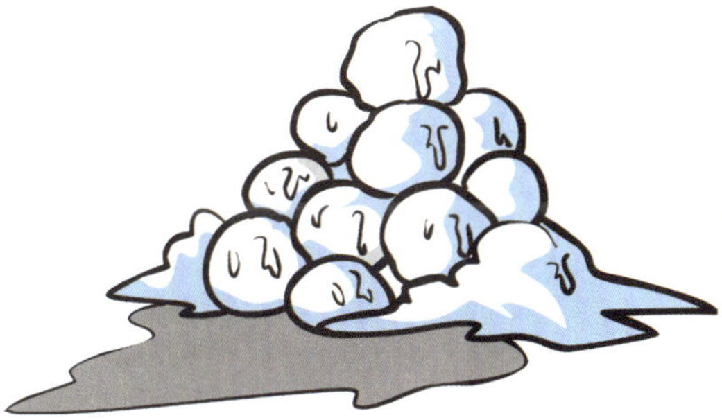

Continents and Oceans

The surface of the earth is covered by continents and oceans. Continents are large land masses. There are seven continents: North America, South America, Europe, Asia, Africa, Australia, and Antarctica. There are five oceans: Atlantic, Pacific, Indian, Arctic, and Southern.

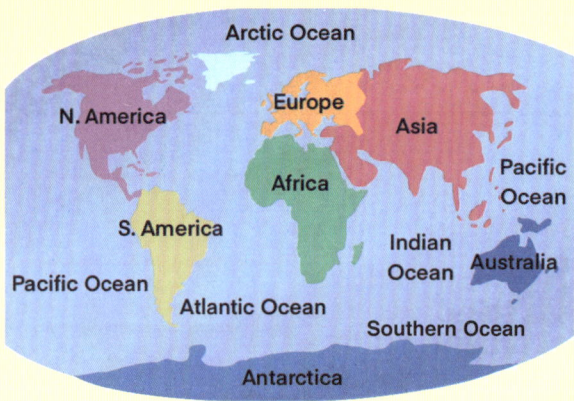

■ Answer the questions.

❶ Name the seven continents.

_____

_____

❷ Name the five oceans.

_____

_____

■ Label the missing continents and oceans on the map below.

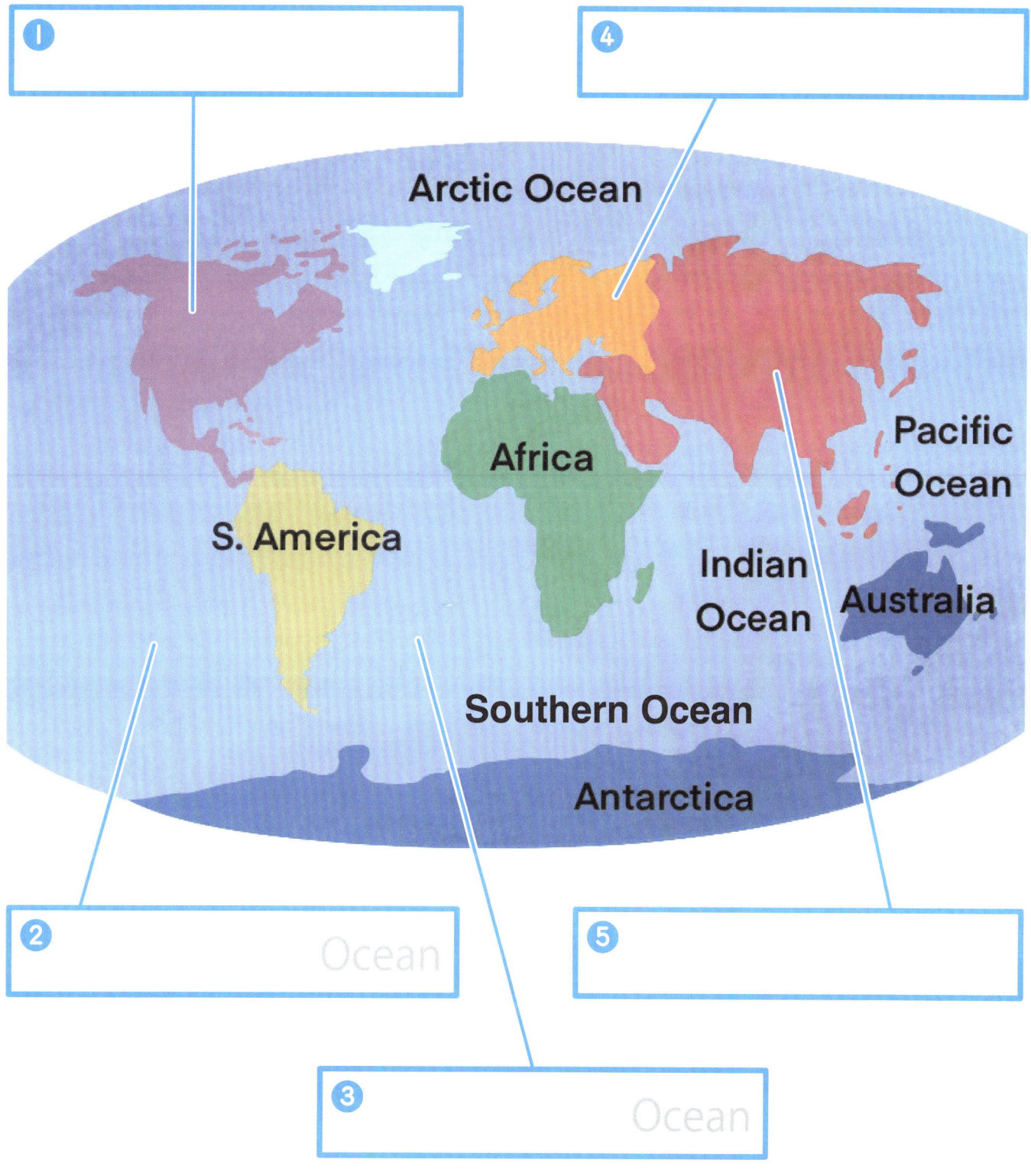

①

④

Arctic Ocean

Africa

S. America

Pacific Ocean

Indian Ocean

Australia

Southern Ocean

Antarctica

② Ocean

⑤

③ Ocean

Landforms

All of Earth's continents have different landforms. Landforms are natural features on the earth's surface. Mountains, rivers, canyons, and valleys are examples of landforms. Some famous landforms are Mount Everest, the tallest mountain in the world, and the Grand Canyon in the United States.

■ Answer the questions.

❶ What is a landform?

❷ Name two types of landforms.

■ Use the world map to write where each landform can be found.

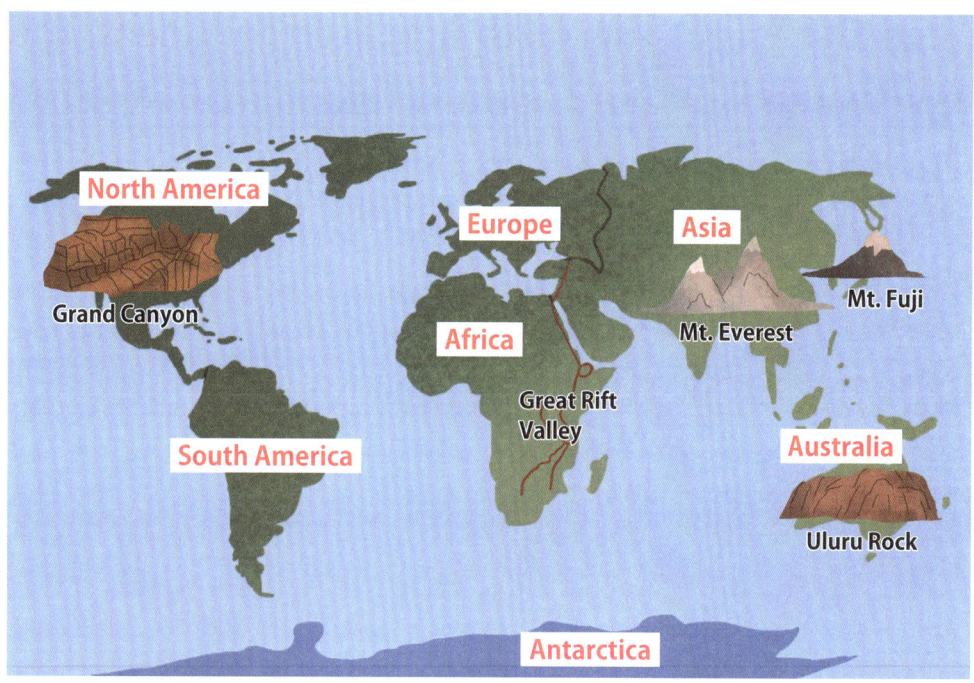

❶Where is Mount Everest?

❷Where is Mount Fuji?

❸Where is the Great Rift Valley?

❹Where is Uluru?

Famous US Landmarks

KEY POINTS

The United States is on the North American continent. The US has many famous landforms, such as the Grand Canyon and the Mississippi River. The US also has many famous landmarks. A landmark is a building or memorial that makes a place easy to recognize.

Here are some examples of US landmarks.

The Gateway Arch is a famous landmark in St. Louis, Missouri.

The Lincoln Memorial is a landmark in Washington, D.C. that honors 16th President Abraham Lincoln.

The Empire State Building is a landmark in New York City, NY. It was once the city's tallest building.

The Golden Gate Bridge is a landmark in San Francisco, CA. It is red to help it stand out from the fog that often surrounds it.

■ Answer the questions using the Key Points.

❶ What is a landmark?

❷ If you saw the Gateway Arch landmark, which city would you be in?

❸ If you saw the Empire State Building which city would you be in?

❹ If you wanted to see the Golden Gate Bridge, what US city would you have to go to?

❺ If you wanted to see the Lincoln Memorial, what city would you have to go to?

The United States is made up of 50 states. Each state has its own famous cities, landmarks, and landforms. Look at the map below for some examples.

Many US states also have a state flower, a state bird, and a state motto!

New York
State Capital: Albany
State Flower: Rose
State Bird: Eastern Bluebird
State Motto: Excelsior

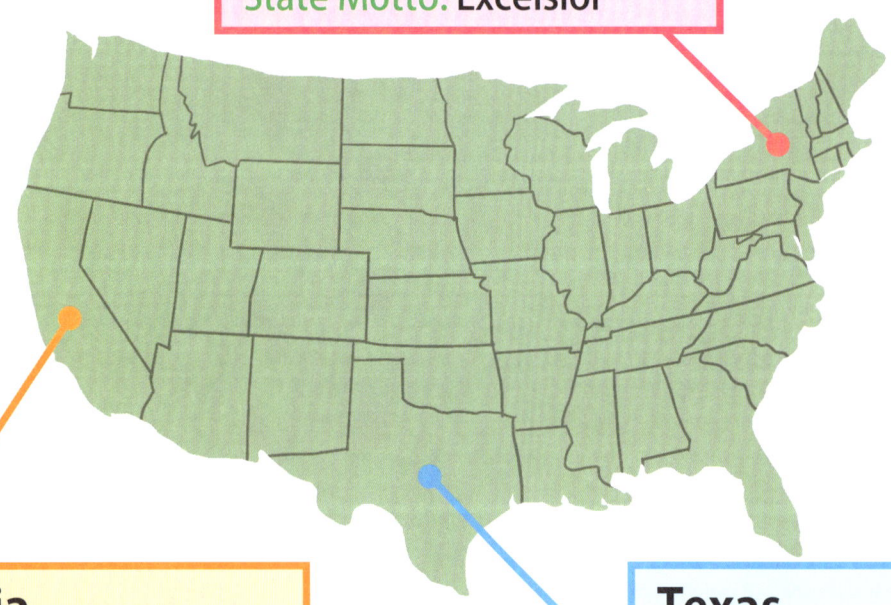

California
State Capital: Sacramento
State Flower: Golden Poppy
State Bird: Valley Quail
State Motto: Eureka!

Texas
State Capital: Austin
State Flower: Blue Bonnet
State Bird: Mockingbird
State Motto: Friendship

■ Answer the questions about your own state. Ask your parent or guardian to help you look up information about the state you live in on the computer or in a book.

My State:

State Capital:

Famous Landmarks:

Famous Landforms:

State Bird:

State Flower:

State Motto:

Brain Break
Word Search

■ Find the words in the word box in the puzzle below.

Continent	Ocean	Asia	Africa
Atlantic	Pacific	Arctic	Europe

C	H	T	D	U	N	M	L	L
O	C	E	A	N	B	W	A	T
N	J	Y	F	P	A	X	T	N
T	N	U	R	O	S	Z	L	H
I	M	I	I	L	I	G	A	F
N	K	O	C	N	A	H	N	C
E	I	P	A	X	Z	N	T	I
N	Q	S	T	V	T	B	I	F
T	W	A	R	C	T	I	C	I
D	E	B	Z	B	Q	V	A	C
F	R	W	X	U	S	C	S	A
G	E	U	R	O	P	E	X	P

■ Color the picture. Focus only on coloring and breathing.

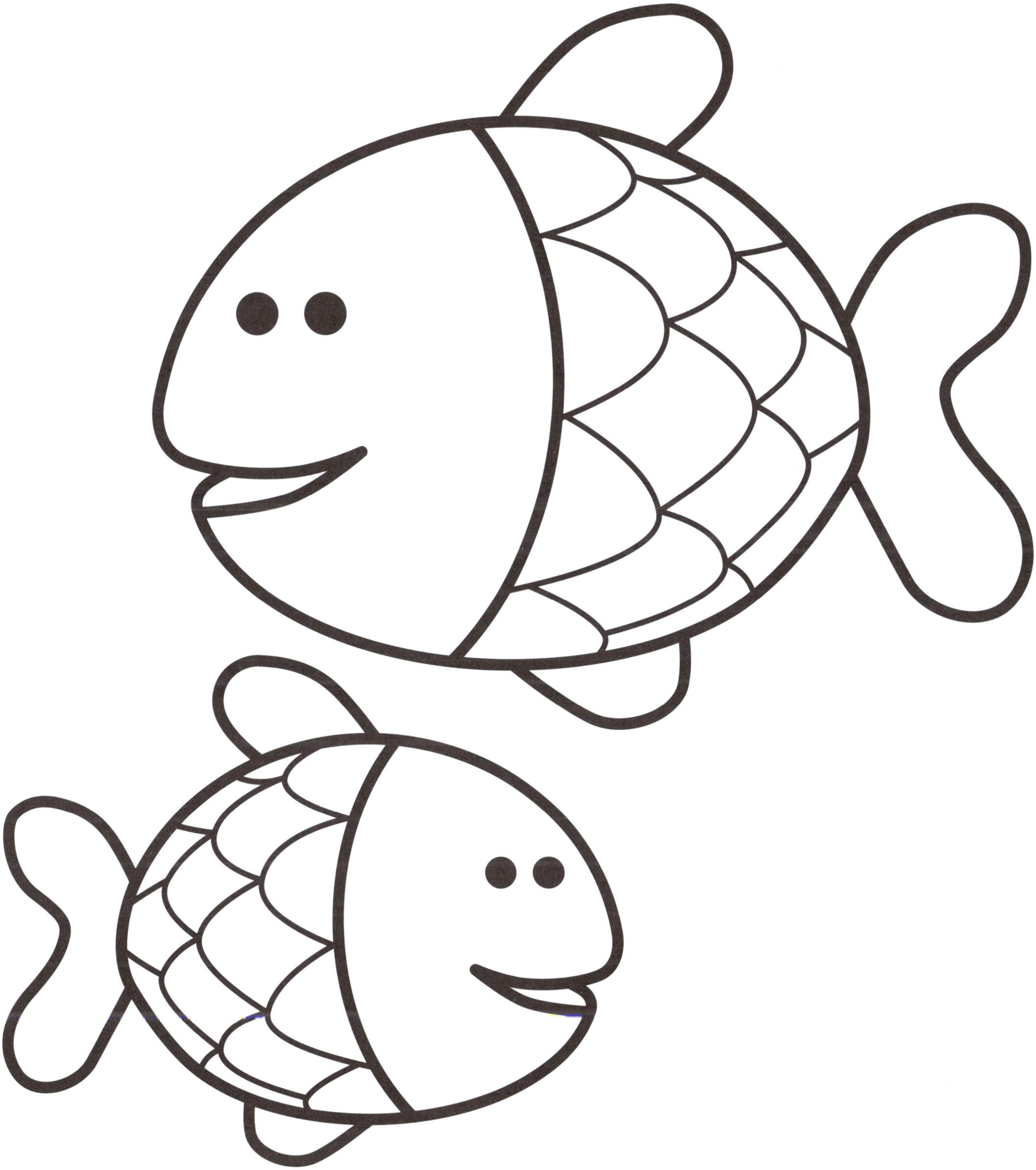

Jigsaw Puzzles 1

■ Fit the missing pieces in the puzzle.

A

B

C

D

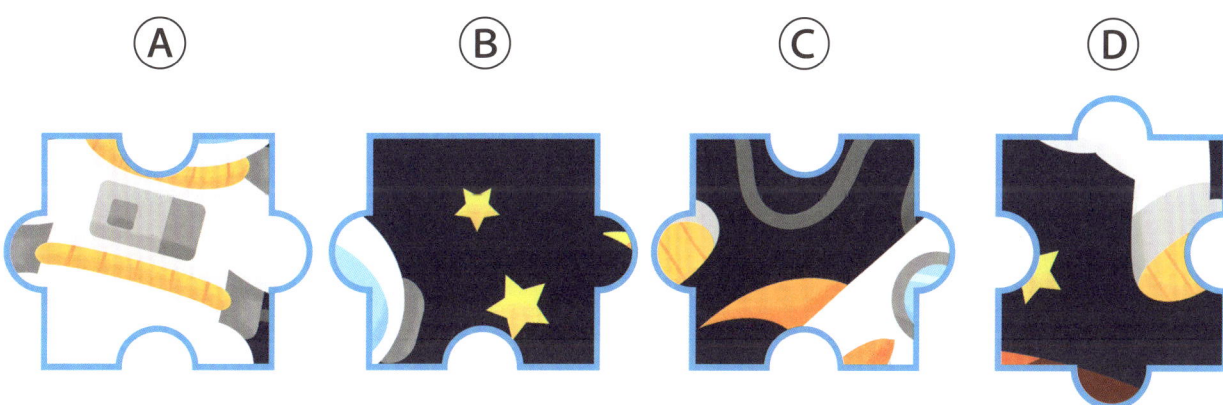

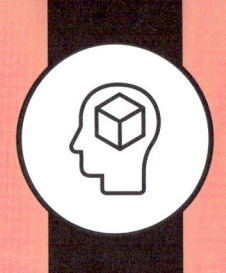

Jigsaw Puzzles 2

■ Place a check mark (✔) by the piece that completes the puzzle.

1

2

3

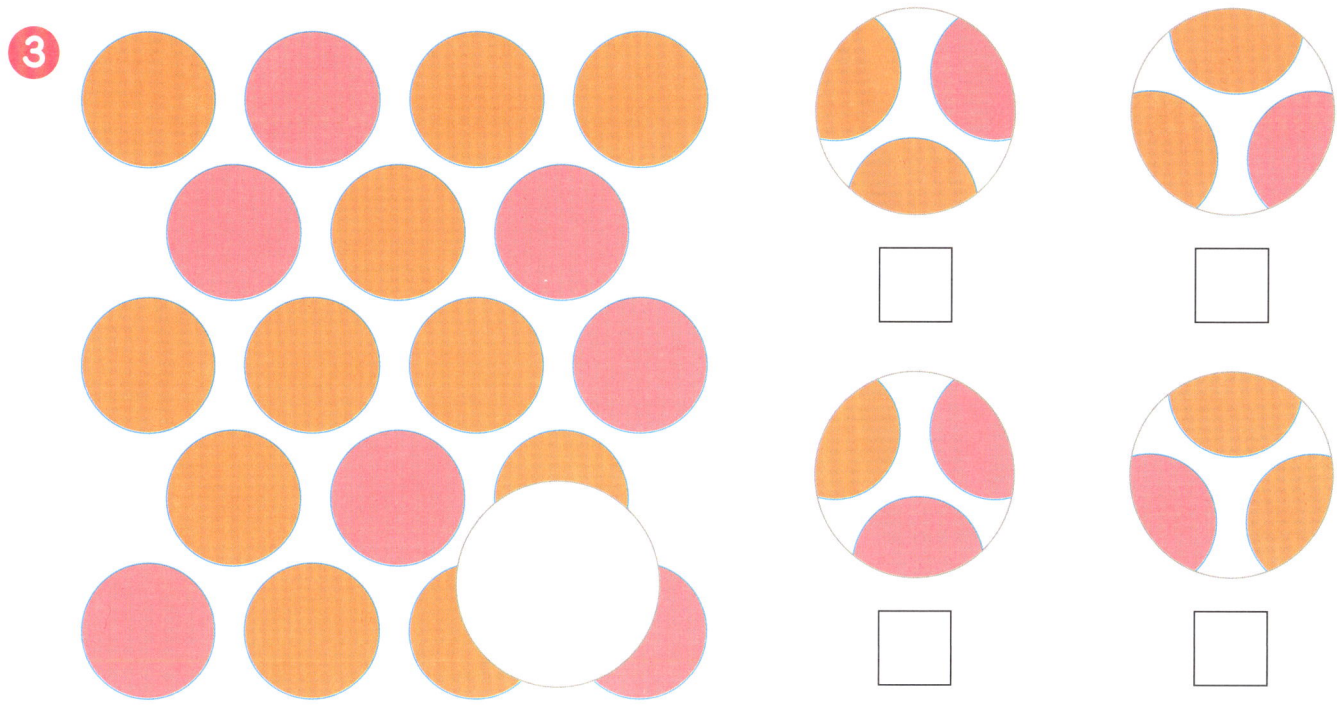

4

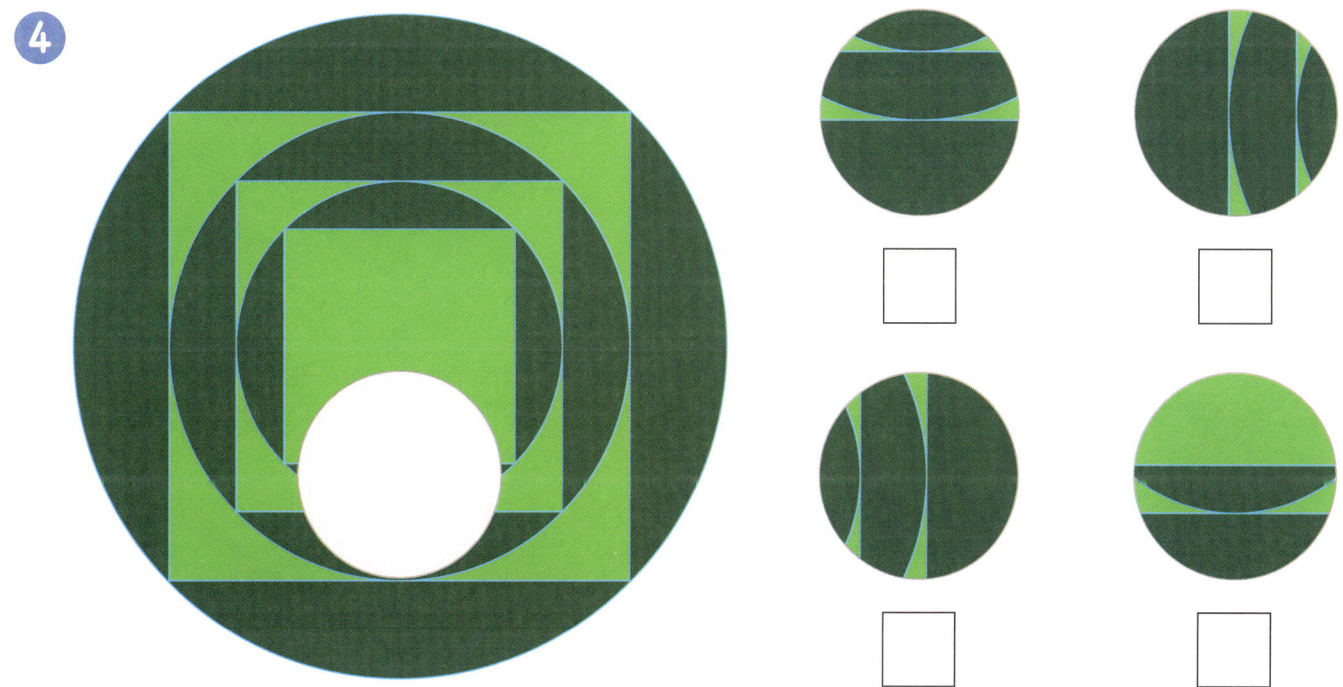

Shadow Pictures

■ Draw a line to match the objects with their shadows.

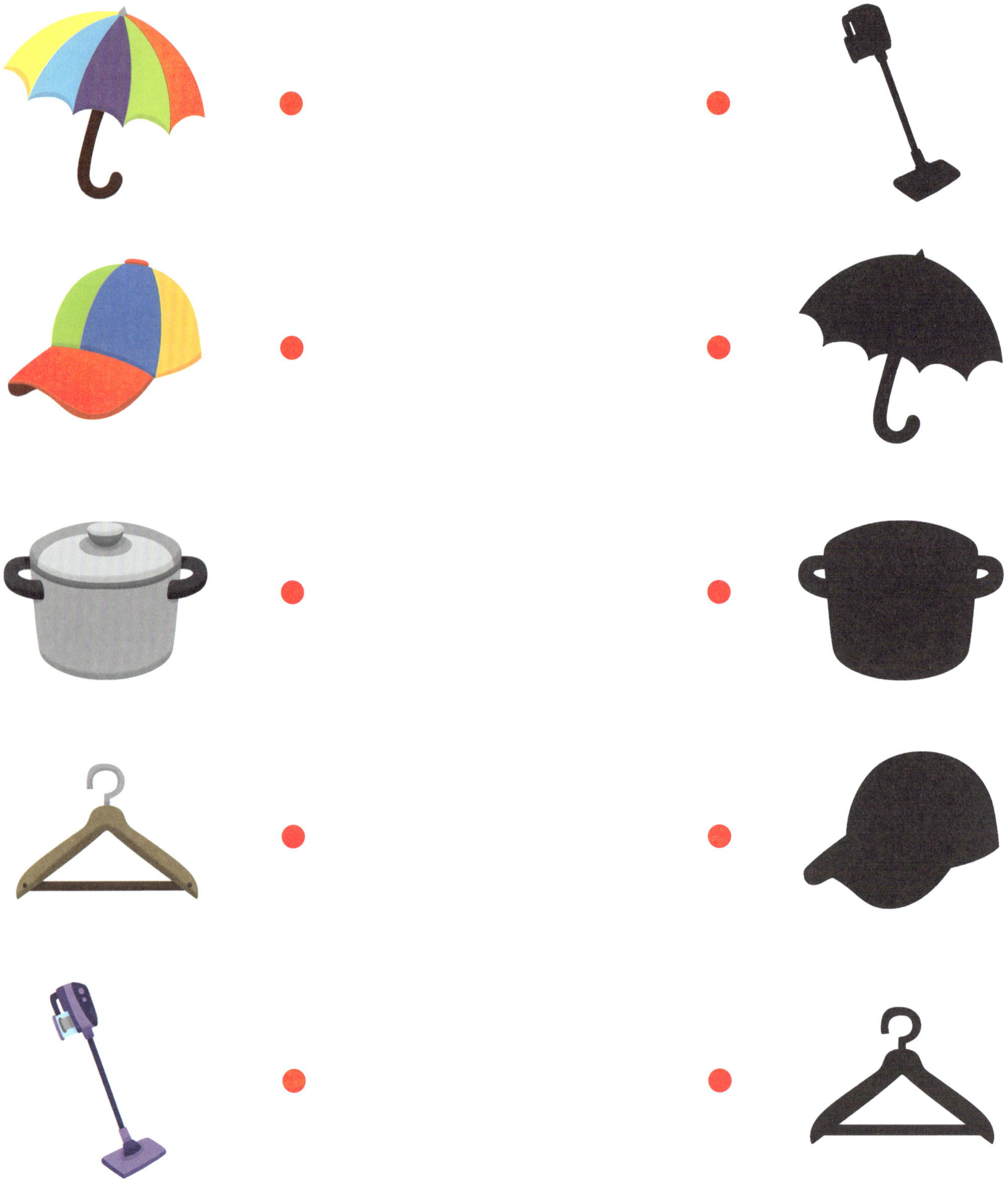

Date

Great Job Sticker

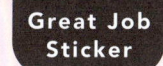

■ Write a check mark (✓) in the box under the blocks that make the shadow.

1

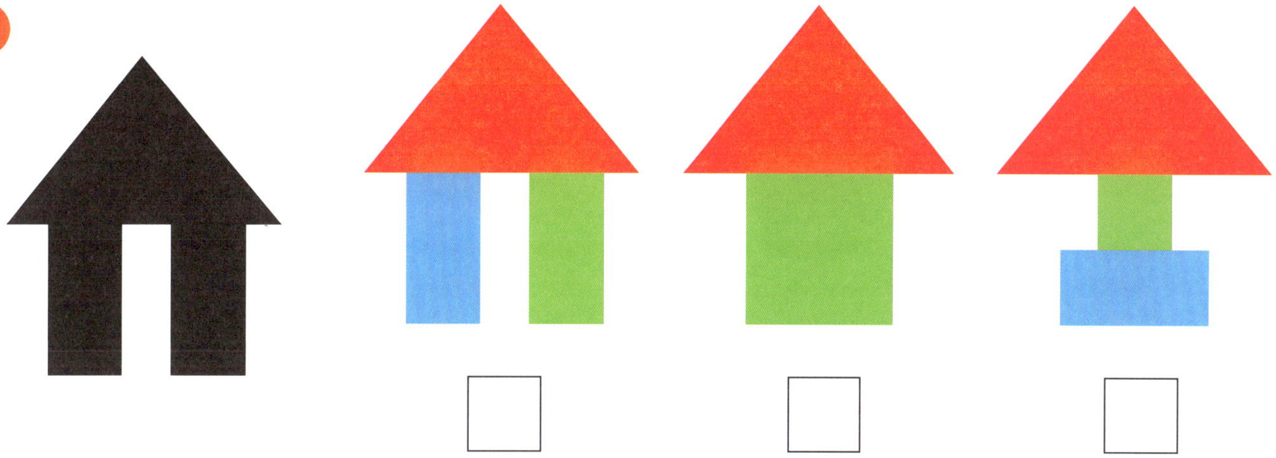

2

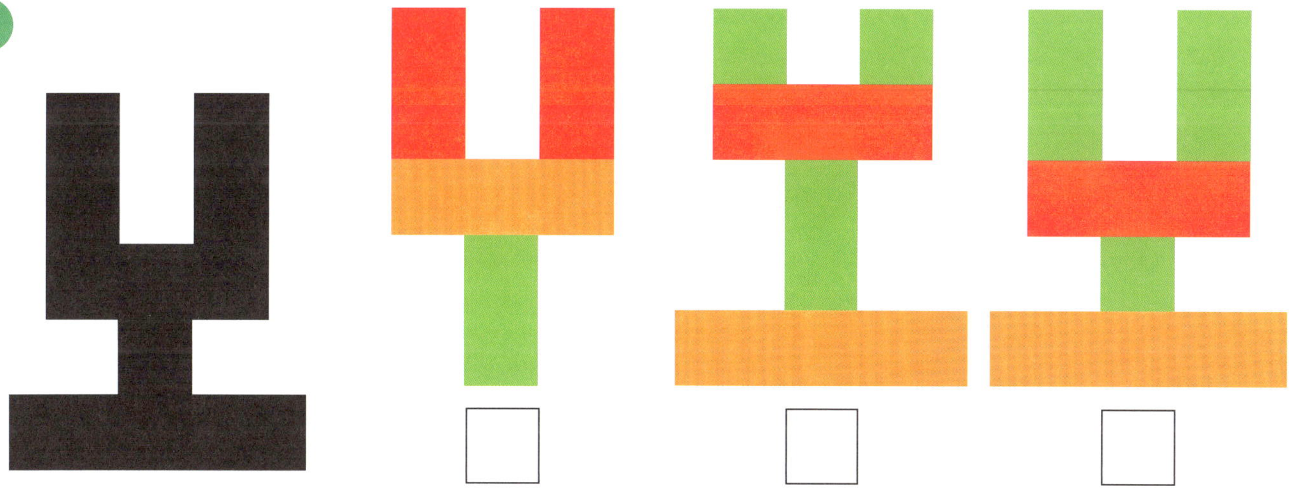

3

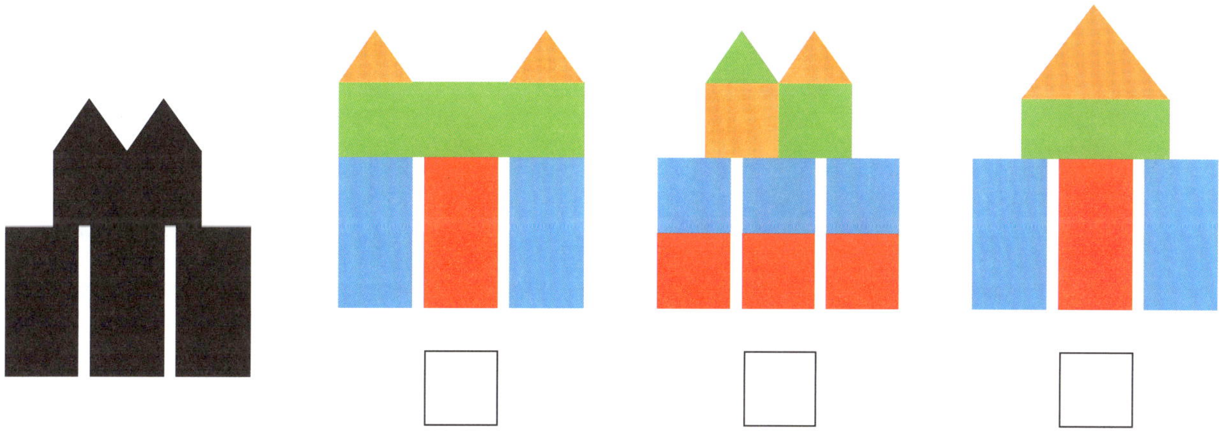

Spot the Difference

■ Only one of the six pictures from Ⓐ to Ⓕ is different from the others. Write the letter in the box for which one is different.

Ⓐ

Ⓓ

Ⓑ

Ⓔ

Ⓒ

Ⓕ

■ Look at the top picture. Then look at the bottom picture. Circle one thing that is different in the bottom picture.

Physical Education Break!

It's important to move your body and exercise!
Try this fun activity below for a study break!

Spell Your Name Exercise Game!

■ Complete the exercise for each letter to spell your name.

A-B-C	D-E-F	G-H-I
5 Jumping Jacks	15 Arm Circles	5 Lunges to the left

J-K-L	M-N-O	P-Q-R
10 High Knees	Run in place for 30 seconds	5 Lunges to the right

S-T-U	V-W-X	Y-Z
10 Toe Touches	10 Jumping Jacks	5 Sit ups

Use this page to keep track of your progress throughout the book. Place a check mark in the box when you have completed a section.

Main Purpose

KEY POINTS

When you read an opinion pieces, try to figure out what the author's opinion is. Often they will say it in the beginning. The opinion is what their piece will be all about.

■ Read the opinion text. Then answer the question.

Winter is the best time of year. It's cold out, but you can be cozy inside. If there is a lot of snow, you might get a day off from school. And you can drink hot chocolate!

What is the author's main opinion? Choose the correct answer.

☐ Winter is the best time of year.

☐ If there is a lot of snow, you might get a day off from school!

☐ And best of all, you can drink hot chocolate!

■ Read the opinion text. Then write the main opinion in the space below.

There are lots of holidays that I like, but the best holiday is Thanksgiving. Thanksgiving is all about food! You don't have to get presents, and you don't have to get dressed up. Thanksgiving is a holiday for family and eating!

What is the author's opinion?

Reasons

■ Read the text below. Then choose the reason that best supports the author's opinion.

> Tacos are the most delicious food. You can have any kind of taco you want: pork, chicken, fish, or vegetables! Tacos are salty, and sometimes spicy. Some people prefer pizza. But I will always choose tacos.

Which of the following best supports the author's opinion?

☐ Tacos are the most delicious food.

☐ You can have any kind of taco you want!

☐ Some people prefer pizza.

■ Read the text below. Then choose the reason that best supports the author's opinion.

> In my opinion, kids should be able to vote for president. Presidents serve for four years. That's a long time! The decisions they make will affect the future, and it's our future, too. Some people think kids shouldn't vote because we might not read the news. And some people think we're just not ready to make choices that are important. But I say, everyone should have their say.

Which of the following best supports the author's opinion?

☐ Some people think kids shouldn't vote because we might not read the news.

☐ The decisions they make will affect the future, and it's our future, too.

☐ And some people think we're just not ready to make choices that are important.

Compare and Contrast 1

All texts can say something different. Even when you read two texts about the same topic, they may tell you different things. Two texts might share different types of information. One may share an opinion. Or the two author's may have opinions that are different.

■ Read the text below. Then choose the correct answer.

> Volcanos are a type of land feature. They are tall, like a mountain. But they are more than just a mountain! Volcanos are a place where hot, melted rock from inside the earth can come up and spill out onto the earth. This is called an erruption. Not all volcanos are active. Some volcanos haven't errupted in many, many years.

What is the author's purpose in this text?

☐ To tell a story about a volcano

☐ To give an opinion about a volcano

☐ To share facts about a volcano

■ Read the text below. Then choose the correct answer.

Volcanoes are the most interesting landform. Sure, mountains are tall. But they just stand there. And lakes are just big puddles. Volcanoes are full of hot melted rock! And sometimes they erupt. Now that's an exciting landform.

This text is also about volcanoes. But what is the author's main purpose?

☐ To give an opinion.

☐ To explain how volcanos work.

☐ To tell a story about visiting a volcano.

Compare and Contrast 2

■ Read the text below. Then choose the correct answer.

July Fourth is a holiday that celebrates American independence. On July 4, 1776, the Declaration of Independence was adopted. This paper said that American no longer wanted to be ruled by England. After this, a war was fought, and the United States became its own country.

What is the author's purpose in this text?

☐ To tell a story about the Fourth of July

☐ To give an opinion about the Fourth of July

☐ To tell the the history of the Fourth of July

■ Read the text below. Then answer the question.

I love the Fourth of July. Every year, my family has a barbecue. My mom grills hamburgers, and my dad cooks corn for us to eat. Then we go to see fireworks with my cousins.

This text is also about the Fourth of July. But what is the purpose of this text? How is it different from the last text? Write your answer below.

Brain Break
Spot the Difference

■ Write three differences between the two pictures on the lines below.

■ Change each negative or bad thought into a postive or good one.

1

Negative I'm bad at math because I got a poor grade on my test.

↓

Positive I didn't do as well as I wanted to, but I will keep working hard and try again next time!

2

Negative My friend didn't sit with me at lunch today, they don't like me anymore.

↓

Positive

3

Negative I can't score a basket in gym class, so I must be bad at everything.

↓

Positive

4

Negative My friend can draw better than me, so I guess I should never draw pictures again.

↓

Positive

Stating Your Opinion

KEY POINTS

Opinion texts always have a clear opinion. As a writer, you need to make sure your reader knows what you believe. This can be done by stating your opinion clearly in the beginning.

Smoking should not be allowed in parks. It creates dirty air for other people to breathe in. It is bad for our health. And it may even cause some people to litter.

■ Write a clear opinion about this topic: having to wear a school uniform.

■ Write an opinion for each topic.

Cats vs. dogs

①

The best month

②

The most delicious food

③

The most interesting subject

④

The funniest movie

⑤

Giving Reasons

KEY POINTS

When you share your opinion, you need to give reasons to support your opinion. These reasons show why you have this opinion. They may also make the reader agree with you.

> It's important to not waste plastic. Lots of things come in plastic. **But plastic is bad for our planet! It is difficult to recycle. A lot of it winds up in the ocean.** It can hurt fish.

■ Which of the following would be the best reason to support the opinion, "students should not get homework"?

☐ Homework helps kids learn.

☐ Kids need time to rest and play.

☐ Some classes give homework.

■ Imagine you are writing an opinion piece about which book you think is the best. Choose the book and write three reasons.

Book

1

2

3

Using Linking Words

Linking words can help your opinion text flow more smoothly. They can also help you link your reasons to your opinion and to each other.

Students should get homework **because** it helps them practice new skills and knowledge.

Students need daily practice **and** there is not enough time during the school day.

Also, some kids enjoy doing homework at home.

■ Choose the correct word.

❶ Dogs play fetch **and • also** they love to go for walks.

❷ Dogs are the best animal **because • and** they help people.

❸ **Because • Also** taking care of a dog teaches responsibility.

■ Write two sentences using each linking word.

because

and

also

Conclusions

Conclusions give the reader a sense of closure.

I think elephants are the cutest animal. They have a long trunk and big ears. They are also very sweet. They spend a lot of time with other elephants and have a community. Not to mention, they're very smart. We've all heard the saying: Elephants never forget!

■ Write a conclusion for an opinion text about your favorite book.

_____

_____

_____

_____

_____

_____

■ Write your opinion text about the best book. Be sure to state your opinion, give reasons, use linking words, and include a conclusion.

Brain Break
Funny Fill-in

■ Fill in the blanks with the correct part of speech to tell an opinion.

In my opinion,

noun

should always

verb

. Some people think

plural noun

are

adjective

. But I think

plural noun

are

adjective

. If you disagree, then you should

verb

. I feel very

adverb

about

this

noun

!

■ Sit comfortably and fill in the boxes based on what is around you.

❶ Write 5 things you can see...

❷ Write 4 things you can touch...

❸ Write 3 things you can hear...

❹ Write 2 things you can smell...

❺ Write 1 thing you can taste...

Data and Graphing 1

■ You were given a bag of three different kinds of cookies. Answer the following questions.

❶ How many round cookies are in the bag? ⬜ cookies

❷ How many triangular cookies are in the bag? ⬜ cookies

❸ How many square cookies are in the bag? ⬜ cookies

4 Write the numbers from the other page in the table below.

Shape of cookie	🍪	🔺	🟧
Number of cookie	5		

5 Color in the correct number of squares in each column of the bar chart.

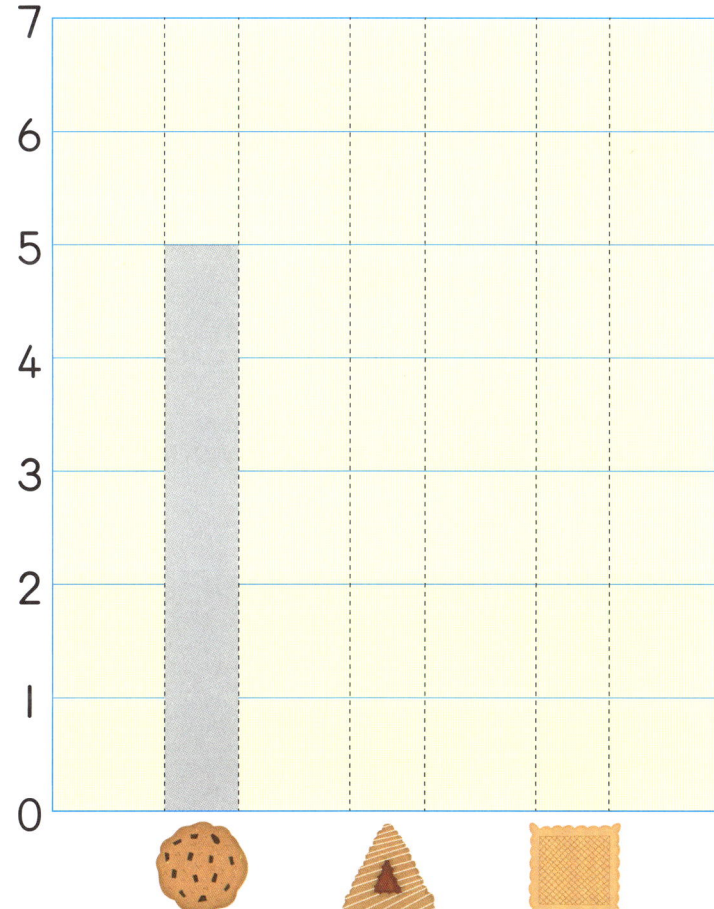

Data and Graphing 2

■ You asked everyone in your class about their favorite fruit. Answer the following questions.

Jim   Olivia   Tim   James   Mary

Liam   Andy   Sophia   Noah   Emma

Fred   Mark   Anna   Bob   Mia

❶ How many people chose apple as their favorite fruit? ☐ people

❷ How many people chose pineapple as their favorite fruit? ☐ people

❸ How many people chose grapes as their favorite fruit? ☐ people

❹ How many people chose banana as their favorite fruit? ☐ people

5 Write the numbers from the other page in the table below.

Favorite Fruit	Apple	Pineapple	Grapes	Banana
Number of people				

6 Color in the correct number of squares in each column of the bar chart.

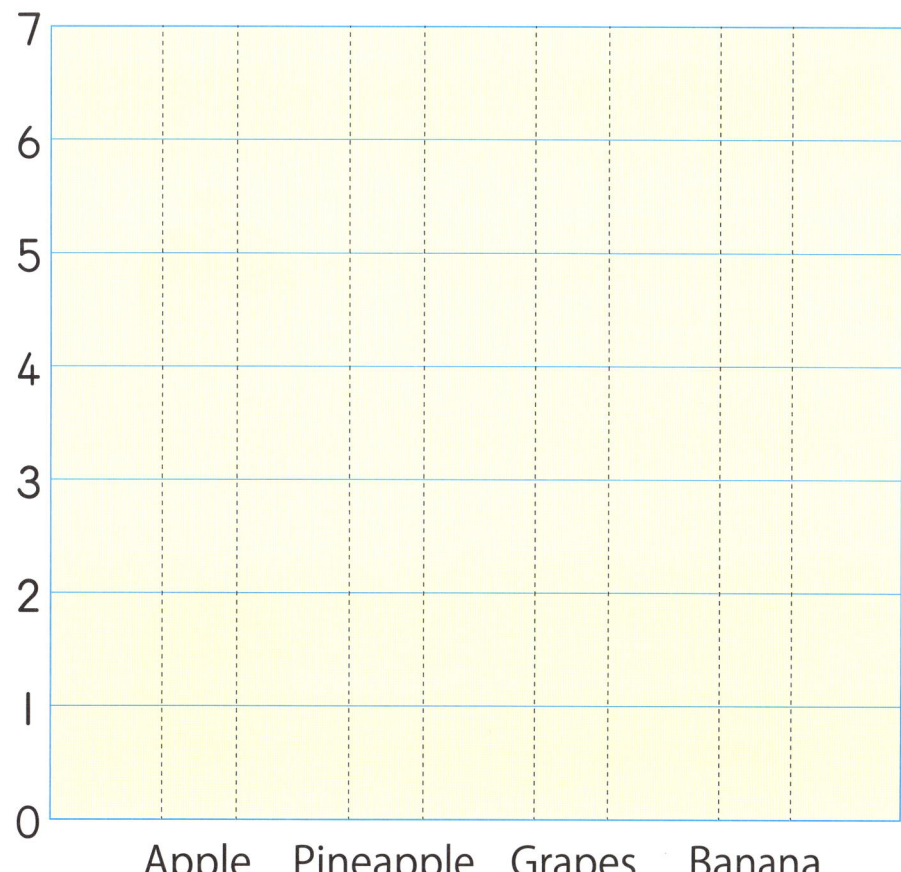

Data and Graphing 3

■ This class is discussing graphs that show their favorite subjects and sports. Write a check mark (✓) for correct or an ✗ for incorrect in each box.

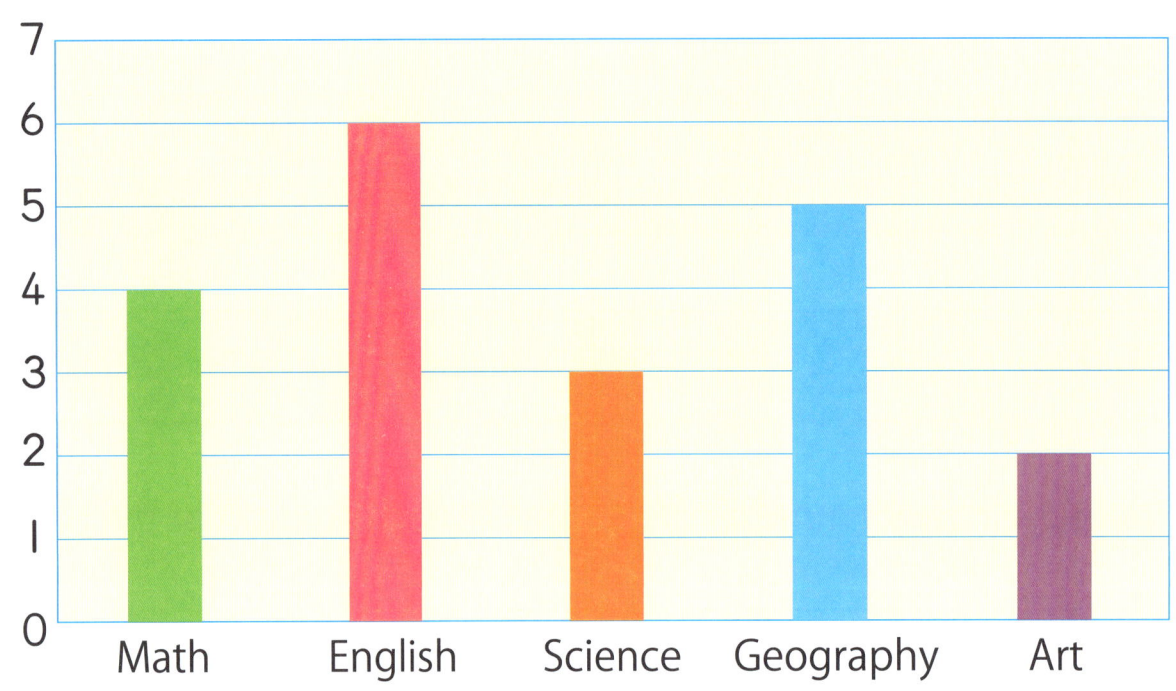

①  Four people answered that their favorite subject is math.

☐

② Six people answered that their favorite subject is geography.

☐

③ The biggest group answered that their favorite subject is English.

☐

④  The smallest group answered that their favorite subject is Science.

☐

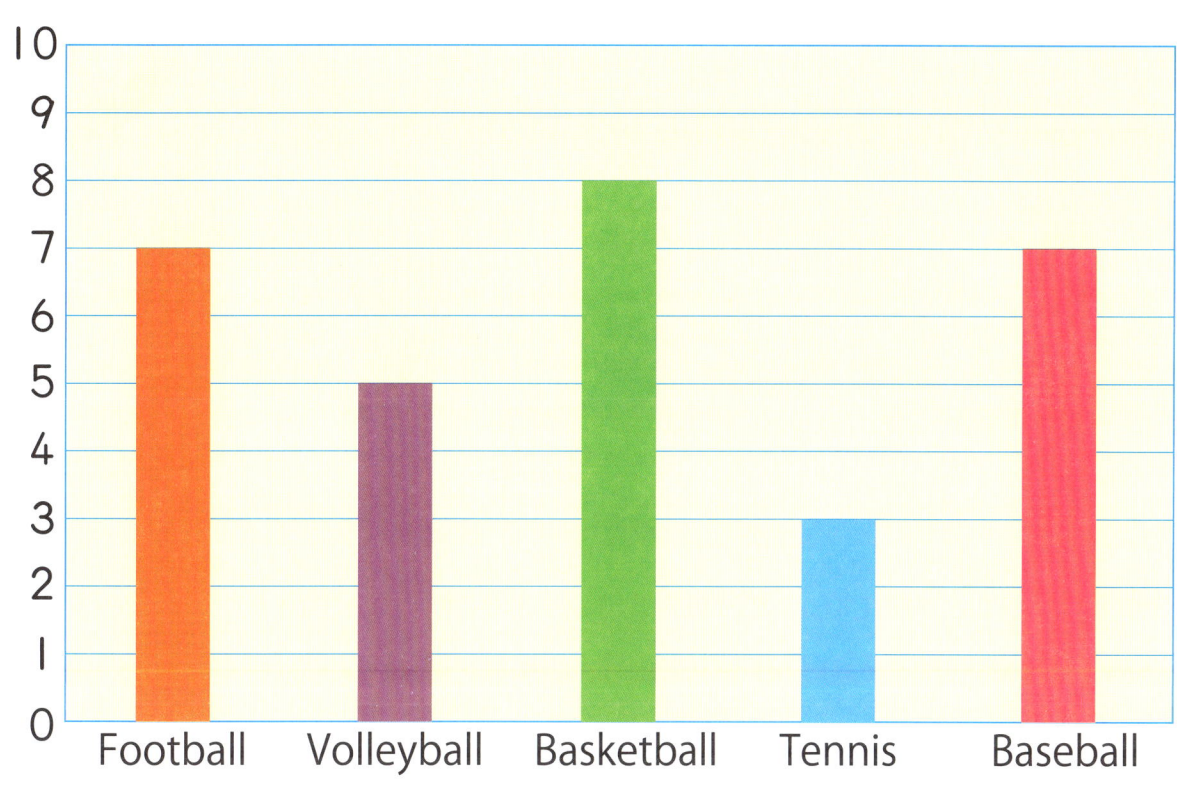

⑤

Seven people answered that their favorite sport is volleyball.

⑥

Seven people answered that their favorite sport is baseball.

⑦

The biggest group answered that their favorite sport is football.

⑧

The smallest group answered that their favorite sport is tennis.

Word Problems 1

■ **Answer the following word problems.**

❶ Elio picked 26 strawberries. Later he picked 7 more. How many strawberries did he pick in all?

Ans. _____ strawberries

❷ Gianna used 35 stickers in her sticker book. She still has 85 left. How many stickers were in her sticker book to start with?

Ans. _____ stickers

❸ Scarlett knitted 19 inches of her scarf and wants to knit 12 inches more today. How long will the scarf be at the end of the day?

Ans. _____ inches

④ Colter had 34 dimes, and then used 16 dimes to buy some candy. How many dimes does he have left?

Ans.   dimes

⑤ The necklace has 70 more beads on it than the bracelet. The necklace has 150 beads. How many beads are on the bracelet?

Ans.   beads

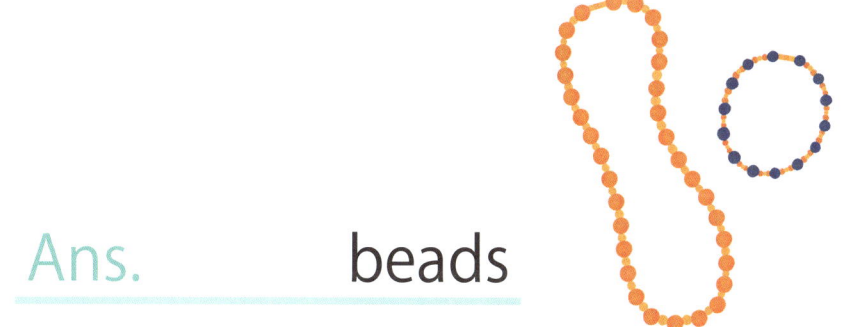

⑥ Flora has a 7-foot rope and an 11-foot rope. What is the difference in length between the two ropes?

Ans.   feet

Word Problems 2

■ **Answer the following word problems.**

1 The cake shop had 78 pounds of sugar this morning. Since then, the chef has used 25 pounds of sugar. How much sugar is left?

Ans. _____ pounds

2 Charlotte got a box of oranges. Yesterday, her family ate 5 and today they ate 8. There are 12 oranges left in the box. How many oranges were in the box to start with?

Ans. _____ oranges

3 Jiraiya got 25 stickers from his brother and 17 from his sister. Now he has 100 stickers. How many stickers did he have before?

Ans. _____ stickers

④ There were 40 passengers on the bus. 15 passengers got off at the train station, and 9 passengers got off at the hospital. How many passengers are still on the bus?

Ans.   passengers

⑤ Emberlynn had 19 chocolate bars. She gave 5 to her sister and also gave 5 to her brother. How many bars does she have left?

Ans.   bars

⑥ Alexander has sheets of colored paper for crafts class. Today, he got 30 more from his teacher, and used 21. Now, he has 16 sheets of colored paper left. How many sheets did he have before class today?

Ans.   sheets

Brain Break
Weather Chart

■ Use the graph below to color in the correct number of circles for each type of weather for the month of January.

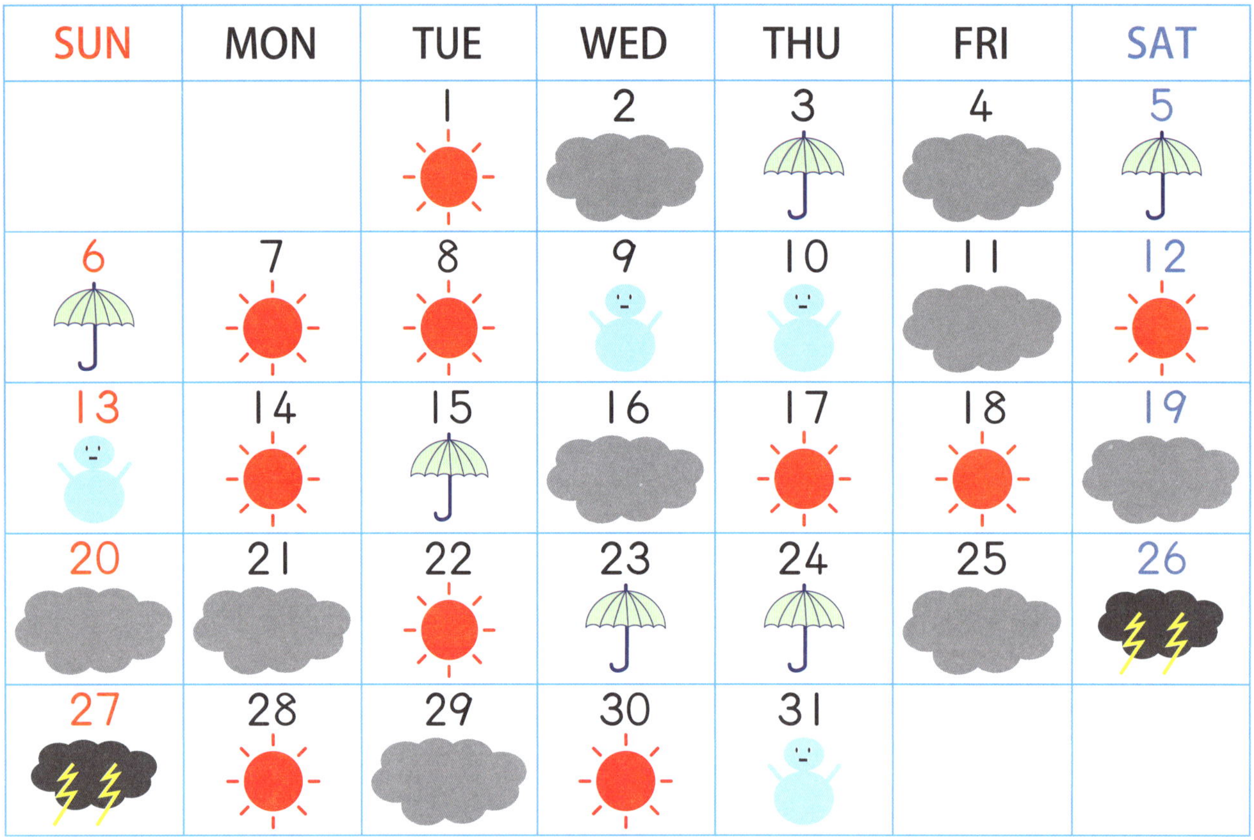

SUN	MON	TUE	WED	THU	FRI	SAT
		1 ☀	2 ☁	3 ☂	4 ☁	5 ☂
6 ☂	7 ☀	8 ☀	9 ⛄	10 ⛄	11 ☁	12 ☀
13 ⛄	14 ☀	15 ☂	16 ☁	17 ☀	18 ☀	19 ☁
20 ☁	21 ☁	22 ☀	23 ☂	24 ☂	25 ☁	26 ⛈
27 ⛈	28 ☀	29 ☁	30 ☀	31 ⛄		

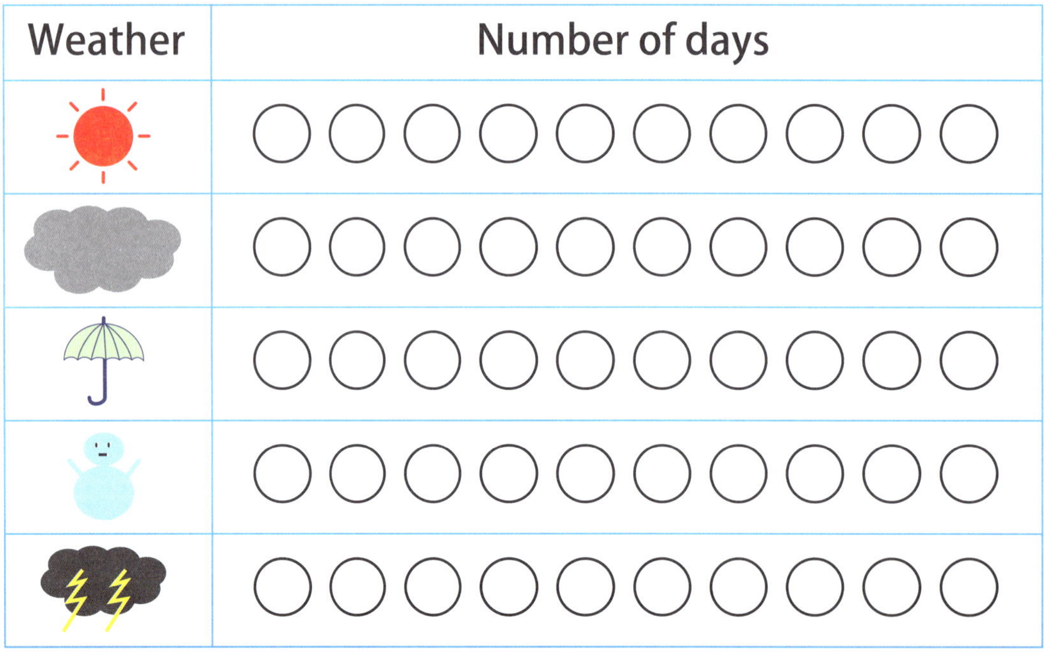

Weather	Number of days
☀	○ ○ ○ ○ ○ ○ ○ ○ ○ ○
☁	○ ○ ○ ○ ○ ○ ○ ○ ○ ○
☂	○ ○ ○ ○ ○ ○ ○ ○ ○
⛄	○ ○ ○ ○ ○ ○ ○ ○ ○
⛈	○ ○ ○ ○ ○ ○ ○ ○ ○

■ Trace the path from start to finish!

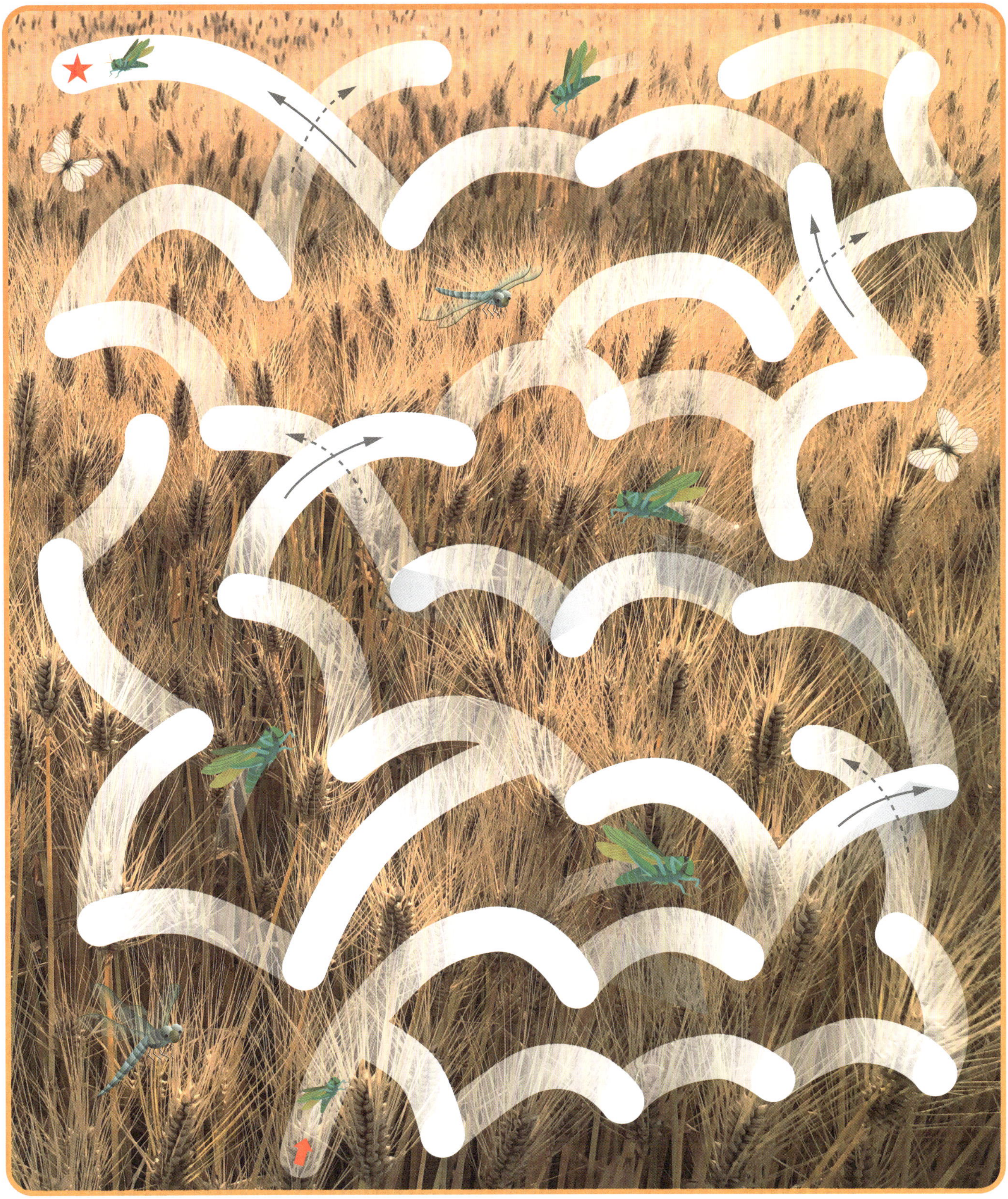

Forces and Motion

When you kick a ball and it begins to roll across the ground, it is in motion. Motion is the change in position of an object. And in order for an object to be in motion a force needs to act on it. A force is anything that can change the motion of an object, like a push or a pull.

■ Answer the questions.

1 What is motion?

_____

2 What is a force?

_____

■ Circle the objects in motion.

Push and Pull

All objects can be moved with either push or a pull. A push is when you use a force to move an object away from you like pushing open a door. A pull is when you use a force to move an object closer to you, like pulling a door shut.

■ **Answer the questions.**

❶ What is a pull?

_____

_____

❷ What is a push?

_____

_____

Date

Great Job Sticker

■ Write push or pull under each picture.

1

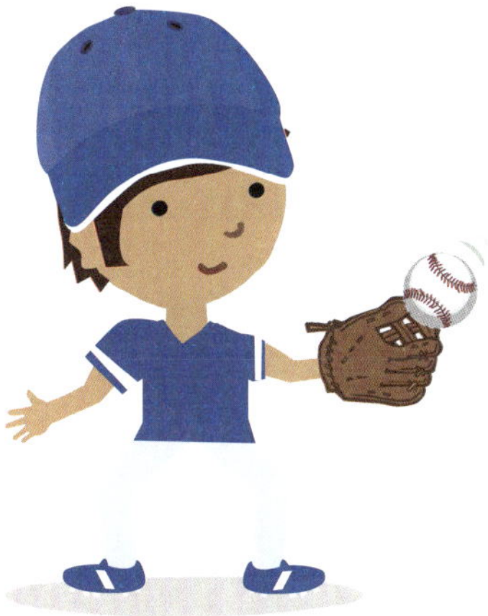

push

2

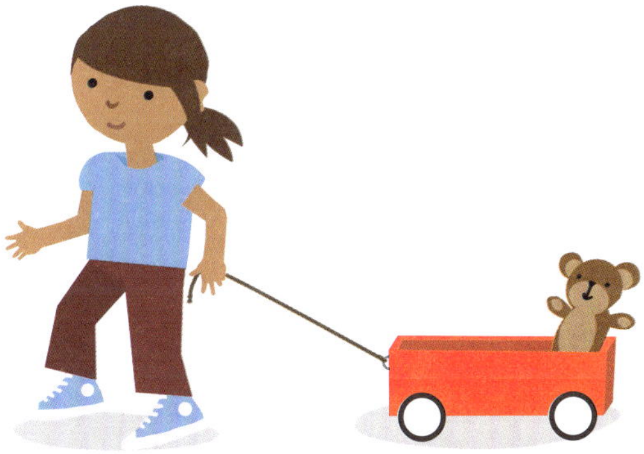

3

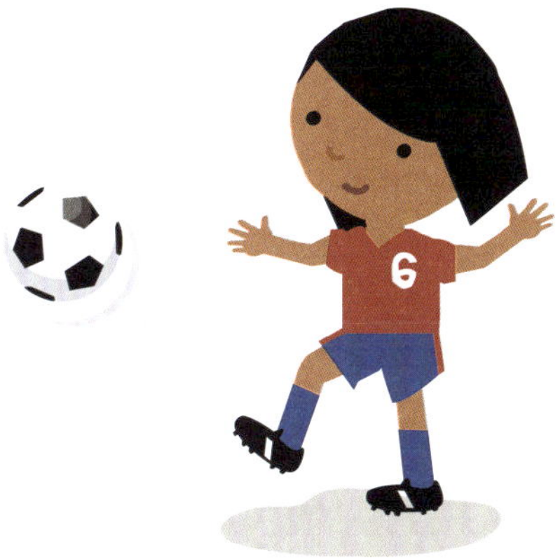

4

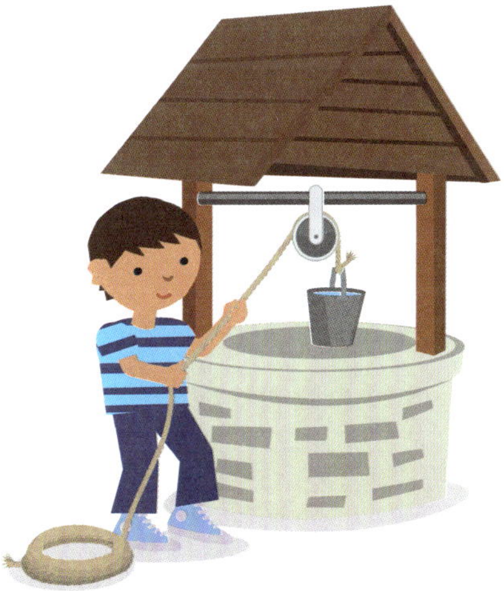

5

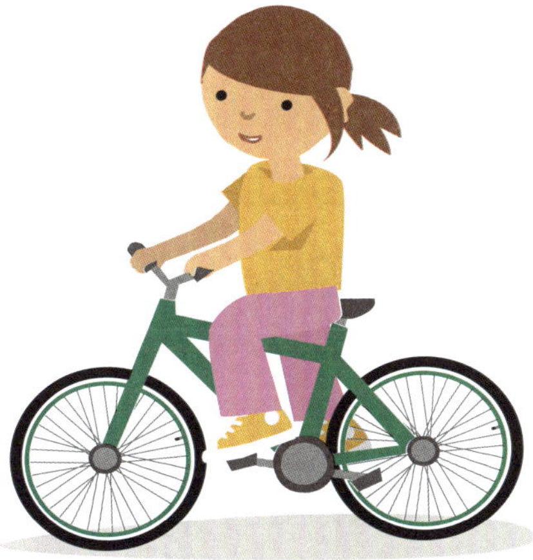

6

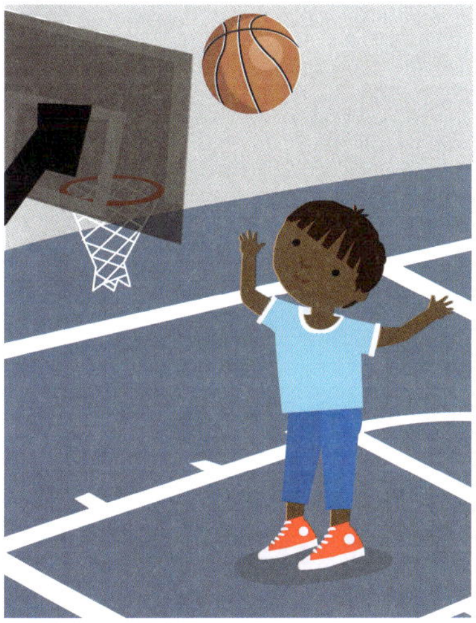

Effects on an Objects

Forces can be described by their direction and strength.

For example, when you kick a ball you are using a certain amount of force to send the ball in a specific direction. The harder you kick the ball, the stronger the force you place on it and the farther it will go.

Another example would be riding a bike. When you ride a bike, your feet push the pedals to move the bike. The harder you push, the faster you go!

■ Answer the questions.

❶ How can forces be described?

❷ What effect can the strength of a force have on a ball?

■ Draw an arrow to show the direction of the force.

1

3

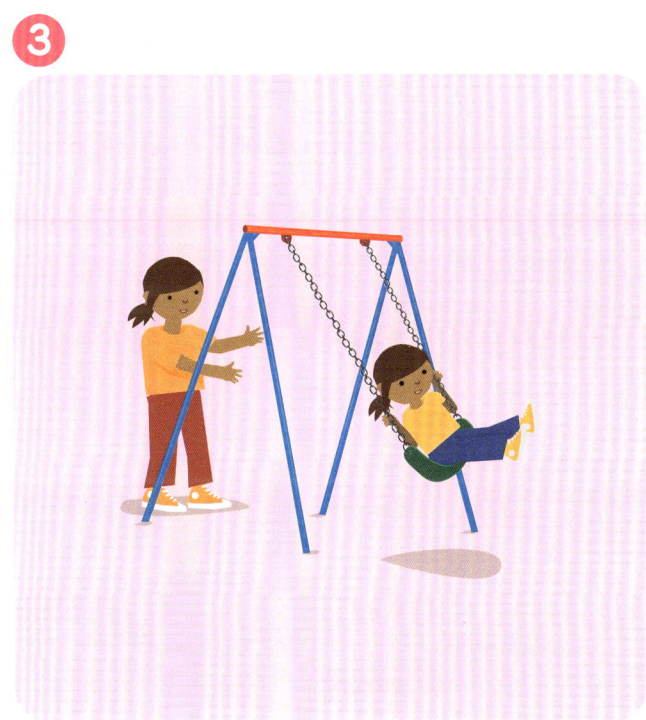

2

A simple machine is any device with few or no moving parts that is used to apply force to an object in order to perform a job. Simple machines were designed to make it easier for people to move objects.

For example, if you carry a heavy object up a set of stairs, you may get tired before you reach the top. But if you roll the object up a ramp, you will use less energy to move the object. A ramp is an example of an inclined plane, which is a type of simple machine.

Here are some other examples of simple machines.

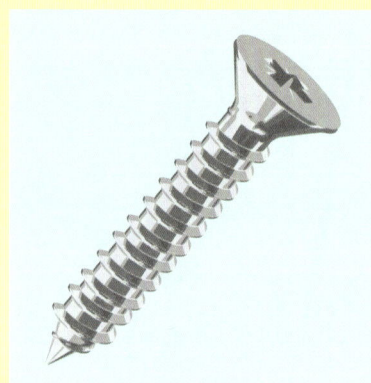

Screw

Inclined Plane

Wedge

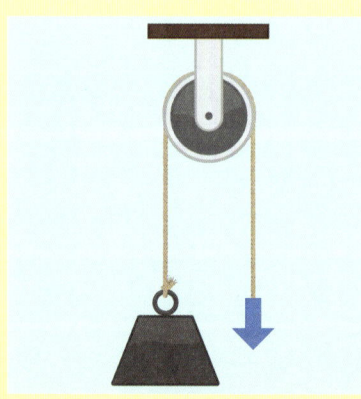

Pulley

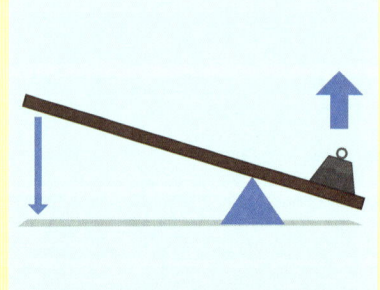

Lever

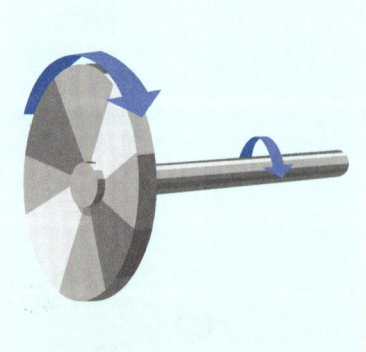

Wheel and Axle

■ Match the simple machine to the task it would help with.

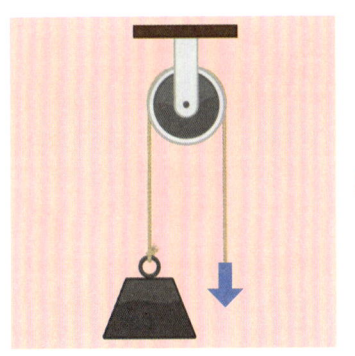

●

● moving a heavy box up stairs

●

● bringing a bucket of water up from a well

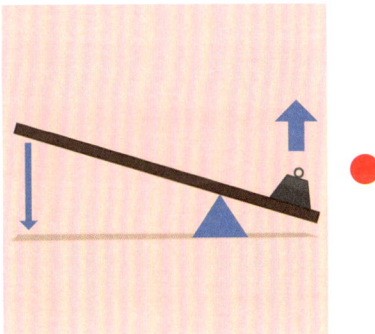

●

● Opening a wooden box

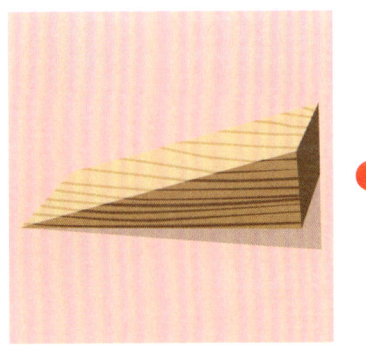

●

● Splitting wood in half.

Build your own pulley!

Supplies : Small plastic container or cup /
Scissors / String / A magnet or two / Paper clips

Step 1 : Have an adult help you poke a hole in each side of the container at the same height.
Step 2 : Thread the string through the holes and tie the ends together to make a handle.
Step 3 : Place the magnet or magnets in the bottom of the container.
Step 4 : Cut a 3-foot long piece of string and tie it to a door handle. Thread the handle of the container onto the string.
Step 5 : Slide the container up and down using the long string and try to pick the paper clips up off the floor!

❶ How many paper clips could you pick up a one time?

_____

❷ Can you think of a way to make your pulley better?

_____

Art Break!

■ Draw a device using simple machines to help save the cat from the tree.

The Economy

The way people spend and make money is called an economy. Economies can be strong or weak.

In a strong economy, there are lots of jobs and people can earn and spend a lot of money. In a weak economy, people may have a hard time finding a job and it can be hard for businesses to make money.

■ Answer the questions.

❶ What is an economy?

_____

❷ What is a strong economy?

_____

❸ What happens in a weak economy?

_____

■ **Read the questions below and check (✓) if the answer is true or false.**

❶ All economies are strong.

True   False

❷ In a strong economy there are lots of jobs and people have extra money to spend.

True   False

❸ In a weak economy, there are not a lot of jobs and businesses shut down.

True   False

❹ When people have more money to spend, the economy is good.

True   False

Goods and Services

People and companies make goods and provide services. Goods are things that are produced. They are physical objects that can be touched. Examples of goods are food, clothing, cars, electronics, and other objects. Services are not physical objects. A service is an act that someone does for money. For example, if a pipe in your home starts leaking, you might hire a plumber to fix it. That plumber does a service, and fixes your pipe.

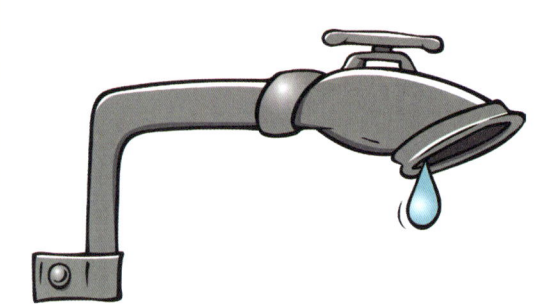

■ Answer the questions.

❶ What are examples of goods?

_____

❷ What is a service?

Date

Great Job Sticker

Circle the examples of goods and draw a square around examples of services in the scene.

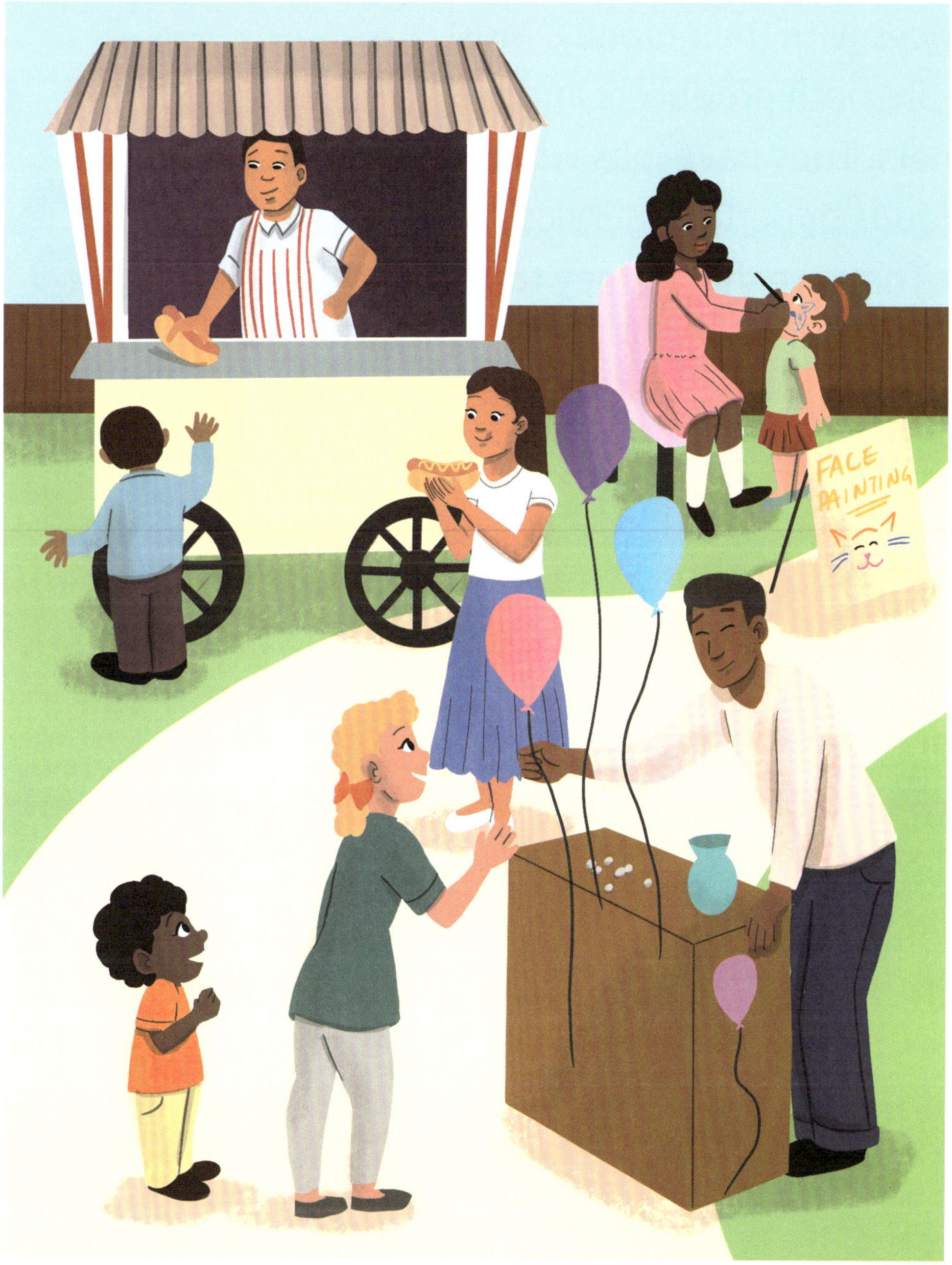
FACE PAINTING

Producers and Consumers

Producers are the people who make the goods or perform services for others. Consumers are people who buy those goods and pay for services with their money. Most people are both producers and consumers. They have jobs where they make goods or perform services for money. They use that money to buy other goods and services.

■ Answer the questions.

❶ What is a producer?

_____

❷ What is a consumer?

_____

Date

Great Job Sticker

Look at each picture and check (✓) the correct one.

1

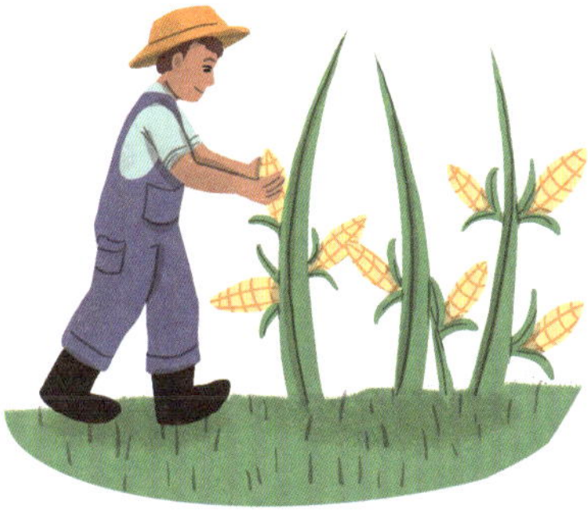

☐ Producer

☐ Consumer

2

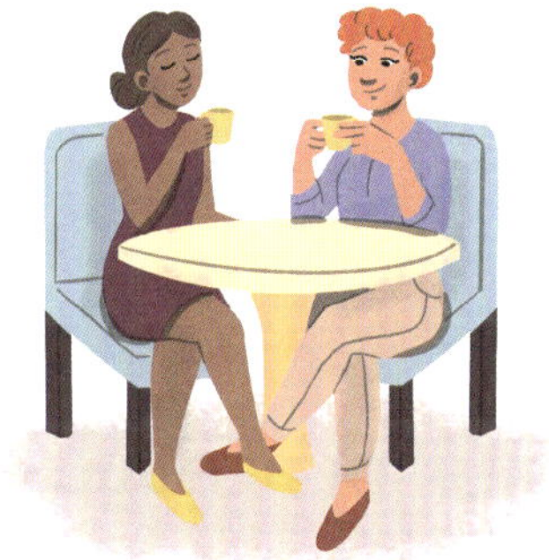

☐ Producer

☐ Consumer

3

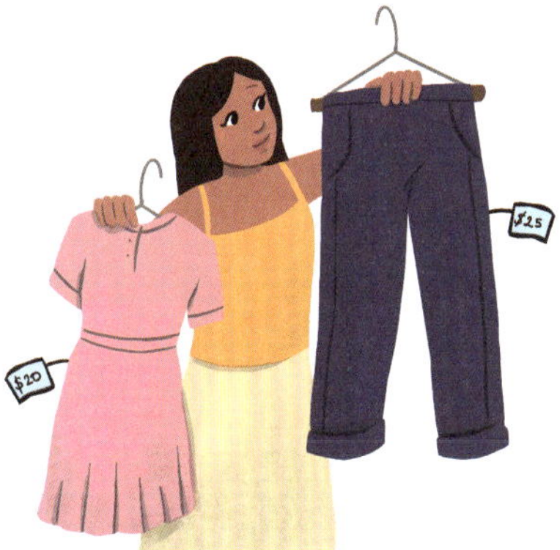

☐ Producer

☐ Consumer

4

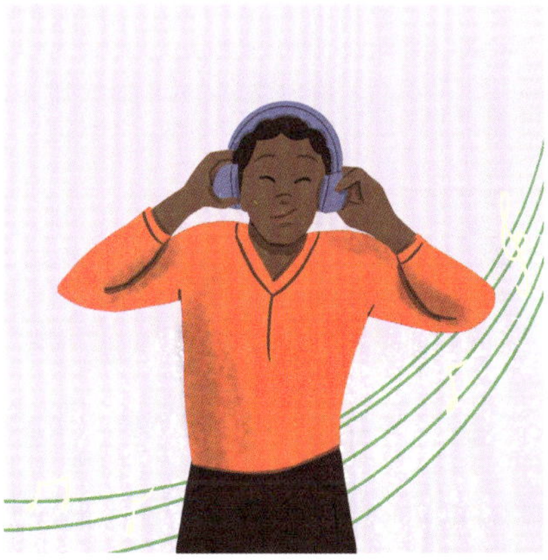

☐ Producer

☐ Consumer

5

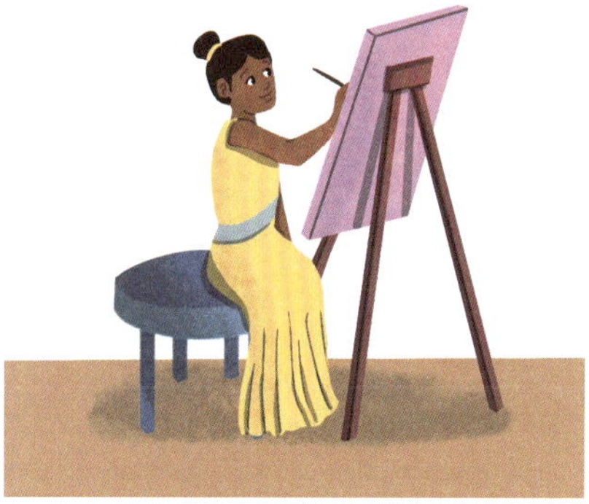

☐ Producer

☐ Consumer

6

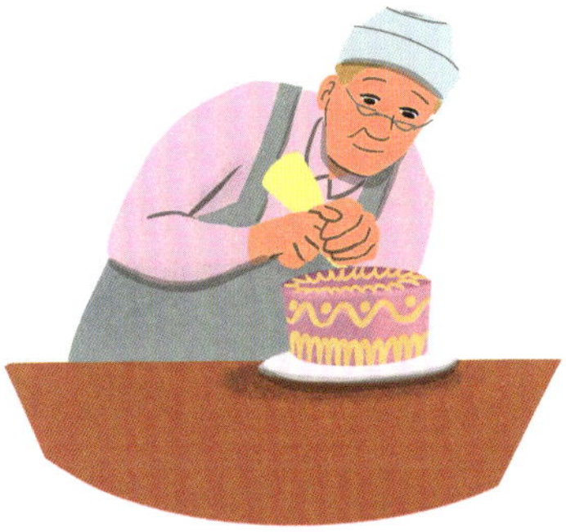

☐ Producer

☐ Consumer

Supply and Demand

In order for a business to make money, they need to understand supply and demand.

Supply is how much of a good is available. Demand is how many people want the good.

Supply and Demand:

❶ Supply high, demand high
➡ There are lots of goods available, but there are also a lot of people buying it.

❸ Supply low, demand low
➡ Not many goods are available, but there isn't a lot of interest anyway.

❷ Supply high, demand low
➡ There are lots of goods available, but not too many people are interested in buying. A business may lower their prices to get more customers.

❹ Supply low, demand high
➡ There aren't a lot of goods available, and lots of people want it! A business may raise its prices, and it will still probably sell out quickly.

■ Read the story. Write what will happen to the price of the product. Will it increase or decrease?

❶ A farmer has a good harvest and there is plenty of corn for everyone.

☐ **Increase**   ☐ **Decrease**

❷ A bakery becomes very popular and everyone wants their cupcakes. But they can only make a small number each day.

☐ **Increase**   ☐ **Decrease**

❸ A toy store decides to sell limited edition action figures.

☐ **Increase**   ☐ **Decrease**

❹ A hardware store sells sleds all year. It is summer now, and they are still selling sleds.

☐ **Increase**   ☐ **Decrease**

Brain Break
Word Search

■ Circle the words in the Word Search.

economy	resource	goods	service
producer	consumer	supply	demand

E	C	O	N	O	M	Y	S
J	Q	L	N	M	Q	L	E
H	W	T	E	R	S	P	V
C	T	K	T	C	U	P	I
O	U	W	Y	S	L	U	C
N	I	S	K	X	P	S	E
S	P	D	P	B	B	V	R
U	D	Y	V	L	N	A	O
M	C	G	G	O	G	X	M
E	X	A	O	I	S	Z	L
R	E	S	O	U	R	C	E
B	K	L	D	A	W	H	O
V	M	Y	S	E	R	J	P
D	E	M	A	N	D	K	M
R	E	C	U	D	O	R	P

■ Draw your design for a new toy that you think would be a best-seller.

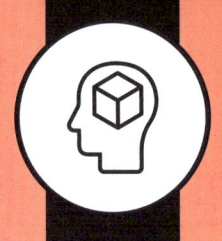

Color and Shape Patterns

■ Write a check mark (✔) below the picture that comes next in the pattern.

1

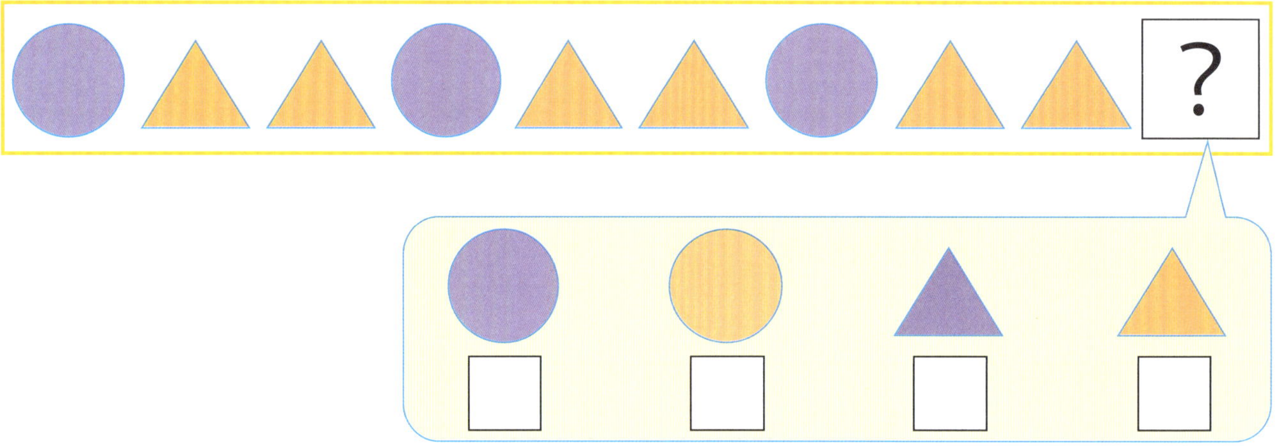

2

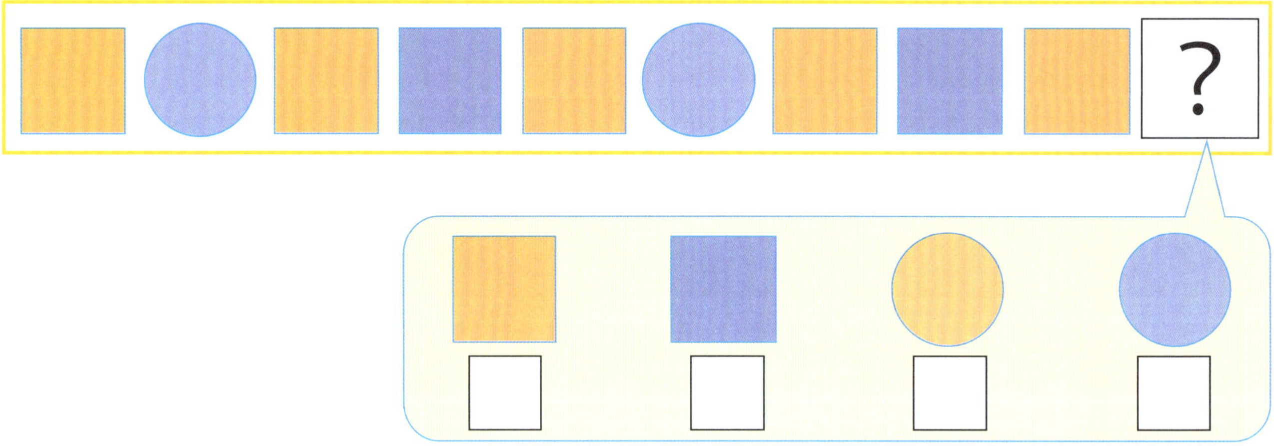

3

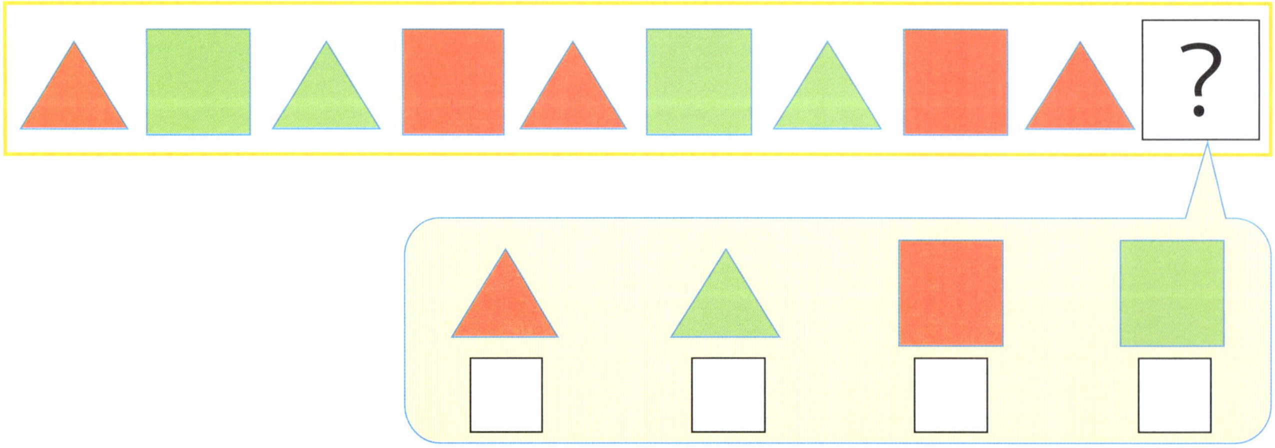

■ **Use the pattern to find the missing shape. Color it the correct color.**

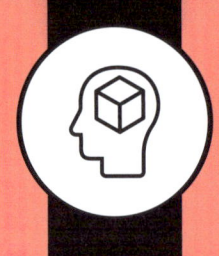

Unit 5 Thinking Skills

Word Search

■ Find and circle the names of the colors in the puzzle below.

R	E	D	E	F	B	L
W	L	L	E	Y	R	O
N	N	W	R	E	T	G
K	W	L	E	L	G	R
E	O	E	B	L	U	E
B	R	Y	U	O	N	E
M	B	L	U	W	I	N

RED

BLUE

GREEN

YELLOW

BROWN

■ Find and circle all the number words in the puzzle below.

N	E	V	E	S	I	C	E
E	I	G	H	K	T	W	V
O	X	I	S	U	H	B	I
A	E	F	O	M	R	O	F
R	I	T	W	O	E	N	I
U	G	H	T	N	E	I	V
O	H	L	S	V	E	N	O
F	T	E	N	I	N	E	I

1 ONE **2** TWO **3** THREE **4** FOUR **5** FIVE

6 SIX **7** SEVEN **8** EIGHT **9** NINE

Secret Words

■ Use the code box to write the letters and write a word in the boxes below.

A	B	D	E	G	K	L	N	P	S	U
●	○	▲	△	▮	▯	※	?	#	!	♪

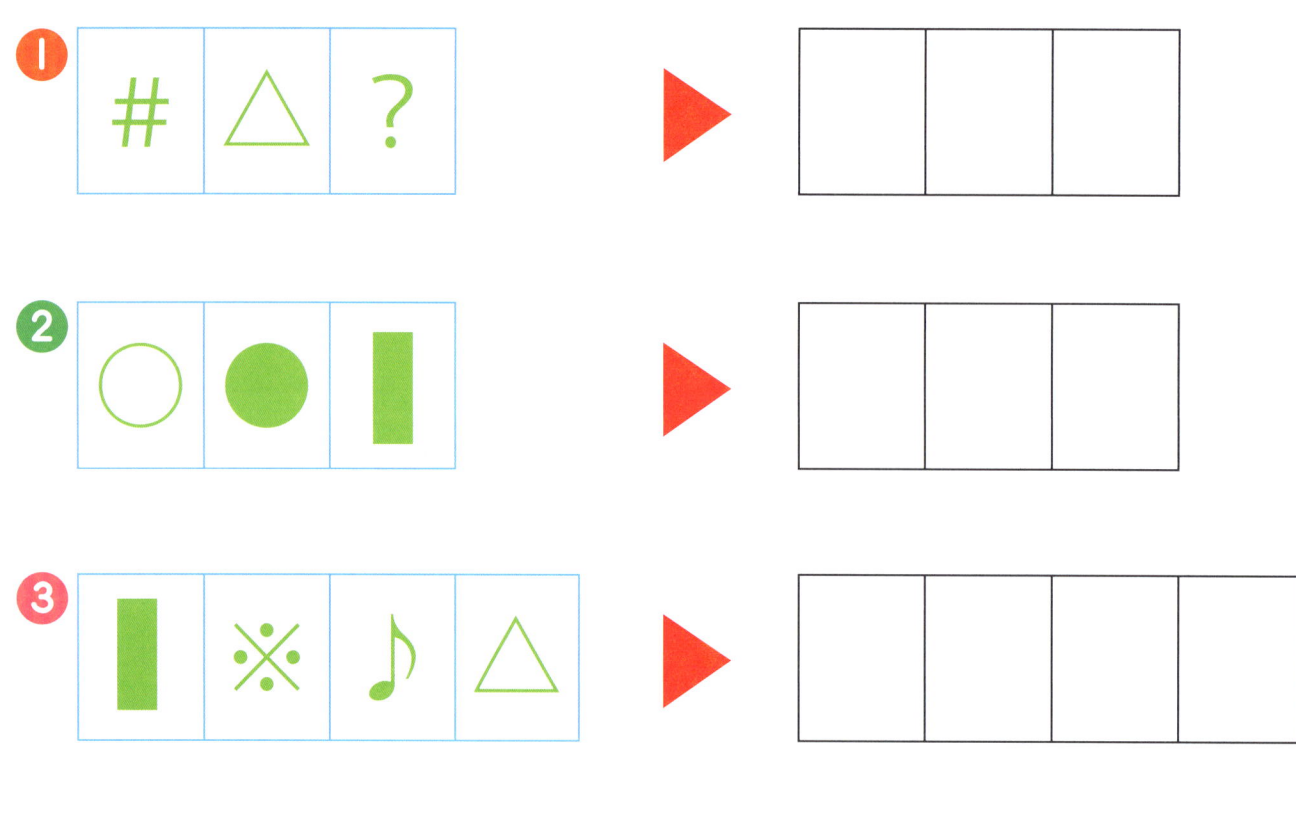

1. # △ ? ▶

2. ○ ● ▮ ▶

3. ▮ ※ ♪ △ ▶

4. ▲ △ ! ▯ ▶

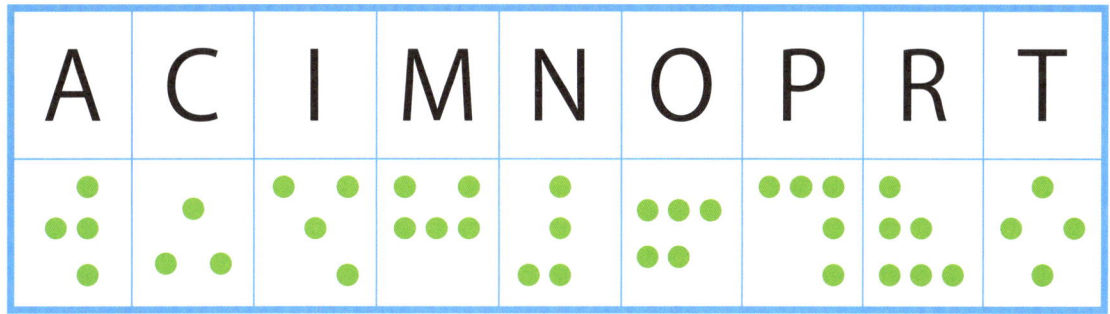

1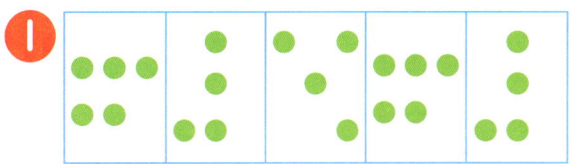

2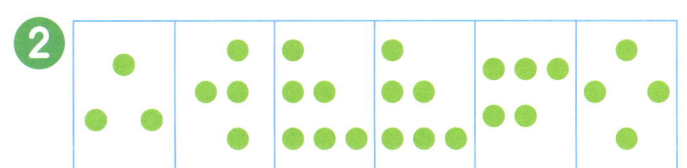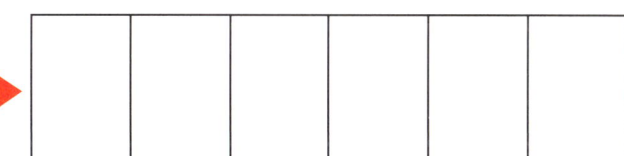

3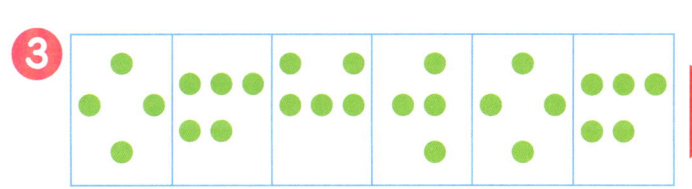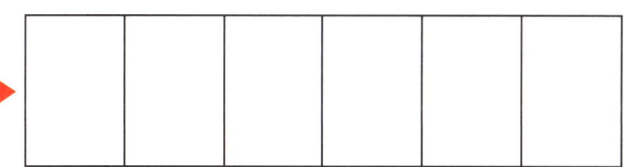

4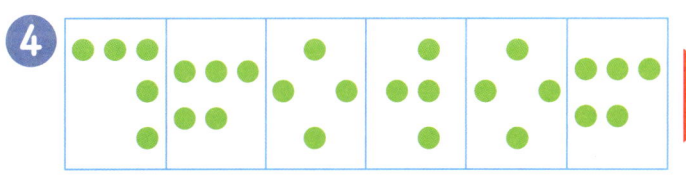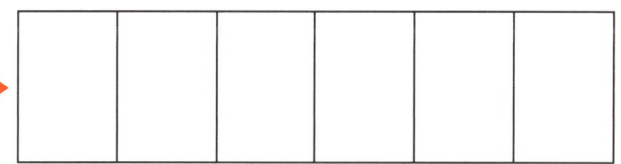

Problem Solving

■ Help the child get her boat back. Draw a solution to getting the boat out of the pond without getting wet!

■ Help the child cross the canyon safely. Draw a solution to help him get to the other side!

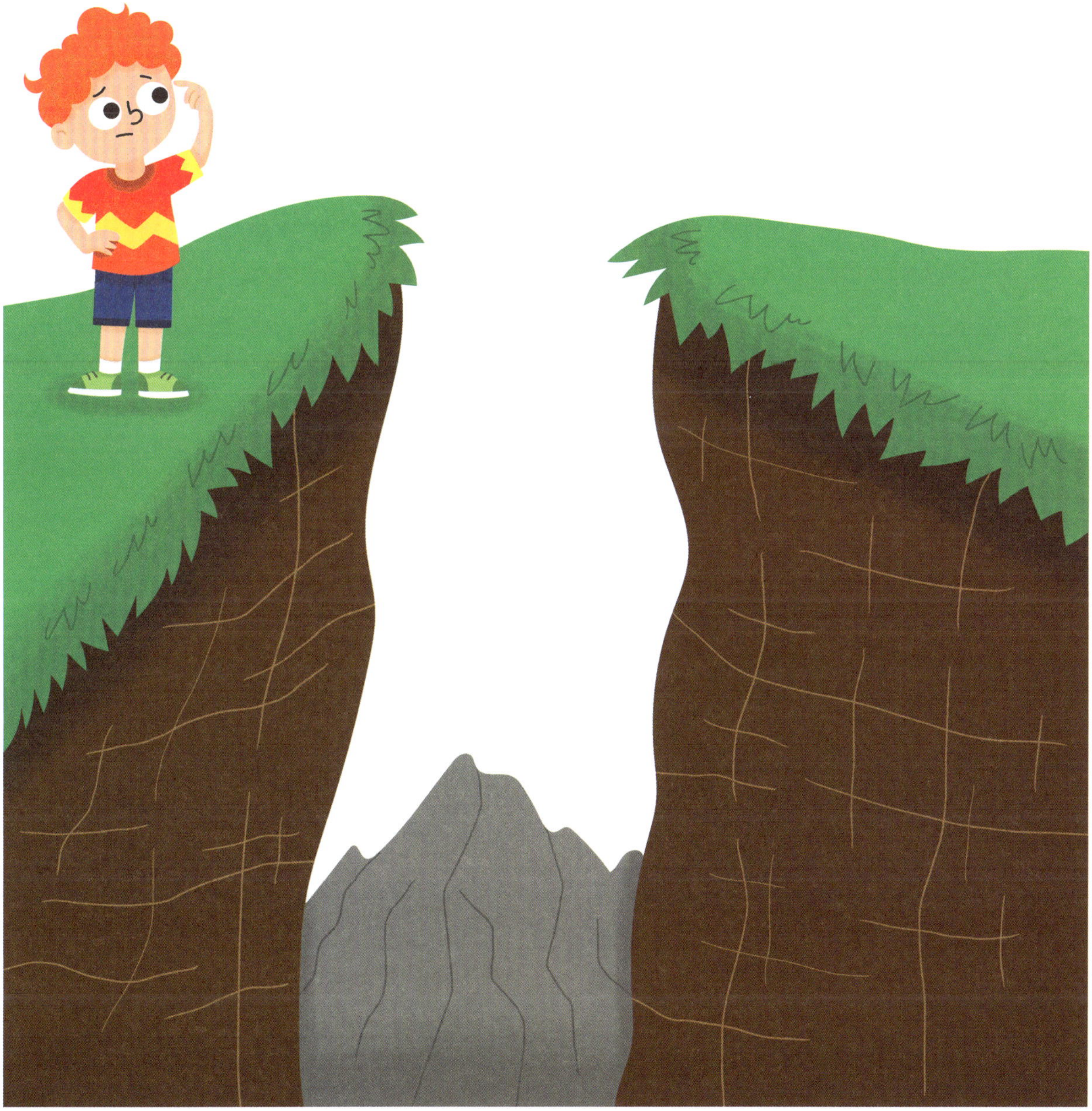

Unit 5

Physical Education Break!

It's important to move your body and exercise!
Try this fun activity below for a study break!

Pick 5 exercises from the list and try to do them daily!
Record your progress in the chart!

10 jumping jacks	5 sit ups	5 squats
1 minute run in place		10 frog hops
1 minute yoga pose		30 seconds high knees
30 seconds marching in place		10 star jumps

Daily Exercise Plan

Exercise	❶	❷	❸	❹	❺
Monday					
Tuesday					
Wednesday					
Thursday					
Friday					
Saturday					
Sunday					

Ace Second Grade

Answer Key

Unit 1 Language Arts

p. 4
❶team ❷class ❸flock ❹bunch

p. 5
❶teeth ❷feet ❸children ❹mice

p. 6
❶herself ❷herself ❸herself

p. 7
❶yourself
❷itself (*himself* or *herself* also ok)
❸ourselves
❹myself

p. 8
❶ran ❷ate ❸told ❹sat

p. 9

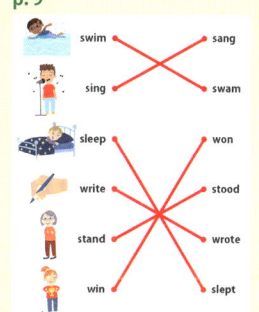

swim — sang
sing — swam
sleep — won
write — stood
stand — wrote
win — slept

p. 10
❶yellow ❷tiny ❸scary ❹loud

p. 11
❶neatly   ❸extremely
❷beautifully   ❹loudly

p. 12
(Answers will vary.)

Unit 1 Reading

p. 14
Long Vowels: like, rake, teeth, wheel
Short Vowels: pack, leg, sick, mint, well, fin

p. 15
Long Vowels: shone, pole, stone
Short Vowels: shut, rock, luck, stuck, rug

p. 16
rain|ing   cool|er
ti|ger   eat|en
spok|en   bik|ing

p. 17
❶feeding   ❷traced   ❸playing
❹spider   ❺voted   ❻student

p. 18
❶ disappear   to go away
❷ unkind   not kind
❸ preview   to see something early
❹ rewrite   to write again

p. 19
❶ thankless   to not receive thanks
❷ kindly   to do something in a nice way
❸ tallest   the most tall
❹ smaller   more small

p. 20
frend → friend
sed → said
coled → cold
sutch → such
agin → again

p. 21
❶what   ❸because   ❺use
❷other   ❹give

p. 22

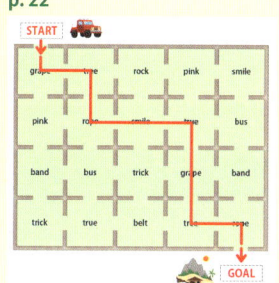

Unit 1 Math

pp. 24–25
❶12   ❹43   ❼146
❷17   ❺60   ❽752
❸25   ❻89   ❾501

p. 26

23 53 14 38
79 30 63 91

67 19 70 77
45 72 31 28

p. 27
❶ 15 23 32   ❹ 407 471 417
❷ 16 86 68   ❺ 931 913 319
❸ 50 5 55   ❻ 24 204 240

p. 28

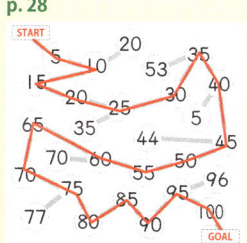

p. 29
60, 140, 270, 310, 430, 550, 700, 780, 820, 990

p. 30

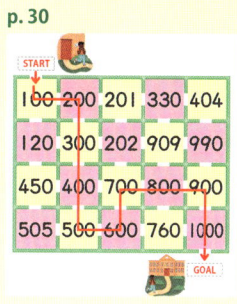

START
100 200 201 330 404
120 300 202 909 990
450 400 700 800 900
505 500 600 760 1000
GOAL

p. 31

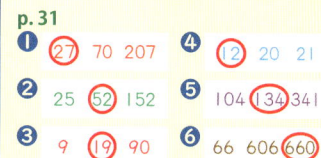

❶ 27 70 207   ❹ 12 20 21
❷ 25 52 152   ❺ 104 134 341
❸ 9 19 90   66 606 660

p. 32
❶✓ ❷✗ ❸✗ ❹✓ ❺✓ ❻✗

p. 33
❶< ❸> ❺> ❼>
❷< ❹< ❻= ❽<

p. 34

❶ 2 1   ❸ 4 6
   3 3   8 6

❷(Answers will vary.)
   5 3
   9 7

Unit 1 Science

p. 36
❶Plants make their food using sunlight and water.
❷Photosynthesis is the process plants use to make their food from sunlight and water.

p. 37
❶True ❷True ❸True ❹False

p. 38
❶An adaptation is a trait that helps a plant survive in its habitat.
❷One example is that plants that grow in hot areas have roots that grow near the surface.

p. 39

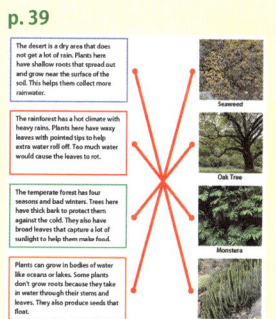

The desert is a dry area that does not get a lot of rain. Plants here have shallow roots that spread out and grow near the surface of the soil. This helps them collect more rainwater.
Seaweed

The rainforest has a hot climate with heavy rains. Plants here have waxy leaves with pointed tips to help extra water roll off. Too much water would cause the leaves to rot.
Oak Tree

The temperate forest has four seasons and bad winters. Trees here have thick bark to protect them against the cold. They also have broad leaves that capture a lot of sunlight to help them make food.
Monstera

Plants can grow in bodies of water like oceans or lakes. Some plants don't grow roots because they take in water through their stems and leaves. They also produce seeds that float.
Cactus

p. 41

Carried by the wind
By sticking to an animal's fur
Falling from the parent plant
Eaten and disposed of by animals

p. 42
❶Pollination is when pollen is moved to a plant so that it can reproduce.
❷Birds and insects.

p. 43

2
3
4
1
5

p. 44
(Answers will vary.)

Unit 1 Social Studies

p. 46
❶Native Americans.
❷All areas of the United States have Native American tribes.

p. 47
❶Native Americans
❷People
❸North / South

p. 48
❶In the Southwest
❷Cherokee and Seminole

p. 49
❶Southeast   ❸Midwest
❷Northeast   ❹Alaska

p. 51
❶Southwest   ❹Seminole
❷Buffalo   ❺Navajo
❸Iroquois

p. 53

She led Lewis and Clark on an expedition across the western United States.
He won two Olympic gold medals in Track and Field.
She was the first Native American prima ballerina.
He led the Sioux people in battle against General Custer.

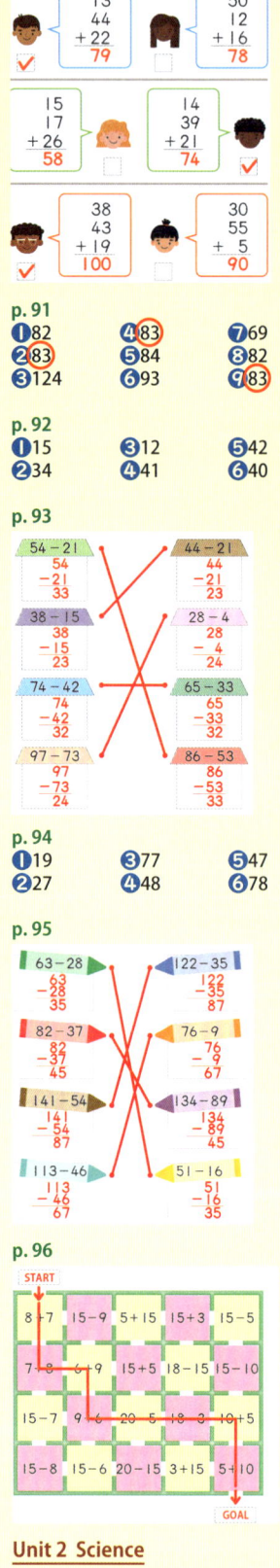

p. 54

```
C W S Q A S C
H T H E C T Q
E J K M R Y I
R X K I E I R
O C X O E U Q
K V N P H O U
E A L W G K O
E N V A J O I
N M P X X L S
V K O H X W P
B O H E K R R
N L I D W I V
I N U I T E A
A R L M E S A
E S I O U X B
```

Unit 1 Technology

pp. 56–57

p. 58

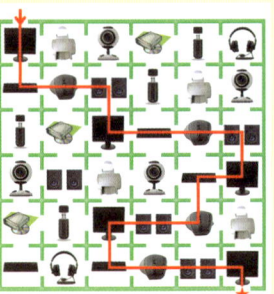

p. 59

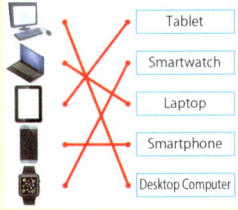

	Tablet
	Smartwatch
	Laptop
	Smartphone
	Desktop Computer

p. 60

p. 61

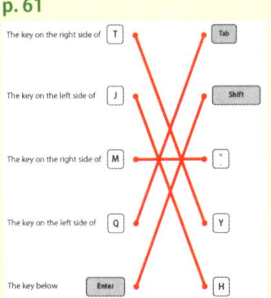

The key on the right side of **T**	Tab
The key on the left side of **J**	Shift
The key on the right side of **M**	,
The key on the left side of **Q**	Y
The key below **[Enter]**	H

p. 62

❶CAT   ❸MILK
❷EGG   ❹CAKE

p. 63

❶juice   ❷tennis   ❸notebook

Unit 2 Language Arts

p. 66

Hi Nate **,**
I can't wait for **h**alloween this year.
I am planning to dress up as a ghost.
My aunt will be visiting from **o**hio.
Your friend **,**
Mindy

p. 67

Dear Aunt Tina **,**
Today is **t**hanksgiving, and I don't have school! This afternoon, my family will drive to **c**hicago to visit my cousins. I am looking forward to playing with **h**enry. Well, that's it for now! I hope you are doing well.
Love **,**
Shanae

p. 68

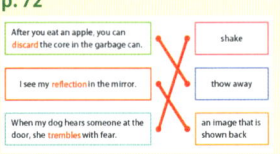

Fire — Smoky
Ocean — Salty
Ice cube — Cold
Orange — Juicy

p. 69

(Answers will vary.)

pp. 70–71

(Answers will vary.)

p. 72

After you eat an apple, you can **discard** the core in the garbage can. — thow away
I see my **reflection** in the mirror. — an image that is shown back
When my dog hears someone at the door, she **trembles** with fear. — shake

p. 73

Canyon: a deep rocky valley, or land feature
park ranger: someone who works in a park and shares safety tips and educational information
desert: a hot and dry place

p. 74

```
T L S R E V P R R C
O V N S S T H R E W P
S C D X U U U F U X
S E D E Z R R Y L P C
E W I S F L R L E A
D R J E T R E O L N
R J R Y Y D K T Y
S U T U Z R L I O
T H P R Y N M O N H
X G B T U A N M O N E
  D I S C A R D M S Q
```

Unit 2 Reading

p. 76

Who: Cinderella
What: didn't have a dress
When: a long time ago
Where: a small town
Why: her family wouldn't help

p. 77

Who: Aleysha
What: won the science fair
When: spring
Where: school
Why: she was prepared

p. 78

Sometimes you have to be patient to get what you want.

p. 79

(Answers will vary.)
Be yourself, and you'll make friends with similar interests.

p. 80

☐ Excited to play with Frank
☑ Sad that Frank was playing with someone else
☐ Angry that he couldn't find Frank

p. 81

(Answers will vary.)
Viviana probably feels good that she is helping her sister.

p. 82

(Answers will vary.)

p. 83

(Answers will vary.)
Maria:
She is worried.
She likes scary movies.
She is good at compromising.
Corey:
He is excited.
He doesn't like scary movies.
He likes funny movies.

Unit 2 Math

p. 86

❶15   ❸39   ❺99
❷38   ❹67   ❻87

p. 87

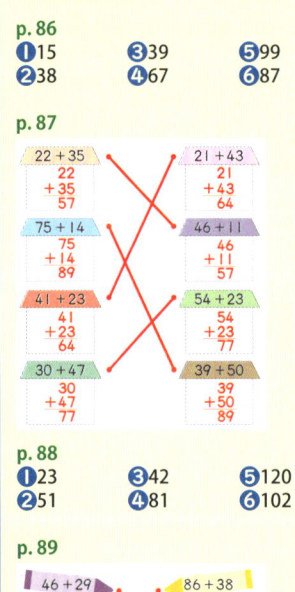

p. 88

❶23   ❸42   ❺120
❷51   ❹81   ❻102

p. 89

46 + 29, 86 + 38, 38 + 47, 66 + 19, 95 + 17, 38 + 37, 59 + 65, 43 + 69

p. 90

```
  13            50
  44            12
+ 22          + 16
  79  ✓         78
```

```
  15            14
  17            39
+ 26          + 21
  58            74  ✓
```

```
  38            30
  43            55
+ 19          +  5
  100  ✓        90
```

p. 91

❶82   ❹83   ❼69
❷83   ❺84   ❽82
❸124   ❻93   ❾83

p. 92

❶15   ❸12   ❺42
❷34   ❹41   ❻40

p. 93

54 − 21, 44 − 21, 38 − 15, 28 − 4, 74 − 42, 65 − 33, 97 − 73, 86 − 53

p. 94

❶19   ❸77   ❺47
❷27   ❹48   ❻78

p. 95

63 − 28, 122 − 35, 82 − 37, 76 − 9, 141 − 54, 134 − 89, 113 − 46, 51 − 16

p. 96

```
START
8+7   15−9  5+15  15+3  15−5
7−6   6+9   15+5  18−15 15−10
15−7  9−6   15+15 18−3  10+5
15−8  15−6  20−15 3+15  5+10
GOAL
```

Unit 2 Science

p. 98

❶A landform is a natural feature on the earth's surface.
❷(Answers will vary.)
Mountains and valleys.

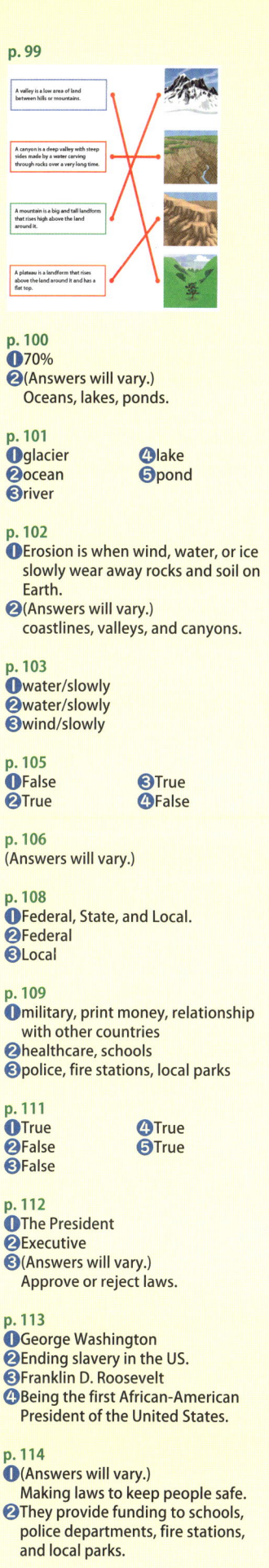

p. 99

p. 100
① 70%
② (Answers will vary.)
Oceans, lakes, ponds.

p. 101
① glacier   ④ lake
② ocean   ⑤ pond
③ river

p. 102
① Erosion is when wind, water, or ice slowly wear away rocks and soil on Earth.
② (Answers will vary.)
coastlines, valleys, and canyons.

p. 103
① water/slowly
② water/slowly
③ wind/slowly

p. 105
① False   ③ True
② True   ④ False

p. 106
(Answers will vary.)

p. 108
① Federal, State, and Local.
② Federal
③ Local

p. 109
① military, print money, relationship with other countries
② healthcare, schools
③ police, fire stations, local parks

p. 111
① True   ④ True
② False   ⑤ True
③ False

p. 112
① The President
② Executive
③ (Answers will vary.)
Approve or reject laws.

p. 113
① George Washington
② Ending slavery in the US.
③ Franklin D. Roosevelt
④ Being the first African-American President of the United States.

p. 114
① (Answers will vary.)
Making laws to keep people safe.
② They provide funding to schools, police departments, fire stations, and local parks.

p. 115

p. 116
Across
① democracy
③ local
⑤ judicial
⑦ federal
Down
② executive
④ legislative

Unit 2 Technology

p. 118
① →→→   ② →↑   ③ →↑

p. 119
①
Repeats ♥ twice.
Repeats ♥♦♥ twice.
✓ Repeats ♥♦ three times.
②
✓ Repeats ★▼● twice.
Repeats ★▼● three times.
Repeats ★▼● three times.

p. 120
①   ②

p. 121
①   ②

pp. 122–123
①   ②   ③   ④

pp. 124-125
①
Move 1 step
✓ Move 2 steps
②
Turn right
✓ Turn left

Unit 3 Reading

p. 128
He knows it is Luna's birthday.
✓ He has a balloon for Luna.
He saw Luna earlier.

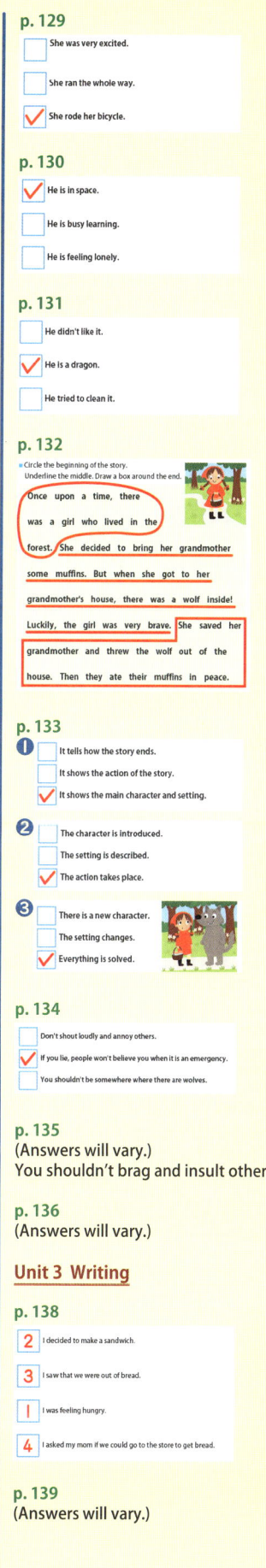

p. 129
She was very excited.
She ran the whole way.
✓ She rode her bicycle.

p. 130
✓ He is in space.
He is busy learning.
He is feeling lonely.

p. 131
He didn't like it.
✓ He is a dragon.
He tried to clean it.

p. 132
■ Circle the beginning of the story. Underline the middle. Draw a box around the end.
Once upon a time, there was a girl who lived in the forest. She decided to bring her grandmother some muffins. But when she got to her grandmother's house, there was a wolf inside! Luckily, the girl was very brave. She saved her grandmother and threw the wolf out of the house. Then they ate their muffins in peace.

p. 133
①
It tells how the story ends.
It shows the action of the story.
✓ It shows the main character and setting.
②
The character is introduced.
The setting is described.
✓ The action takes place.
③
There is a new character.
The setting changes.
✓ Everything is solved.

p. 134
Don't shout loudly and annoy others.
✓ If you lie, people won't believe you when it is an emergency.
You shouldn't be somewhere where there are wolves.

p. 135
(Answers will vary.)
You shouldn't brag and insult others.

p. 136
(Answers will vary.)

Unit 3 Writing

p. 138
2 I decided to make a sandwich.
3 I saw that we were out of bread.
1 I was feeling hungry.
4 I asked my mom if we could go to the store to get bread.

p. 139
(Answers will vary.)

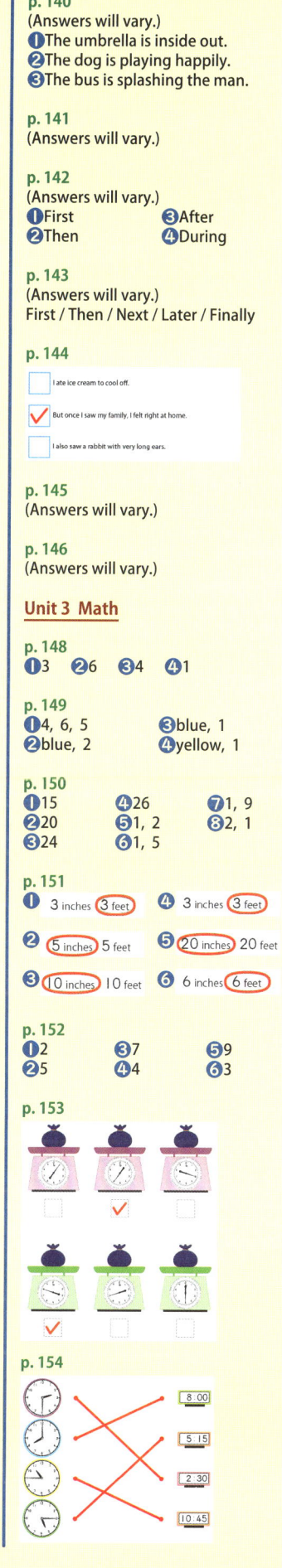

p. 140
(Answers will vary.)
① The umbrella is inside out.
② The dog is playing happily.
③ The bus is splashing the man.

p. 141
(Answers will vary.)

p. 142
(Answers will vary.)
① First   ③ After
② Then   ④ During

p. 143
(Answers will vary.)
First / Then / Next / Later / Finally

p. 144
I ate ice cream to cool off.
✓ But once I saw my family, I felt right at home.
I also saw a rabbit with very long ears.

p. 145
(Answers will vary.)

p. 146
(Answers will vary.)

Unit 3 Math

p. 148
① 3   ② 6   ③ 4   ④ 1

p. 149
① 4, 6, 5   ③ blue, 1
② blue, 2   ④ yellow, 1

p. 150
① 15   ④ 26   ⑦ 1, 9
② 20   ⑤ 1, 2   ⑧ 2, 1
③ 24   ⑥ 1, 5

p. 151
① 3 inches (3 feet)   ④ 3 inches (3 feet)
② (5 inches) 5 feet   ⑤ (20 inches) 20 feet
③ (10 inches) 10 feet   ⑥ 6 inches (6 feet)

p. 152
① 2   ③ 7   ⑤ 9
② 5   ④ 4   ⑥ 3

p. 153

p. 154

p. 155

7:00 | 1:45
4:00 | 5:15
11:30 | 9:45

p. 156

① 7:05   ③ 9:20   ⑤ 4:45
② 2:35   ④ 12:10   ⑥ 10:50

p. 157

p. 158

p. 160

① Weather is the state of the Earth's atmosphere.
② Rain, snow, sunshine.

p. 161

① True   ② True   ③ True   ④ False

p. 162

① Severe weather is weather that is dangerous and causes damage.
② Sample answer: Hurricanes, thunderstorms.

p. 163

① Hurricane
② Heavy rains, fast winds, flooding, and damage to homes.
③ Stay inside and stay away from windows that could break.
④ Tornado
⑤ Very fast winds and damage to land and homes.
⑥ Stay inside and go down in a storm cellar or basement.

p. 165

This event forms when very strong winds spin around very fast.

This event is a severe storm with strong winds and heavy rain. It forms over the ocean.

This event happens when pieces of Earth's crust shift or move against each other.

This event happens when a lot of water rushes into an area.

This event is a large, uncontrolled fire that spreads very fast through forest or grasslands.

p. 167

(Answers will vary.)

p. 168

(Answers will vary.)

Unit 3 Social Studies

p. 170

① Culture is the shared way of life of a society.
② (Answers will vary.)
Language, food, clothing

p. 171

(Answers will vary.)

p. 172

① In February
② To honor the past presidents of the United States and their accomplishments.

p. 173

George Washington
President from 1861-1865
This US president is best known for leading the country during the Civil War and signing the Emancipation Proclamation to free all enslaved people in the US.

Abraham Lincoln
President from 1933-1945
This US president is best known for signing the New Deal, which created many services for people in the United States during the Great Depression. He also led the country during World War II.

Franklin D. Roosevelt
President from 1789-1797
This US president is best known for leading the Continental Army during the American Revolutionary War and for becoming the first President of the United States.

Thomas Jefferson
President from 1801-1809
This US president is best known for writing the Declaration of Independence, which declared the United States a free country separate from England. He is also one of the founding fathers.

p. 174

① The Fourth of July is a US holiday that celebrates the signing of the Declaration of Independence.
② American celebrate with BBQs, parades, and fireworks.

p. 175

① True   ③ False   ⑤ True
② False   ④ True

p. 176

① Juneteenth is a United States holiday that celebrates the end of slavery in the US.
② People celebrate by going to parades, prayer services, and getting together with family and friends.

p. 177

What? Slavery
Who? African-Americans
When? June 19th
Why? Emancipation Proclamation

p. 178

Across
① Juneteenth
③ freedom
⑤ culture
⑦ July Fourth
Down
② Jefferson
④ president
⑥ Lincoln
⑧ Washington

Unit 3 Personal Finance

p. 180

p. 181

$2.03
$2.25
$1.15

p. 182

① No   ② Yes   ③ Yes   ④ No

p. 183

①

②

p. 184

① $0.01   ② $0.20   ③ $0.03   ④ $0.05

p. 185

① French Fries   ③ Ice Cream
② Salad

p. 187

① Budget   ③ Charity   ⑤ Save
② Spend   ④ Earn

Unit 4 Reading

p. 190

(Answers will vary.)
Who: Martin Luther King, Jr.
What: fought against unfair treatment of Black people
When: 1950s and 1960s
Where: the United States
Why: He believed everyone should have equal rights.

p. 191

(Answers will vary.)
Who: Amelia Earhart
What: was the first woman to fly across the Atlantic
When: 1932
Where: the US
Why: She was determined to prove that women were just as talented as men.

p. 192

What rainbows look like
How rainbows are made
Why rainbows are beautiful

p. 193

(Answers will vary.)
There are many types of waterfalls, and they all are formed differently.

p. 194

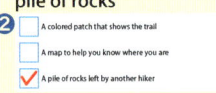

Put sauce on it.
Knead the dough.
Add cheese.

p. 195

(Answers will vary.)

p. 196

① (Answers will vary.)
hikers, interesting spot, tricky turn, pile of rocks
②
A colored patch that shows the trail
A map to help you know where you are
A pile of rocks left by another hiker

p. 197

① (Answers will vary.)
get around, sound, listening, hearing
②
Not seeing well.
Using sound to know where things are.
Sleeping during the day.

p. 198

(Answers will vary.)

Unit 4 Writing

p. 200

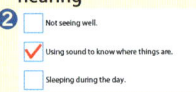

Some people see squirrels as pests, but they're a special animal.
Squirrels hide acorns so that they can come back and eat them later.
Newborn squirrels are only an inch long.

p. 201

Pandas have black and white fur.
Pandas are a very interesting animal.
Pandas can climb trees.

p. 202

(Answers will vary.)
Whales are the largest mammal.
Mammals are warm-blooded animals.
Blue whales can be almost one hundred feet long.
Blue whales only eat tiny fish.

p. 203

(Answers will vary.)

pp. 204–205

(Answers will vary.)

pp. 206–207

(Answers will vary.)

p. 208

```
R S F H G R F Z I H R
D I V C D E V U L G P
I N F O R M A T I O N
P T V N P T K O V S L
A R E C E O F P E X L
T O W L G R D I D S I
H D V U S U R C P R G
W U F Z S Z Y Z O E V S
B C I I O R E I L I B
R T W N L K E B F X X F
X I W N G E V V B H V
U O O D S H F A C T S
W N E W R D H G V V B
H K F X H J L J S K
R W P K F X C K E U R
```

Unit 4 Math

p. 210

Pentagon
Square
Trapezoid
Triangle
Circle
Hexagon
Rectangle

p. 211

p. 212
❶
❷
❸
❹

p. 213

Cylinder
Pyramid
Sphere
Cube
Rectangular prism
Cone

p. 214

p. 215

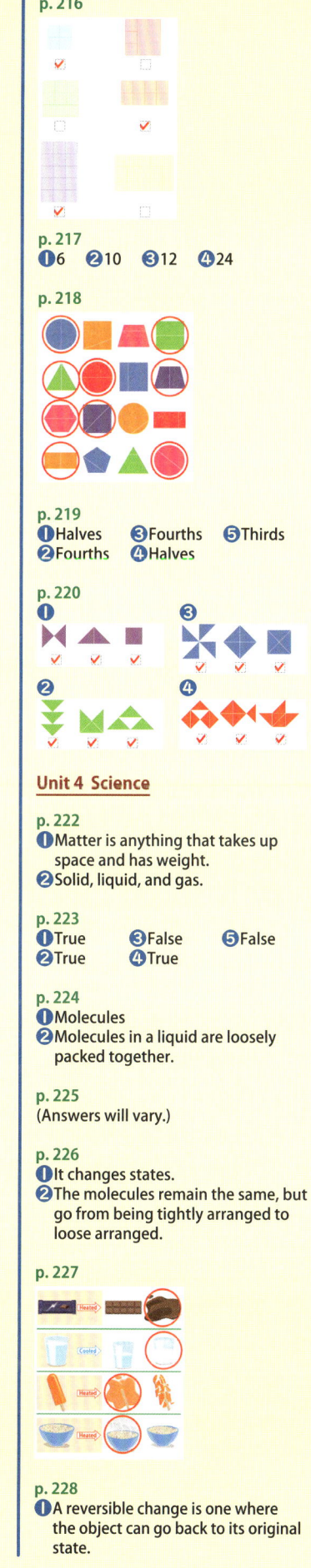

p. 216

p. 217
❶ 6 ❷ 10 ❸ 12 ❹ 24

p. 218

p. 219
❶ Halves   ❸ Fourths   ❺ Thirds
❷ Fourths   ❹ Halves

p. 220
❶   ❸
❷   ❹

Unit 4 Science

p. 222
❶ Matter is anything that takes up space and has weight.
❷ Solid, liquid, and gas.

p. 223
❶ True   ❸ False   ❺ False
❷ True   ❹ True

p. 224
❶ Molecules
❷ Molecules in a liquid are loosely packed together.

p. 225
(Answers will vary.)

p. 226
❶ It changes states.
❷ The molecules remain the same, but go from being tightly arranged to loose arranged.

p. 227

p. 228
❶ A reversible change is one where the object can go back to its original state.

❷ An irreversible change is one in which the object cannot go back to its original state.

p. 229
❶ R   ❷ I   ❸ I   ❹ R   ❺ R

p. 230
❶ The chocolate bar will melt.
❷ The chocolate bar will harden.

Unit 4 Social Studies

p. 232
❶ North America, South America, Europe, Asia, Africa, Antarctica, and Australia.
❷ Atlantic, Pacific, Indian, Arctic, and Southern.

p. 233
❶ North America   ❹ Europe
❷ Pacific Ocean   ❺ Asia
❸ Atlantic Ocean

p. 234
❶ A landform is a natural feature on the Earth's surface.
❷ (Answers will vary.) Mountain and canyon.

p. 235
❶ Asia   ❸ Africa
❷ Asia/Japan   ❹ Australia

p. 237
❶ A landmark is a man-made feature that makes a place recognizable.
❷ St. Louis, MO
❸ New York City
❹ San Francisco
❺ Washington, D.C.

p. 239
(Answers will vary.)

p. 240

C	H	T	D	U	N	M	L	L
O	C	E	A	N	B	W	A	T
N	J	Y	F	P	A	X	T	N
T	N	U	R	O	S	Z	L	H
I	M	I	I	L	I	G	A	F
N	K	O	C	N	A	H	N	C
E	I	P	A	X	Z	N	T	I
N	Q	S	T	V	T	B	I	F
T	W	A	R	C	T	I	C	I
D	E	B	Z	B	Q	V	A	C
F	R	W	X	U	S	C	S	A
G	E	U	R	O	P	E	X	P

Unit 4 Thinking Skills

p. 242
❶ A   ❷ D   ❸ C   ❹ B

p. 243
❶ A   ❷ D   ❸ B   ❹ C

pp. 244–245
❶   ❸
❷   ❹

p. 246

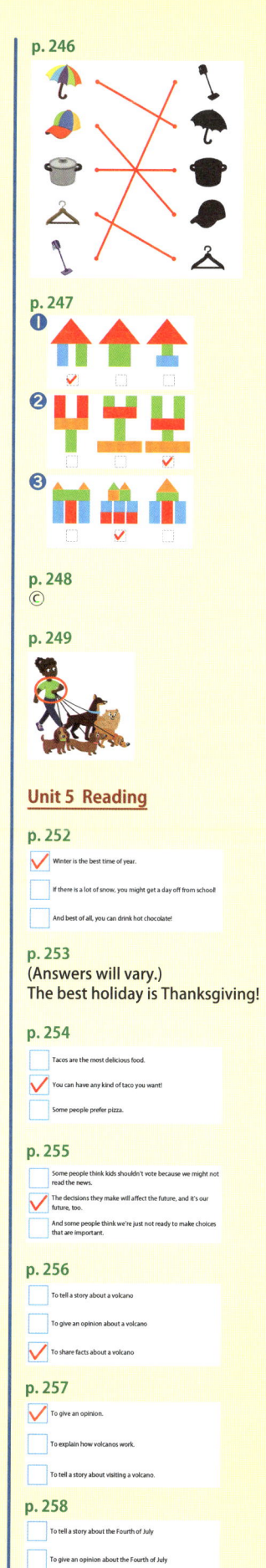

p. 247
❶
❷
❸

p. 248
Ⓒ

p. 249

Unit 5 Reading

p. 252
☑ Winter is the best time of year.
☐ If there is a lot of snow, you might get a day off from school!
☐ And best of all, you can drink hot chocolate!

p. 253
(Answers will vary.)
The best holiday is Thanksgiving!

p. 254
☐ Tacos are the most delicious food.
☑ You can have any kind of taco you want!
☐ Some people prefer pizza.

p. 255
☐ Some people think kids shouldn't vote because we might not read the news.
☑ The decisions they make will affect the future, and it's our future, too.
☐ And some people think we're just not ready to make choices that are important.

p. 256
☐ To tell a story about a volcano
☐ To give an opinion about a volcano
☑ To share facts about a volcano

p. 257
☑ To give an opinion.
☐ To explain how volcanos work.
☐ To tell a story about visiting a volcano.

p. 258
☐ To tell a story about the Fourth of July
☐ To give an opinion about the Fourth of July
☑ To tell the the history of the Fourth of July

p. 259
(Answers will vary.)
This text tells about someone's experience celebrating the Fourth of July.

p. 260
number of sneakers
color of backpack
water in glass

Unit 5 Writing

pp. 262–263
(Answers will vary.)

p. 264

☐ Homework helps kids learn.

☑ Kids need time to rest and play.

☐ Some classes give homework.

p. 265
(Answers will vary.)

p. 266
❶and　　❷because　　❸Also

p. 267
(Answers will vary.)

pp. 268–269
(Answers will vary.)

p. 270
(Answers will vary.)

Unit 5 Math

pp. 272–273
❶5　　❷3　　❸6
❹

Shape of cookie	🍪	🔺	🟧
Number of cookie	5	3	6

❺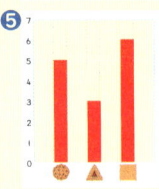

pp. 274–275
❶5　❷4　❸2　❹4
❺

Favorite Fruit	Apple	Pineapple	Grapes	Banana
Number of cookie	5	4	2	4

❻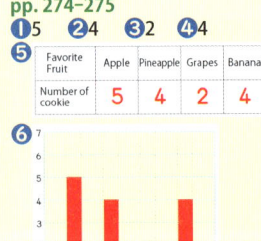

pp. 276–277
❶✓　　❸✓　　❺✗　　❼✗
❷✗　　❹✗　　❻✓　　❽✓

pp. 278–279
❶26+7=33　　Ans. 33 strawberries
❷35+85=120　Ans. 120 stickers
❸19+12=31　　Ans. 31 inches
❹34−16=18　　Ans. 18 dimes
❺150−70=80　Ans. 80 beads
❻11−7=4　　　Ans. 4 feet

pp. 280–281
❶78−25=53　　Ans. 53 pounds
❷5+8=13, 13+12=25
　　　　　　　　Ans. 25 oranges
❸100−17=83, 83−25=58
　　　　　　　　Ans. 58 stickers
❹40−(15+9)=16
　　　　　　　　Ans. 16 passengers
❺19−(5+5)=9　Ans. 9 bars
❻16+21=37, 37−30=7
　　　　　　　　Ans. 7 sheets

p. 282

Unit 5 Science

p. 284
❶Motion is the change in position of an object.
❷A force is the movement on an object to put it in motion.

p. 285

p. 286
❶A pull is when you use force to move an object closer to you.
❷A push is using a force to move an object away from you.

p. 287
❶push　　❸push　　❺push
❷pull　　❹pull　　❻push

p. 288
❶Forces can be described by their direction and strength.
❷Force can change a ball's speed and direction.

p. 289
❶ 　　❸
❷

p. 291

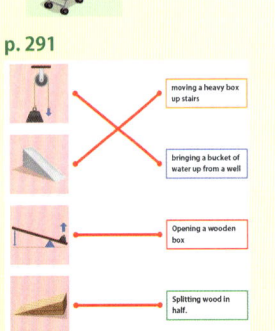

moving a heavy box up stairs

bringing a bucket of water from a well

Opening a wooden box

Splitting wood in half.

p. 292
(Answers will vary.)

Unit 5 Social Studies

p. 294
❶An economy is the way people make and spend money in a society.
❷A strong economy is where people have jobs and money to spend.
❸In a weak economy people lose jobs, businesses close, and people make less and spend less money.

p. 295
❶False　　　❸True
❷True　　　❹True

p. 296
❶Examples of goods are food, clothing, cars…etc.
❷A service is an act someone performs for money, like a job.

p. 297

p. 298
❶A producer is someone who makes things.
❷A consumer is someone who buys or uses goods.

p. 299
❶Producer　　❹Consumer
❷Consumer　　❺Producer
❸Consumer　　❻Producer

p. 301
❶Decrease　　❸Increase
❷Increase　　❹Decrease

p. 302

E	C	O	N	O	M	Y	S
J	Q	L	N	M	Q	L	E
H	W	T	E	R	S	P	V
C	T	K	T	C	U	P	I
O	U	W	Y	S	L	U	C
N	I	S	K	X	P	S	E
S	P	D	P	B	B	V	R
U	D	Y	V	L	N	A	O
M	C	G	G	O	A	Z	M
E	X	A	O	I	S	X	L
R	E	S	O	U	R	C	E
B	K	L	D	A	W	H	O
V	M	Y	S	E	R	J	P
D	E	M	A	N	D	K	M
R	E	C	U	D	O	R	P

Unit 5 Thinking Skills

p. 304
❶
❷
❸

p. 305
❶ ⭐ ♡ ◆
❷ ⭐ ♥ ◇
❸ ☆ ♡ ◆

p. 306

R	E	D	E	F	B	L	O
W	L	L	E	Y	R	O	G
N	N	W	R	E	T	G	R
K	W	L	E	L	G	R	E
E	O	E	B	L	U	E	E
B	R	Y	U	O	N	E	N
M	B	L	U	W	I	N	

p. 307

N	E	V	E	S	I	C	E
E	I	G	H	K	T	W	V
O	X	I	S	U	H	B	I
A	E	F	O	M	R	O	F
R	I	T	W	O	E	N	I
U	G	H	T	N	E	I	V
O	H	L	S	V	E	N	O
F	T	E	N	I	N	E	I

p. 308
❶PEN　　　　❸GLUE
❷BAG　　　　❹DESK

p. 309
❶ONION　　　❸TOMATO
❷CARROT　　　❹POTATO

pp. 310–311
(Answers will vary.)

Ace Second Grade

Unit 1

COMPLETED!

Unit 2

COMPLETED!

Unit 3

COMPLETED!

Unit 4

COMPLETED!

Unit 5

COMPLETED!

All Pages Completed!

Excellent Work!

CERTIFICATE
OF ACHIEVEMENT

is hereby congratulated on completing

Kumon Ace Second Grade

Date

Parent or Guardian